The PLO and World Politics

To my Parents and Josephine

The PLO and World Politics

A Study of the Mobilization of Support for the Palestinian Cause

Kemal Kirisci

 Frances Pinter (Publishers), London.

First Published in Great Britain in 1986 by
Frances Pinter (Publishers) Ltd,
25 Floral Street, London WC2E 9DS

British Library Cataloguing in Publication Data
Kirisci, Kemal
    PLO and world politics : study of the
    mobilization of support for the Palestinian
    cause.
    1. Palestine Liberation Organization
    2. Palestine-International status
    I. Title
    322.4′2′095694   DS119.7
    ISBN 0-86187-585-0

Typeset by Joshua Associates Limited, Oxford
Printed by SRP Ltd., Exeter

Contents

List of Tables   vi
List of Figures   vii
List of Abbreviations   viii
Preface   ix
Acknowledgements   xii

1 Historical Background and the Research Problem   1
2 Paradigms and the Research Problem   11
3 The Analytical Framework   20
4 Mobilization of Support at the Palestinian Level   34
5 The Arab Governmental Level   54
6 Mobilization of Support Among Third World Regional and Political
  Groupings   69
7 Mobilization of Support for the Palestinian Cause Among East and
  West European Countries   93
8 Mobilization of Support at the UN Level   127
9 Conclusion   152

Appendices   167
    I Operationalizing the Concept of 'Political Support' for the
      Palestinian Cause   167
   II List of Membership of Regional and Political Groups   175
  III List of Palestinian National Council Meetings   180
   IV List of PLO Offices Abroad by Early 1980s   181
    V   184

Bibliography: theory and methodology   185
Bibliography: substantive   188
Index   193

List of Tables

1.1 Distribution of Votes on the Partition Plan by Regional Groupings   5
1.2 Expansion of Israeli Diplomatic Representation Abroad between 1951 and 1966   7

4.1 Estimated Distribution of Palestinians in 1977   35
4.2 Matrix of Access Routes to the Palestinians   46

5.1 Access Routes to Arab Governments   60

6.1 Level of Average Anti-colonial Voting Scores for Groups of Countries   74
6.2 Distribution of Highly Anti-colonial and Pro-Palestinian Votes in each Group across Three Sessions   76
6.3 Access Routes to Third World Governments   78
6.4 PLO Offices by Third World Regional and Political Groupings   80
6.5 Distribution of Non-Aligned Support   83
6.6 Distribution of African Support for the Palestinian Cause   85
6.7 Distribution of Islamic Support at the 24th Session by ICO and Sub-group Membership   86
6.8 Distribution of Latin-American Support   88

7.1 Access Routes to European Agendas   106
7.2 Distribution of Support across Sessions for West European Countries Outside the EC   117

8.1 Change in the Distribution of United Nations' Membership by Region between 1945 and 1980   128
8.2 Geographical Distribution of Vice-Presidents before and after Resolutions 1990 (XVIII) and 33/138   129
8.3 Distribution of Main Committee Chairmanship before and after Resolutions 1990 (XVIII) and 33/138   129
8.4 Number of Countries Sponsoring PLO's Participation in the Work of the Special Political Committee   133
8.5 Distribution of Support by Regional Groupings at the 24th Session   139
8.6 Distribution of Support by Regional Groupings at the 26th Session   140
8.7 Distribution of Support by Regional Groupings at the 28th Session   140
8.8 Distribution of Support by Regional Groupings across the 29th and 35th Sessions   145

A1.1 Distribution of Roll-calls by Sessions and by Sub-issues   168
A1.2 Distribution of Weights by Period and by Issues   171
A1.3 Unweighted and Weighted Versions of the Distribution of Support by Groups at the 29th Session   173
A4.1 Distribution of PLO Offices by Regions   183

List of figures

3.1 Model for Studying the Mobilization of Support for the Palestinian
    Cause   26

8.1 The UN System as it Relates to the Palestinian Problem   144

9.1 Growth of Support across Different Levels Represented as
    Multi-step-Function   152
9.2 Convergence of Issue Positions on the Palestinian Question   159

List of abbreviations

ACR	African Contemporary Record
AHC	Arab Higher Committee
ALF	Arab Liberation Front
ANM	Arab Nationalist Movement
ARR	Arab Report and Record
EC	The European Community
GAOR	Official Records of United Nations General Assembly
ICO	Islamic Conference Organization
OAU	Organization of African Unity
OAS	Organization of American States
PDFLP	Popular Democratic Front for the Liberation Front
PFLP	Popular Front for the Liberation Front
PLA	Palestine Liberation Army
PNC	Palestine National Council
SCOR	Official Records of United Nations Security Council
UN	United Nations
UNRWA	United Nations Relief Works Agency

Preface

After having worked with Kemal Kirisci while he was doing the research for this book, it is a pleasure and a compliment to be asked to write a preface for it. The overwhelming majority of the existing work on the international relations of the Middle East has an empirical, historical approach and either uses no theory or is, implicitly rather than explicitly, in the Realist theoretical school. The virtue of this book is that it focuses directly on the theoretical questions raised by the success of the Palestine Liberation Organization in gaining recognition and support for its cause. The Realist approach is abandoned in favour of the Global Politics approach.

Those working with the Global Politics approach have moved away from the idea that the study of international relations is simply concerned with the diplomatic and military relations between supposedly coherent units called states. More attention is given to non-governmental organizations, of which the PLO is one of the most dramatically prominent. There is also stress on the independent impact of interactions within intergovernmental organizations such as the United Nations, which has been involved in all aspects of the 'Question of Palestine'. More attention is given to economic, social and moral issues, as well as the diversity among what have been traditionally viewed as political issues. Most people in the past, and some people still today, see the conflicts in the Middle East as being centred on the different 'national interests' of Israel and the Arab 'states'. But it is economic and social questions and, above all, the moral questions of individual human rights and collective self-determination which have made an issue of Palestine. The Global Politics approach does not see international relations as a struggle for 'power' between 'states', but as contention over issues by a diverse range of political actors.[1]

As Kemal Kirisci compellingly argues in Chapter 2, the support the Palestinians have obtained for their claim to a right of self-determination cannot be explained adequately under the traditional Realist approach to international relations. Firstly, the creation and increase in status of the Palestine Liberation Organization violates the assumption that the relations between 'states' are fundamental to all important issues. Governments may in practice act on the assumption that only other governments have to be considered. An extreme example of this approach inspired the Camp David Agreements, but they could only be partially implemented because they failed to take into account the PLO and the impact of intergovernmental organizations such as the Islamic Conference, the Arab League, the Non-Aligned Movement and the United Nations. The result was that the Sinai withdrawal had to be laboriously renegotiated, President Sadat was assassinated and the framework for settling the future of the West Bank collapsed. Secondly, the increased isolation of the Israeli government violates the assumption that 'power', particularly military power, can determine outcomes. Israel has achieved overwhelming victory in each of the wars in 1948, 1956, 1967, 1973 and 1982 and the PLO has never presented a military threat of any significance, yet the Palestinian political challenge has grown successively stronger.

Once one is no longer assuming that 'states' are the only significant actors in world politics, it is apparent that the elements of the system are continually changing. An important theoretical question is 'how are new actors created?' The simple answer for the PLO is that it was established by the Arab League, but Kemal Kirisci goes on to explore the more fundamental question of how the PLO gained support among the Palestinians to become an effective organization. It was first necessary that certain changes occurred—modernization of young Palestinians, setbacks to the Nasserite ideas of Arab unity and an alternative example being provided by the Algerian nationalists' war against France—before the political environment became conducive to mobilization among the Palestinians. Then there had to be access channels from the PLO to its constituency. This access came both via direct contact, with the guerrilla groups and the other organizations within the Palestinian community which were invited to participate in the Palestine National Council, and indirectly via the attention generated by violence against Israel. Patterns of political thought were changed by the development of a Palestinian identity separate from the previous emphasis on pan-Arab nationalism and by placing the Palestinian cause in the general context of decolonization. With this access and changes in cognitive patterns the PLO was able to mobilize support.

A fundamental assumption of the Global Politics approach is that there is no difference between politics within countries and politics at the international level, whereas the Realists believe there is order within countries and anarchy in relations between countries. Thus Kemal Kirisci is able to see the growth of the PLO as being just like the rise of any other pressure group (with the exception that most pressure groups will not countenance the use of violence). For the Realists the PLO is a problem, as a truly transnational group with an ordered structure, which is not dependent upon being based in any one country and drawing support from Palestinians and other people living in many countries. But Kemal Kirisci denies the existence of a boundary between domestic and international politics in a more far-reaching way. His theoretical framework for considering the rise in support for the PLO among the Palestinians is also applied at the regional and global level. The concepts of a conducive environment, access routes and cognitive linkages as the requirements for the mobilization of support are also applied to the PLO gaining recognition and support for its cause from Arab governments, Third World regional groups, Eastern and Western European governments and at the United Nations.

Kemal Kirisci has not covered the more recent events, such as the divisions in the PLO and the break with King Hussein in February 1986 which seem to cast doubt upon the ability of the PLO to maintain its position. The strength of his theoretical framework is that it can be used to explain the decline, as well as the increase, in support. Changes in the environment—notably the handover from President Carter to President Reagan in the United States in 1981, the outbreak of the Iran–Iraq war and the spillover of the Lebanese civil war into the Sabra–Chatilla massacres—were detrimental rather than conducive to the Palestinian cause. Access routes to the United States government, which had been opening up, were closed off; cognitive stress was produced in the guerrilla movements, leading to challenges to Arafat's leadership; and both factors led to an increased use of violence to claim the world's attention. As there is no sign that loyalty to the PLO has diminished in the core group of the West Bank Palestinians, one can presume the mobilization process will recover from these setbacks.

This is an original and creative book. It should be of value both to those with an interest in Middle Eastern politics and to those developing the Global Politics theoretical approach to the study of international relations.

Peter Willetts
The City University
London

Note

1 The most important contributions to the Global Politics approach are:

Mansbach, R. W. and Vasquez, J. A. *In Search of Theory: A New Paradigm for Global Politics* (New York: Columbia University Press, 1981).

Keohane, R. O. and Nye, J. S. (eds) *Transnational Relations and World Politics* (Harvard University Press, Cambridge, Mass. 1971) and their more ambiguous *Power and Interdependence: World Politics in Transition* (Little, Brown and Co., Boston, 1977).

Rosenau, J. N. *The Study of Global Interdependence: Essays on the Transnationalisation of World Affairs* (Frances Pinter, London, 1980).

An attempt to develop the approach through theoretically conscious empirical studies has been made with the Global Politics Series of books:

Chetley, A. *The Politics of Baby Foods: Successful Challenges to an International Marketing Strategy* (Frances Pinter, London, 1986).

Suter, K. *An International Law of Guerrilla Warfare: The Global Politics of Law-making* (Frances Pinter, London, 1984).

Willetts, P. *The Non-Aligned in Havana: Documents of the Sixth Summit Conference and an Analysis of their Significance for the Global Political System* (Frances Pinter, London, 1981).

Willetts, P. *Pressure Groups in the Global System: The Transnational Relations of Issue-Orientated Non-Governmental Organizations* (Frances Pinter, London, 1982).

Acknowledgements

The research process can be a long and arduous one. However, it is never a lonely one, for, during the years of preparation, many people contribute in ways that not only make the task lighter but also enhance the final result. Many have helped and supported me during the past six years and to all of them I shall always be deeply grateful. Space precludes me from naming them all individually, but there are some to whom I must convey my special thanks. To Mrs R. Al-Fattal (Khalidi) and Dr. B. Hammad for the insight they have given me into the decision-making process of the United Nations, an insight I could never have gained solely from the records of the UN; to Pat Fraquhar, the librarian at the United Nations in London, in particular for patiently guiding me through the wealth of UN documentation in the initial stages of the research; to Rauf Obeid and Vedat Kirisci for the seminar they organized for me at the University of Texas, Dallas, during which the idea of constructing an index of support germinated; to the Institute of Jewish Affairs for allowing the generous and friendly use of their library; to the Council for the Advancement of Arab and British Understanding for the use of their library facilities; to the City University library, in particular to Sheila, for their help; to Doreen Schlesinger and the secretarial team for their help and support; finally, to Dr. Peter Willetts, for his generous support, advice and friendship, from which I have greatly benefitted.

1 Historical Background and the Research Problem

The origins of the Palestinian Question

Our purpose in this chapter is twofold. First, we shall give a brief account of some of the major historical developments that appear to constitute the origins and background of the Palestinian Question. Second, from this summary analysis we shall derive and introduce the research problem that this book intends to examine.

The historical background of the Palestinian Question will be studied with particular attention to politics at the international level. The turn of this century seems to form a natural starting point. It was then that the world saw the birth of Zionism and Zionist efforts to rally world support for a 'Jewish homeland'. The chapter will stress, particularly, these energetic efforts to mobilize international support towards the establishment of a 'Jewish homeland' and contrast it with the unsuccessful Arab counter efforts. The chapter will also note how Zionist goals were achieved within half a century while the Arabs and Palestinians found themselves in total disarray at the end of this period. It is in light of this background that the gradual re-emergence of the Palestinian Question in the late 1960s, from relative obscurity to the forefront of world politics, becomes puzzling. This puzzlement constitutes the basis of our research problem and our efforts to explain it.[1]

The origins of the Palestinian problem lie in the persecution of Jewish populations in modern times and a growing realization on the part of Jewish intellectuals, particularly from Eastern Europe, of the need to respond to it. In the late 1880s, this response to the so-called 'Jewish problem' began to transform itself into Jewish nationalism. Jewish nationalism, often referred to as Zionism, considered the solution to be the settlement of the Jewish people on a piece of land governed by themselves. This idea would appear to have been articulated in the first place by T. Herzl, in 1896. In his famous pamphlet *Der Judenstaat*, Herzl expressed this very view.[2]

Herzl's idea of a Jewish state together with the need to secure international support was taken up and endorsed by the First Zionist Congress in August 1897.[3] In an effort to bring about the creation of a Jewish state, Herzl set out to gain the support of various leaders such as Sultan Abdul Hamid, Kaiser Wilhelm II and Czar Nicholas.[4] The reluctance of these leaders to lend their support in any concrete manner turned Herzl towards the British. However, to his dismay early British offers of territory in East Africa were not well received by Zionist circles.[5] In July 1905, the Zionist movement refused to accept any offer outside Palestine.[6] The need to accommodate divisions[7] within the various politically active Jewish communities, as well as fears expressed about Arab rights in Palestine, led the Zionist Congress, in 1911, to replace their earlier goal i.e. that of a state by, 'a publicly recognized legally secured home in Palestine'.[8]

This reconsidered Zionist position was taken up by Chaim Weizmann with the British. As a result of both external and internal considerations, the British government became favourable to the idea of a Jewish homeland and this culminated in the Balfour Declaration.[9] This Declaration, issued on 2 November, 1917, was the first British public recognition and support of the Jewish claims for a homeland in Palestine. When the British took over responsibility for Palestine under a League of Nations Mandate, this recognition became an international commitment. The revised British draft Mandate approved by the Council of the League of Nations, in July 1922, stated that: 'The Mandatory shall be responsible for placing the country under such political, administrative and economic conditions as will secure the establishment of the Jewish national home . . .'[10]

The Zionists did not limit their efforts simply to receiving British support and ensuring the inclusion of the provisions for a 'Jewish homeland' in the draft Mandate. An international campaign directed towards the League of Nations was initiated during the period preceding the League Council's decision on the terms of the Mandate. The intensity of this campaign is evidenced in the roughly 350 telegrams sent by Jewish organizations from all around the world calling for the ratification of the Mandate with the Balfour Declaration.[11] These efforts far outweighed the modest Arab and Palestinian efforts against the Mandate[12] as well as the Vatican's objections to 'the privileged and preponderating position' given to the Jewish people in the Mandate.[13]

In accordance with the term of the Mandate Britain facilitated Jewish immigration into Palestine and the development of a Jewish community. However, as a result of mounting discontent among the Palestinian Arabs and the changing international climate, Britain began to revise her position. This was particularly evident between 1936–9.[14] The Royal Commission, which was set up in response to Palestinian Arab disturbances directed against British rule during the summer of 1936, recommended the abandonment of the Mandate and the division of Palestine into three parts; a Jewish state, an Arab state and a British mandatory zone including Jerusalem.[15] The negative Palestinian Arab reaction led to increased violence. Britain, after having suppressed this violence, was forced to abandon the Peel partition scheme and tried instead to reconcile all the parties involved through two conferences held in London. The failure of these efforts coupled with the changing strategic-military and political considerations brought about by the approaching war led the British government to declare that it had no intention of making Palestine a Jewish state.[16]

Britain's policy towards the 'Jewish homeland' had neither been stable nor continuous and did not always represent a unified stance. British commitments to Arab nationalism together with tensions between the British executive in Palestine and the Foreign Office in London complicated this policy and at times made it incoherent. Although Churchill's speech, in June 1922, reiterated the Government's commitment to the Mandate provisions and the 'Jewish homeland', by the late 1920s the Passfield White Paper, issued as a result of Arab disturbances, urged restrictions on Jewish immigration and land sales to Jews.[17] This new statement was bitterly denounced by the Zionists as a violation of the Mandate and, in 1931, the government had to respond to these pressures in the form of the Macdonald letter assuring Britain's commitment to the terms of the Mandate.[18]

This marked departure, however, from Britain's earlier statements precipitated two major changes in Zionist politics. First, the use of violence to achieve a Jewish state became increasingly central to the Zionist movement. Apart from a lull, brought about by an Axis military threat to the Middle East during the major part of the Second World War, this violence continued unabated until 1948. Second, the Zionists took this shift in Britain's policy towards Palestine to the Permanent Mandate Commission and succeeded in achieving a decision critical of the British government.[19] Equipped with the support of the Permanent Mandate Commission they sought the British government's reconsideration of the White Paper. Although Churchill sympathized with the Zionist demand the government was not prepared to change its position.[20] Hence, a second, important period of mobilization of support at the international level was initiated. These efforts were directed primarily towards the American government and American Jewry.[21]

The United States government had endorsed the British Mandate, in 1922, on the condition that Britain did nothing prejudicing the rights of non-Jewish communities in Palestine. As late as May 1943, President Roosevelt had assured Ibn-Saud that 'no decisions altering the basic situation of Palestine should be reached without full consultation with both Arabs and Jews'.[22] This situation changed very drastically, however, during the period preceding the establishment of Israel. Having succeeded in gaining the support of the American Jewry in May 1942, the World Zionist Organization, in the form of the Biltmore programme, embarked on an intense period of political lobbying in the United States.[23]

In 1944 these efforts culminated in the tabling of draft resolutions in the American Congress calling for unrestricted Jewish immigration and the establishment of a Jewish Commonwealth.[24] Although these resolutions were never adopted because of intense War Department objections that they would incite violence in Palestine and undermine American war efforts, it did not prevent the question of a Jewish Palestine from becoming an important item on the agendas of the Presidential election campaigns of both Democrats and Republicans.[25] Election campaigns and growing public awareness about the Holocaust were successfully used by Jewish politicans to strengthen links between the solution to the 'Jewish refugee problem' and the establishment of a Jewish Commonwealth in Palestine.[26]

For example, Zionist efforts to mobilize American support for their cause were reflected in a July 1945 petition, widely supported by Governors of the states and many members of Congress, calling on President Truman to give formal governmental support to a Jewish Palestine.[27] In the face of strong State Department and British opposition President Truman reluctantly resisted domestic pressure until just prior to the United Nations vote on the Partition Plan 'when he yielded to Jewish pressure and instructed the US delegation to assure the attainment of the two-thirds majority'.[28]

In contrast to Zionist political successes, particularly at the international level, the Palestinian Arabs were in disarray. Although the Arab uprising in Palestine between 1936 and 1939 played an important part in getting the British government to change its policy towards Palestine, it also precipitated such a fierce reaction that the backbone of the Palestinian Arab political structure was broken.[29] This left the Palestinian Arab community with two disadvantages. First, at the local level they lacked the political and administrative institutions that the Jewish community possessed.[30] Second, at the international level they lacked a well organized movement with access to major governments. They were, thus, unable to match Zionist success in gaining the support of the American government.[31] To make matters worse, while the Zionist managed to mobilize a government which was to play a very central role in the drawing up of the post-war order, some prominent, local Arab political leaders associated themselves with Nazi Germany in the hope of receiving Axis support to achieve independence.

The only politically favourable development for the Palestinian Arabs came at the regional level. The Arab states with the support of the British government met in Alexandria in September 1944 and, among others, adopted a resolution supporting the independence of Palestinian Arabs. In March 1945, this was followed by the inclusion of a Palestinian Annex to the Covenant of the newly founded Arab League. This provided for the possibilty of a Palestinian representative at the Arab League Council meetings.[32] It is possible that as a result of Arab League lobbying Zionist efforts to achieve representation at the United Nations Conference on International Organization in San Fransisco in April 1945 were thwarted.[33] However, this rather simple procedural success achieved by the Palestinian Arabs did not significantly change the course of events in the coming years.

The problem reaches the United Nations

In the aftermath of the Second World War the Zionists were in direct conflict with British authorities in Palestine. The Jewish population had increased from 83,790 in 1922 to 554,329 in 1945,[34] thus enabling the Zionists to make a formal bid for a Jewish state. In August 1946, in Paris, the Jewish Agency proposed a plan demanding a Jewish state in an available area of Palestine.[35] These developments, together with domestic pressures and military exhaustion caused by the Second World War, led the British government in February 1947 to place the Palestinian problem before the United Nations General Assembly.

Britain's decision precipitated intense political activity in both the Arab and Zionist camps. The Arab League, at the start of the Special Session of the General Assembly on Palestine in April 1947, tried to place: 'The termination of the mandate over Palestine and the declaration of its independence' as an additional agenda item.[36] The Zionists, for their part, requested the right to be heard by the Assembly and lobbied extensively in an attempt to link the problem of Jewish refugees in Europe to the Palestinian problem.[37]

Despite forceful Arab arguments, the General Committee of the Assembly rejected the Arab proposal for the inclusion of an additional item on the agenda of the Special Session.[38] Symbolically, the Zionists faired much better. The Jewish Agency was granted the right to address the Assembly, setting a precedent for non-governmental organizations to participate in the work of the Assembly.[39] Although this decision opened the way for the Palestinian Arabs to put their case to the Assembly too, this was achieved only after a dispute arising from an Arab procedural protest over the unequal treatment of the cases for representation was settled.[40] Probably the greatest achievement for the Zionists was the adoption of an amended American Draft Resolution authorizing the United Nations Special Commission on Palestine to conduct investigations anywhere it considered necessary.[41] The Special Session Resolution 106 (S-1), 15 May 1947, opened the way for United Nations Special Committee on Palestine (UNSCOP) visits to refugee camps in Europe and hence the potential to link the Jewish refugee problem to the future of Palestine.

The Partition Plan

The UNSCOP presented its report to the General Assembly at the end of August. The report declared the Mandate unworkable and presented two competing plans for Palestine's independence: a majority plan, 'Partition with Economic Union' and a minority plan, 'A federal state of Palestine'.[42] These two plans precipitated intense Arab and Zionist efforts to gain support for their respective positions before the final Assembly decision. As a result of effective Zionist lobbying invoking the Holocaust and the Jewish refugee problem in Europe, coupled with

American pressure on smaller states and the Soviet decision to support the Partition Plan, the General Assembly adopted Resolution 181 (II) on 29 November 1947. This recommended the establishment of a Jewish state and an Arab state with an economic union between them.

As Table 1.1 suggests the Partition Plan received practically the full support of all delegations belonging to the Western European, Eastern European and Latin American groups. One could argue that the 10 delegations that abstained lent implicit support to the resolution by allowing a two-thirds majority to hold. The Arabs, on the other hand, were joined by only six other countries, four of them with significant Muslim populations.

Table 1.1. Distribution of votes on the Partition Plan by regional groupings [43]

	Yes	Abstain	No
W. European	12	1	2
E. European	5	1	—
L. American	14	6	1
Africa	1	1	—
Asia	1	1	4
Arabs	—	—	6
Total	33	10	13*

* 10 Islamic

The establishment of Israel

The UN decision to endorse the establishment of a Jewish state brought the Zionists one important step closer to the realization of their goal. Two major obstacles, however, still remained—the withdrawal of Britain from Palestine and the opposition of the Arabs to the Partition Plan. The first obstacle did not constitute a serious problem. Although the British Government had not given its full support to the Partition Plan, this did not prevent it from announcing that it would terminate its responsibilities in Palestine on 14 May 1948. The second obstacle proved more challenging. The Zionists responded to the challenge by channelling their military capabilities against the Arabs.

The Arabs had made it clear that they would regard the Partition Resolution as illegal and that they would resist it by all means. They too, therefore, took the struggle to the military plain. First, Arab irregulars came to the support of the Palestinian Arabs during late 1947, followed by the regular Arab armies after the departure of Britain from Palestine. This military struggle did not, however, prevent the proclamation and the early consolidation of Israel.[44] When, in early 1949, armistices between the belligerents were finally signed, the Arabs had not only failed to stop the partition of Palestine but were now faced with a Jewish state that was 21 per cent larger than the UN Partition Plan had envisaged and more than half a million Palestinian Arabs had been displaced.[45]

The research problem

In just about 50 years the Zionist movement had resolved Herzl's 'Jewish Question' by establishing Israel. The ability of the Zionist movement to mobilize not only the Jewish people but a variety of actors in the international political system played a central role in the establishment of Israel. This is well demonstrated in the various Zionist groups skill in lobbying and pressure-group politics transcending state boundaries. They worked closely with the British government and mobilized various groups to their cause during the 1920s and most of the 1930s. They continued their alliance with Britain as long as it served their interests. Once the protection and assistance of Britain for Jewish immigration and the Jewish community in Palestine started to diminish they replaced Britain with the United States. Furthermore, the successful linking of the solution of the 'Jewish refugee problem' in Europe to the future of Palestine appears to have favourably influenced the attitudes of various actors towards a Jewish state. Finally, the strategic interests of the two emerging 'superpowers' were favourably disposed towards Israel.

On the Palestinian Arab side the picture was very different. During the Mandate, the Palestinian Arab community never had a political-administrative infrastructure as complex and elaborate as that of the Jewish community. British attempts to establish an Arab Agency similar to the Jewish Agency had not been well received.[46] This lack of internal organization may well have played an important part in the breakdown of the Palestinian Arab society in the aftermath of the 1948 war. Even though the Partition Plan recognized the political rights of the Palestinians to form an Arab state, with more than half of its population displaced they were far from establishing one. A tentative attempt to set up an 'All Palestine Government' in September 1948 received recognition from Egypt, Iraq, Lebanon and Syria but never achieved the status of a politically independent unit.[47] Of the areas remaining outside Israel, the Gaza strip remained under Egyptian military rule while the West Bank was annexed by Jordan despite tremendous Arab League opposition.

The situation at the international level was no better. The Palestinian Arabs as well as members of the Arab League lacked the degree of accessibility to the governments and domestic politics of important countries that the Zionists enjoyed. This lack of influence was particularly evident during the debates and decisions over Palestine. Most of the countries that did support the Arab position had done so as a result of Islamic solidarity.

As Israel gained admission to the UN in May 1949 the Palestinian Problem looked set to be relegated to the status of a 'refugee problem'. Although the 'right of refugees to return to their homes' was supported by a series of resolutions, including the resolution admitting Israel to the UN, the issue began to lose its political nature. This was particularly evident in the growing number of resolutions of a 'technical and humanitarian' nature pointing to the plight of refugees and noting the need to offer them technical and financial assistance.[48]

In this context, two developments at the UN appear to have played a central role in bringing about the eventual change in attitudes that redefined the nature of the Palestinian Question away from one of 'self-determination'. The first change came in the content of resolutions referring to the refugee problem. Until the fifth session of the Assembly resolutions concerning refugees had stressed speedy 'repatriation'. However, starting with Resolution 394 (V) on 14 December 1950, Assembly resolutions began to add to their recommendations 'resettlement' and 'rehabilitation'. These recommendations were supported by Israel and certain Western governments. They maintained that the solution to the refugee problem would not be achieved by repatriation but instead through their resettlement in neighbouring Arab states. The Arab governments saw these developments as an attempt to erase the problem of Palestine by removing the refugees from the area. At the UN these developments had their impact by further pushing the political rights of the Palestinian Arabs into obscurity and in some ways prepared the groundwork for the second change.

The second change came in the form of the exclusion of the 'Question of Palestine' from the Assembly's agenda. When the Secretary-General chose, in 1952, not to include this in the provisional agenda, the Arab delegations attempted to get the Assembly to discuss the political aspects of the Palestinian problem. During the debates at this session the changing attitude of the Assembly became even more conspicuous. A draft resolution by Western and Latin American countries argued that previous UN Resolutions on Palestine constituted an obstacle to direct negotiations for achieving peace.[49] Although this resolution, recommended by the *Ad Hoc* Political Committee, did not meet the Assembly President's two-third majority request for the plenary the damage was done. The Palestinian problem lost its independent existence as an item on the agenda and became instead an obscure issue pushed behind items concerning the refugees of the Near East.

In the meantime, Israel appeared to be dominating the international scene outside the UN as well. As Table 1.2 shows, Israel during the 1950s and 1960s expanded substantially her diplomatic relations with the outside world. Particularly significant were her growing diplomatic and economic ties with the newly emerging Third World:[50] Israel's preparedness to share her developmental and technical experience with the Third World made her sought after. These bilateral relations were supplemented by a sympathetic attitude towards problems of great concern to the Third World such as decolonization and apartheid. Israeli success in maintaining such a high level of prestige did play its role in perpetuating the status quo during the 1950s and early 1960s.

From the early 1960s, however, the beginnings of a change, particularly at the local level became evident: an awakening Palestinian national movement could be seen. Until then, the Palestinian national movement, mostly as a result of the traumatic experience of the 1940s, had remained disunited. Both Al-Fatah and the

Table 1.2. Expansion of Israeli diplomatic representation abroad between 1951 and 1966[51]

	1951		1967	
	Embassy	Diplomatic representation	Embassy	Diplomatic representation
W. European	1	16	15	7
E. European	1	4	2	5
L. American	—	6	16	5
Africa	—	—	25	4
Asia	—	1	6	4
Total	2	21(23)	64	25(89)

early PLO sponsored by the Arab League played an important role in providing the Palestinian national movement with an institutional-organizational background. During the late 1960s and 1970s the movement, centred around the PLO, gained increasing support and legitimacy among both the Palestinians and the Arabs.

This mobilization of support for the PLO and the Palestinian cause was not confined to the local and regional levels. A similar process at the international level also became evident. At the United Nations General Assembly an increasing number of delegations drew attention to the political nature of the Palestinian Question. As early as 1969 resolutions referring, in one form or the other, to the political rights of the Palestinians began to receive majority votes. Third World governmental forums such as the Islamic Conference Organization (ICO), the Non-Aligned Movement and the Organization of African Unity (OAU) began to recognize and lend their support to the Palestinian cause. This was followed by a recognition of the PLO's authority and legitimacy to represent the Palestinian cause. This growing base of support took concrete form at the 29th General Assembly session which, in 1974, re-introduced the 'Palestine Question' as a separate item on its agenda, adopted resolutions in support of the Palestinians' right to self-determination and granted the PLO observer status.

Within less than a decade of the reappearance of the indigenous Palestinian national movement a significant section of the international political system had changed its attitude towards the Palestinian problem. The problem was no longer simply perceived as a 'refugee problem' but one of 'self-determination'. The Palestinian dimension of the Arab–Israeli conflict that had previously been ignored was restored.

The globalization of the support and the recognition of the Palestinian cause enabled the PLO to consolidate its role as the representative of the Palestinian people, both locally and internationally. Hence, the image of the PLO held by a great majority of the governments and other actors, as 'terrorists' changed. Furthermore, many governments did not simply recognize the PLO as the representative of the Palestinians but also granted this organization varying degrees of diplomatic status. This newly acquired legitimacy and status as an actor in world politics gave the PLO the opportunity to work directly with a large number of governments and international organizations and enabled it to increase the salience of the Palestinian issue to a variety of actors.

It is to the factors and processes that led various actors in the international political system to change their perceptions about the nature and salience of the Palestinian problem that this book is devoted.

Notes

1 For an examination of the role of 'puzzlements' in the study of world politics, see Rosenau, J. 'Puzzlements in Foreign Policy' in *The Scientific Study of Foreign Policy* (Revised and Enlarged Edition, Frances Pinter, London, 1980).

2 Herzl, T. 'From "The Jewish State"' in Laquer, W. (ed.) *The Israel-Arab Reader: A documentary history of the Middle East Conflict* (Penguin Books, London, 1970).

3 Vital, D. *The Origins of Zionism* (Clarendon Press, Oxford, 1975) p. 368.

4 Vital, D. *Zionism, The Formative Years* (Clarendon Press, Oxford 1982).

5 For Herzl's acceptance of the first British offer see Vital (1982: 129–62).

6 Ovendale, R. *The Origins of the Arab–Israeli Wars* (Longman, London, 1984) p. 7.

7 For divisions within the Zionist movement over the offer see Vital (1982: 267–341).

8 For the debate whether to use the label 'state' or 'home' see Vital (1975: 366–8).

9 For a general analysis of British interest in the Balfour Declaration see Tibawi, A. L. *British Interest in Palestine* (Oxford University Press, London, 1961).

10 *League of Nations Official Journal* 3rd Year no.8 (August 1922) pp. 823–5.

11 See League of Nations Docs. C.104.M.57.1921; C.226.M.165.1921.VI[A]; C.252(e.) 1922 VI[A].

12 See League of Nations Documents; C.21/4/44.VIA, C.67.M.32.1921.VIA; C.372 M.260 1921(VIA).

13 League of Nations Document C.332.1922 VI[A].

14 For a detailed account of changing British attitudes towards Palestine during this period see Bethell, N. *The Palestine Triangle. The Struggle between the British, the Jews and the Arabs 1935–1948* (Andre Deutsch, London, 1979).

15 *Palestine Royal Commission Report* (Cmd. 5479, 1937) pp. 380–6.

16 White Paper May 1939, Cmd.6019, in Laquer (1970: 88, 101).

17 For W. Churchill's statement in 1922, see Laquer, 1970: 67–72. White Paper, October 1930, Cmd. 3692. This Paper is also known as the Passfield Paper after the then Colonial Secretary, Lord Passfield.

18 In Laquer (1970: 73–9).

19 Sachar, H. M. *Europe Leaves the Middle East, 1936–1954* (Cox and Wyman, London, 1972) pp. 105–6.

20 Davis, J. *The Evasive Peace: A Study of the Zionist–Arab Problem* (John Murray, London, 1968) p. 31.

21 For a detailed study of these efforts see Lilienthal, A. M. *The Zionist Connection II* (North American, N.J., 1982) ch. II; Bain, K. R. *The March to Zion: United States's Policy and the Founding of Israel* (Texas University Press, College Station, 1969); Glick, E. *The Triangular Connection: America, Israel and American Jews* (George Allen and Unwin, London, 1982).

22 Ovendale (1984: 75).

23 For detailed analysis of Zionist influences on American domestic politics during this period see Ovendale (1984: 75–87); Lilienthal, 1982: Chs. 6 and 7; Glick (1982).

24 Lilienthal (1982: 37–9); Glick (1982: 65).

25 Glick (1982: 70).

26 Sachar (1972: 452–7).

27 Glick (1982: 78).

28 Quoted in Glick (1982: 88).

29 See Bethell, 1979; Kayyali, N. *Palestine: A Modern History* (Croom Helm, London, 1978); for a detailed study of the destruction of the Palestinian Arab political infrastructure by British authorities.

30 For information on both communities' political administrative institutions see *Great Britain and Palestine 1915–1945* (Royal Institute of International Affairs, London, 1946); Quandt, W., Jabber, F. and Lesch, A. *The Politics of Palestinian Nationalism* (University of California Press, London, 1973) pp. 5–42. For a detailed and informative study of the political and administrative structure of the Jewish community in Palestine see Horowitz, D. and Lissak, M. *Origins of the Israeli Polity* (University of Chicago Press, Chicago, 1978).

31 For an analysis of the degree of meticulous organization achieved by the Zionist Movement in mobilizing grass-root support to bring pressure on the United States' legislature and government see Stevens, R. *American Zionism and U.S. Foreign Policy (1942–1947)* (Pageant, New York, 1962).

32 Macdonald, R. *The League of Arab State: A Study in the Dynamics of Regional Organization* (Princeton University Press, Princeton, 1965) p. 87.

33 Ovendale (1984: 82).

34 Survey of Palestine (Government Publication, Jerusalem, 1946: 142)

35 For various plans including the one approved by the WZO see Khalidi, W. *From Heaven to Conquest* (Institute for Palestine Studies, Beirut, 1971), pp. LXVI and LXXX.

36 *General Assembly Official Records*, First Special Session, Docs. A/287 to A/291.

37 *GAOR*, First Committee, 54th, p. 252.

38 *GAOR*, General Committee, vol. II, 29th to 31st meetings.
39 *GAOR*, ibid., 32nd meeting, pp. 92–3.
40 *GAOR*, First Committee, vol. III, 46th to 50th meetings.
41 *GAOR*, First Committee, vol. III, 56th meeting.
42 The majority plan, 'Partition with Economic Union' and the minority plan, 'A Federal state of Palestine' (*GAOR*, Second Session, Document A/364).
43 The table was prepared from the distribution of votes for Resolution 181 (II). See appendix II for membership of regional groupings.
44 For an account of the fighting between the Jewish and Arabs forces see Davis, 1968; Dupuy, T. N. *Elusive Victory: The Arab Israeli Wars* (Harper and Row, London, 1978).
45 Israel at the end of armed hostilities covered an area of 20,724 km. sq. instead of 14,260 km. sq. as envisaged by the Partition Plan. There were 726,000 Palestinian refugees as a result of the war (United Nations Conciliation Commission for Palestine, Document A/AC.25/6, p. 19).
46 For an account of British attempts to set up an Arab Agency and Arab refusal to co-operate see Kayyali, (1978: 130); Davis (1970: 27–8); Abu-Lughod, *Transformation of Palestine* (Northwestern University Press, Evanston, 1971) p. 223. The Jewish Agency was set up in accordance with Article 4 of the Mandate.
47 Sachar (1972: 562); Quandt (1973: 41–2).
48 Resolution 212 (III), 19 November 1948; Resolution 302 (IV), 8 December 1949; Resolution 393 (V), 2 December 1950.
49 A/AC.61/L.23/Rev.3, 8 December 1952 also in *The Yearbook of the United Nations*, 1952, p. 250.
50 For extensive literature on Israel's relations with Africa see Decalo, S. 'Israel and Africa: A Selected Bibliography' *The Journal of Modern African Studies* vol. 5 (1967), no. 3 and Jansen, G. J. *Zionism, Israel and Asian Nationalism* (The Institute of Palestine Studies, Beirut,1971).
51 Source: *The Jewish Yearbook*, 1951: pp. 301–5 and 1967: 160–3). 'Diplomatic representation' covers other forms of diplomatic relations, such as legations, consulates and non-resident Ambassadors.

2 Paradigms and the Research Problem

Paradigms in the study of international relations

Waltz warns us of the futility of starting research without 'at least a sketchy theory'[1]. Any theory, however sketchy, has to rely on some existing body of knowledge. Then, the first task, in formulating this theoretical framework to understand and explain the problem, is to identify a suitable body of knowledge.

According to Kuhn in *The Structure of Scientific Revolutions*, paradigms provide the ground knowledge needed to further our understanding of the world around us. Scholars turn to a paradigm for guidance in selecting a research question and constructing a suitable theoretical framework to study a problem. Here, it would be appropriate to think of a paradigm as supplying a scientific community with a set of conceptual and instrumental tools[2] which help the members of that community identify and resolve certain puzzles. These would then become evident in the work they produce.[3]

There are roughly four different ways of picturing world politics. By far the dominant paradigm in international relations' literature is the Realist or the Power-politics paradigm which has inspired most of the work produced in international relations since World War II. Morgenthau, a major and early contributor, typically sees the international political system as anarchic thus inducing states, which are assumed to be unified, to struggle for power in an attempt to satisfy their 'national interest'.[4]

The second most evident paradigm in international relations' literature originated in the United States around the early 1970s.[5] The Global Politics paradigm has questioned and empirically demonstrated the weakness of focusing on states as the only important actors in world politics.[6] Instead, this paradigm claims that world politics is better depicted by a multitude of issues imperfectly linked receiving the attention of a variety of actors and parts of the state.

The remaining two paradigms in the study of world politics are less comprehensive in their scope. For the World Society paradigm, the unit of analysis is the 'system' rather than the state and it envisages a world depicted by means of a 'cobweb' model.[7] This model pictures a world that is characterized by a great variety of exchanges ranging from economic to cultural. It is around these exchanges that the boundaries of the 'relevant' system are drawn and its structure investigated. This paradigm limits its area of concern to the cooperative aspects of international relations and to the need to study structures that would increase cooperation in the international system.[8]

Finally, there is the Marxist paradigm. Here, the level of analysis is lowered from state-to-state interactions to the relations between socio-economic classes. The state is given a secondary importance being a superstructure which simply reflects the prevailing economic relationships in a society.

The fact that so many paradigms exist in the study of world politics may not necessarily be the sign for a protracted and fractionalized revolution in the Kuhnian sense but rather that the discipline is a multi-paradigm one.[9] In such a discipline a scholar's decision to work with one of these paradigms will be political and cultural. The following section will examine closely the first two dominant paradigms in relation to our research problem.

The research problem and the Global Politics paradigm

If 'Understanding ... means nothing more than having whatever ideas and concepts are needed to recognize that a great many different phenomena are part of a coherent whole,'[10] then it seems that it is the ideas, concepts and theories associated with the Global Politics paradigm which provide the most fertile ground upon which to construct our theoretical framework in order to explain our research problem. This would appear to be the case for the following theoretical and methodological reasons.

Theoretical considerations

We have already mentioned that puzzlements, which form the basis of a research problem, are paradigm bound. An analysis of two of the three central Realist assumptions should demonstrate that it would be difficult to place our research problem within the context of that paradigm.[11]

The first central assumption in Realist thinking is that the state is the only important actor in world politics and, rather like billiard-balls, these states are assumed to be hard-shelled and monolithic. This assumption produces a number of problems with regard to our research problem. The first part of the assumption manages to squeeze out the potential role of non-state actors, such as the PLO, so central to our problem. It also ignores the independent impact that the United Nations, the Non-Aligned and other political groupings can have on world politics, particularly in attitude formation.[12] This particular aspect of Realist thinking also makes it difficult to account for the processes that lead to the creation of new actors as well as the impact such new actors may have on the structures and processes particular to a system.

To treat the state as a monolithic unit makes the conceptualization of various aspects of our research problem rather difficult if not impossible. It seems that the only way to alleviate this problem is to disaggregate the state into its constituent parts. It is by drawing a distinction between the state, the nation and the government that we can begin to account for the characteristics of some of the more important actors and the nature of the interactions between them. Otherwise if one worked within the Realist paradigm it would not be possible to talk about the Palestinian nation scattered across a number of states. Equally, it would not be possible to account for the effects that certain political processes at the international level can have on different parts of either a government or a country.[13]

In terms of this research, within the Realist framework, it would be very difficult to account for the emergence of an independent modern Palestinian identity as a transnational represented by a non-state actor, the PLO. Although the PLO was created by the decisions of the Arab governments it nevertheless was a response to growing signs of Palestinian nationalism and within a few years came under the influence of Palestinian guerrilla groups. This development played an important role in the mobilization of the Palestinian community but also precipitated a process that changed the perceptions and attitudes of the outside world towards the definition and nature of the Middle Eastern Conflict. The definition of the problem was revised in such a way that the conflict was no longer perceived as one between Arab states and Israel but, instead, one between the Palestinian people and Israel.

The second assumption central to the Realist paradigm is that world politics can be pictured as a struggle for power. This struggle constitutes a single issue in a single system and entails a ceaseless and repetitive competition for a single stake of power. In such a system the major source of power becomes military strength and the ultimate use of force remains as an omnipresent concern in the minds of statesmen.

Naturally, with such a conflictful image of world politics, where strategic-security considerations dominate the political agenda, it is not surprising that this assumption fails 'to accommodate the multiplicity of values and stakes for which actors both cooperate and compete',[14] making it difficult to consider situations where new issues can make their way on to the global agenda. The Realist paradigm, by introducing a distinction between high and low politics, treats any issue that fall outside national security, power and strategic considerations as being of minor significance in world politics.

There are two problems, one general and the other particular to our research, associated with this distinction between high and low politics. The first and general problem is a methodological one caused by the subjective nature of how to decide or define what constitutes 'high politics' at any one time or location. An issue that may be treated as low politics by one government may well be of crucial importance to other governments: 'For many governments of the Third World, such as Jamaica, Ghana or Sri Lanka, there may be no significant problems of 'national security' affecting their international relations. ... For them the high politics of international relations lies in trade and aid issues'.[15] Similarly, an issue that was not regarded as high politics may, at a later point in time, come to be redefined as of paramount significance. Wallace points out how the question of Britain's relations with the EC was redefined from being a matter of foreign trade policy to a matter of high policy.[16]

The second problem caused by this distinction is more central to the substance of our research problem. The question of how the political and human rights of the Palestinian people became a major issue on the political agendas of numerous governments, international organizations and other actors could not be raised within the Realist paradigm, as self-determination and human rights would typically constitute issues of low policy.

The Global Politics paradigm is not plagued with these problems. Instead, the Global Politics paradigm, with the help of a concept like 'issue-salience', resolves the methodological problems associated with the concept of high and low politics. Hence, it by-passes the difficulties associated with defining, once and for all, what constitutes high policy for a government by enabling the researcher to determine, empirically, how much salience a government or an actor attaches to an issue.[17] Furthermore, this paradigm allows scholars to view a world politics from a point which is not simply dominated by one issue and accompanying conflict behaviour. Instead, it demonstrates that world politics is not uni-dimensional and that behaviour varies according to the issues.[18]

These characteristics of the Global Politics paradigm make it possible to postulate that the Palestinian issue could have varying degrees of salience for a variety of actors in world politics and that these actors will interact with each other in ways that will produce different kinds of behaviour. While the Palestinian issue for leading Arab-African governments, Israel, the PLO, the Special Committee on Palestine will be of high salience this may not be the case for the

Bahamas' government, the Friends of the Earth or Commonwealth Summits. During the decision making process for allocating the various values and stakes associated with the Palestinian issue, some of these actors may cooperate and form coalitions, other opposed actors may follow policies to undermine this cooperation. This process will be influenced by the changing salience of the Palestinian issue for different actors.

Hence, according to the Global Politics paradigm world politics is not seen as a uni-dimensional activity in which the players are states struggling for power in an anarchic international environment. Instead, an alternative view is argued which defines politics as contention over issues. The participants are actors ranging from governments to non-governmental organizations. Each actor may attach different degrees of salience to a wide range of issues that may be on the world political agenda. The process of interaction between these actors is not characterized by a competition to acquire as much power as possible. Instead actors are seen to interact with each other in order to influence the composition of the agenda as well as mobilize support for positions they hold on issues of salience to them.

The third and final assumption in Realist thinking is centred around separating domestic politics from international politics. This assumption is based on the idea that states are simply responding to stimuli from the international environment and that a state's response will not be influenced by domestic factors, just as the internal politics of a particular state will not be affected by events outside a country. Rosenau was one of the first scholars to question this assumption and point out the linkages existing between issues transcending the boundary between the two systems. Rosenau noted that:

Almost every day incidents are reported that defy the principles of sovereignty. Politics everywhere, it would seem, are related to politics everywhere else.... One can no more comprehend the internal political processes of a Latin American country without accounting for the United States presence (or, more accurately, the multiple United States presences) than one can explain the dynamics of political life in Pakistan or India without reference to the Kashmir issue.[19]

Inherent in this assumption is the Realist proposition that while domestic politics is characterized by order and stability, international politics is dominated by anarchy and lack of order.[20] This, Realists say, is caused by the absence of a centralized authority in the international system capable of performing the role of governments in maintaining law and order. Increasingly, however, incidents around the world show that not all national political systems are stable and peaceful. The frequency of political unrest and civil wars in an ever growing number of countries makes it rather diffcult to separate the two political systems on the basis of order versus anarchy.[21] Furthermore, just as not all parts of the international system are unstable and violent, the international system does have a growing number of collaborative arrangements and legal regimes governing the allocation of values in an ordered and peaceful manner.

Such an assumption also affects our research problem in a number of ways, although not in as direct a manner as the previous two because the study's general focus is at the international level. Without undermining the last assumption of the separability of international politics, it would be difficult to understand the dynamism behind some of the central processes characterizing the mobilization of support for the Palestinian cause. The interplay between international and national politics makes itself, to a certain degree, evident in understanding the attitude of certain governments towards the Palestinian cause. It would be difficult

to understand American attitudes towards the Palestinian issue without considering how the Jewish lobby influences American foreign policy toward the Middle
East.

Similarly, to understand the attitude of Non-Aligned governments particularly
towards the Palestinian issue one would need to explore the cognitive linkages that
are formed in the minds of the policy makers between the situation in southern
Africa and the Palestinian Question. In the other direction, although not of immediate interest to this study, the internal politics of the PLO as well as of the
Palestinian community appear to have been influenced by political developments
at the international level. This is particularly evident in the changing nature and
the intensity of violence employed by the PLO in response to growing international recognition for the organization and the cause it represents.

So far, we have tried to elaborate the theoretical reasons for choosing the
Global Politics paradigm to tackle the core of our research problem. Now, we shall
examine certain methodological considerations that are better satisfied by the
Global Politics paradigm.

Methodological considerations

The Global Politics paradigm has, in a number of ways, better potential for guidance in methodological matters because the paradigm's behaviouralist origins
encourage the researcher to use knowledge from other disciplines and its theoretical (substantive) composition encourages the use of data that would otherwise be
considered unimportant.

Behaviouralism, from its very inception in the early 1950s, found fertile ground
in the study of politics and at a later stage triggered a lively debate between the followers of the historical approach (the traditionalists) and the scientific approach
(the behaviouralists) in international relations.[22] For a long time, however, the
academic community confused the attempts to employ scientific methods in
theory building and testing in international relations with a substantive-
theoretical breakthrough.[23] Instead, this led to a situation whereby there were
Realist scholars such as Morgenthau and Bull following a traditionalist methodology on the one hand and scholars such as Singer and Kaplan employing a
scientific methodology on the other hand. But they all worked from a similar
theoretical basis about the nature of the international system.[24]

It should, however, be noted that behaviouralism, 'means more than scientific
techniques, more than rigour'.[25] It is not simply an attempt to employ sophisti-
cated and rigorous techniques for accumulating, interpreting and analysing data.
According to Easton one of the crucial tenets making up behaviouralism is:
'Integration: Because the social sciences deal with with the whole human situation,
political research can ignore the findings of other disciplines only at the peril of
weaking the validity and undermining the generality of its own results'.[26]

It is particularly this aspect of behaviouralism that, at large, distinguishes the
Global Politics paradigm. Scholars working within this paradigm have not only
tried to employ scientific techniques and methods in their research but they have
also made a conscious effort to use knowledge from different disciplines. The evidence for this is particularly great in two areas that are strongly related to our
research problem. These two areas among others from which the Global Politics
paradigm has borrowed ideas and concepts are psychology (social-psychology)
and comparative government.

Jonsson notes that in recent years there has been growing interest in using cognitive approaches in International Relations in an attempt to develop theories that

can account for the gap between the 'perceptual world' of actors and the actual world.[27] Willetts too has tried to think of interdependence in terms of psychological resources where the cognitive realm of actors become important.[28] He argues that Festinger's 'cognitive consistency theory'[29] is applicable to the study of global politics. This stems from the idea that not only individuals but also collectivities can have a drive to make their perceptions of the world harmonious.

Comparative government is another area from which the Global Politics literature has drawn ideas. This has been facilitated by a preparedness not to treat domestic and international political systems as completely different. Breaking down the distinction between domestic and international politics has enabled the possibility of assuming that certain political processes within and between countries have similarities. When Mansbach and Vasquez[30] define politics as the raising and resolving of issues by actors they stress the central importance of understanding the agenda process. But they also note that this problem of 'how issues are born, how and why they are placed on the agenda, how they are removed, and how and why the content of agendas change overtime' has not been investigated in the Global Politics literature.[31] Lack of a body of knowledge on this phenomenon has led them to borrow ideas particularly from the work of Cobb and Elder who have studied the dynamism of agenda building in American politics.[32]

The hard-core Realists have always been reluctant to make use of knowledge from other disciplines, a result of defining international relations strictly as the study of state-to-state interactions, setting it apart from all other disciplines. Some Realists have openly questioned the usefulness of explaining international relations in terms of psychological or social-psychological factors. Their position is that such 'reductionist theories' cannot provide better explanation than theories of international politics.[33]

Although this view may be broadly supported it should, however, be noted that Realists are not that monolithic a group. Among them there have been, particularly in the area of decision making, scholars who have employed ideas from psychology and socio-psychology particularly.[34] Their readiness to make use of knowledge from other disciplines may well have been a result of the influence of the then emerging behaviouralism. It seems that behaviouralism not only led this sub-set of Realist scholars to be more rigorous and precise in their work but also to integrate ideas from other disciplines. These scholars appear to have been brought to the fringes of the Realist paradigm by discovering the weaknesses of some of the Realist assumptions and concepts.[35] However, by and large the Realist paradigm has not encouraged its followers to employ concepts and ideas from other areas of study.

The final methodological issue we wish to consider concerns the kind of data we intend to use for operationalizing the more central concepts in our theoretical framework. Vasquez shows how data-making in international relations has been wholly dominated by the Realist paradigm. He does note, however, that some of this data has been used by people within the Marxist and, in a very limited way, the Global Politics paradigms.[36] The major sources of data we intend to use will be from voting at the UN and diplomatic exchanges. Both are highly government-centred but most data used in international relations are in one way or another based on or derived from government collected data. This will probably remain so until the Global Politics paradigm develops and accumulates its own data. The data on UN voting has not been put into significant use by the Realist paradigm because the theoretical considerations within the Realist paradigm do not attribute any significance to UN voting. However, as Alker[37] has shown and Vasquez[38] has argued there does not appear to be any reason why this data-set could not be used for testing non-Realist hypotheses.

As the above theoretical and methodological considerations show, our research problem falls firmly within the realm of the Global Politics paradigm. In the following section we intend to develop an analytical framework which will draw not only from an already existing body of theory in the Global Politics paradigm but also from mobilization theory.

Notes

1 Waltz, K. *Theory of International Politics* (Addison-Wesley, Reading, Mass., 1979) p. 17.

2 Kuhn, T. *The Structure of Scientific Revolutions* (University of Chicago Press, Chicago, 1970) p. 37. For a discussion of paradigms as conceptual frameworks see Nicholson, M. *The Scientific Analysis of Social Behaviour* (Frances Pinter, London, 1983) pp. 10–16.

3 Kuhn (1970: 43).

4 Morgenthau, H. *Politics Amongst Nations* (5th ed., Alfred A. Knopf, New York, 1973) p. 5.

5 Possibly as a reflection of the rather unsettled nature of this paradigm there is not yet one common agreed label for it. Here we shall employ Willetts label 'global politics paradigm' first used in 'The United Nations and the Transformation of the Inter-State System' in Buzan, B. and Jones, B. (eds.) *Change and The Study of International Relations: The Evaded Dimension* (Frances Pinter, London, 1981) pp. 104–8.

6 Vasquez, J. *The Power of Power Politics; An Empirical Evaluation of the Scientific Study of International Relations* (Rutgers University Press, New Brunswick, 1981) and Mansbach, R., Ferguson, I. and Lampert, D. *The Web of Politics: Non State Actors in the Global System* (Prentice Hall International, London, 1976).

7 Burton, J. *International Relations: A General Theory* (Cambridge University Press, Cambridge, 1965) and Burton, J. *World Society* (Cambridge University Press, Cambridge, 1972).

8 The normative aspect of this paradigm is particularly evident in the work of the founding father of Functionalism; see Mitrany, D. *The Functional Theory of Politics* (Martin Robertson and Company, London 1975).

9 Lakatos, I. and Musgrave, A. *Criticism and the Growth of Knowledge* (Cambridge University Press, Cambridge, 1970) p. 74.

10 Quoted in Waltz (1971: 9).

11 These three assumptions project a picture of high coherence among those scholars working within the Realist paradigm. However, to say that all Realist scholars strictly work within these assumptions may be rather too simplistic. The reality is more complex and diversified. There are a great number of scholars who have regarded themselves, or have been regarded, as Realists. These have produced analyses that have gone beyond at least two of the above assumptions. With the emergence of behaviouralism in the late 1950s there has been some work, for example, Snyder, G., Bruck, H. and Sapin, B. *Foreign Policy Decision Making* (Free Press, New York, 1962) and Allison, G. *Essence of Decision* (Little Brown, London, 1971) that has relaxed the assumptions that the state is monolithic and that there is no interaction between domestic and international politics. However, it appears that even the above scholars have remained confined to a state centric and unidimensional view of world politics. Furthermore, there also appears to be some degree of agreement in the international relations literature that these three assumptions are quite central to the Realist paradigm. See for example, Mansbach, R. and Vasquez, J. *In Search of Theory; A New Paradigm for Global Politics* (Colombia University Press, New York, 1981) p. 9.

12 For detailed discussions of the role of non-state actors in world politics see Mansbach, R. *et al.* (1976); Willetts, P. *Pressure Groups in the Global System: The Transnational Relations of Issue-Orientated Non-Governmental Organizations* (Frances Pinter, London, 1982). For non-Realist studies of the role of the United Nations in world politics see

Kaufmann, J. *United Nations Decision Making* (Sitjhoff and Noordhoff, Alphen aan den Rijn, 1980); Jacobsen, K. *The General Assembly of the United Nations* (Universitat-forlaget, Oslo, 1978) and for an illuminating comparision of the Realist and Global Politics views of the United Nations see Willetts in Buzan and Jones (eds) (1981).

13 For example if one did not disaggregate the United States' government into its various bureaucratic constituent parts, including the separate analysis of the American delega-tion to the United Nations, it would not be possible to understand and explain the frequent disagreements and conflicting behaviour between the State Department and the American United Nations' delegation, each being exposed to and participating in rather different political processes. For a discussion of this particular phenomenon see Finger, M. *Your Man at the United Nations: People, Politics and Bureaucracy in the Making of Foreign Policy* (New York University Press, New York, 1980), particularly ch. 2 and Beichman, A. *The 'Other' State Department, The United States Mission to the United Nations: Its Role in the Making of Foreign Policy* (Basic Books, New York, 1967).

14 Mansbach and Vasquez (1981: 11).

15 Willetts (ed.) (1982: 22).

16 Wallace, W. *The Foreign Policy Process in Britain* (George Allen and Unwin, London, 1977) p. 13.

17 Willetts, P. (ed.) (1982: 22); see also Willetts's introduction to Chetley, A. *The Politics of Baby Foods* (Frances Pinter, London, 1986).

18 O'Leary, M. 'The Role of Issue', in Rosenau, J. (ed.) *In Search of Global Patterns* (The Free Press, New York, 1976) pp. 318-26.

19 Rosenau, J. 'Introduction: Political Science in a Shrinking World', in Rosenau (ed.) *Linkage Politics* (Free Press, New York, 1969) p. 2.

20 Alger, C. 'Comparision of Intranational and International Politics', *American Political Science Review*, vol. 57 (June 1963), No.2, pp. 40-69.

21 Riggs, F. 'International Relations as a Prismatic System', in Knorr and Verba (eds) *The International Systems: Theoretical Essays* (Princeton University Press, Princeton, 1961).

22 For a detailed study of this debate see Knorr, K. and Rosenau, J. (eds) *Contending Approaches to International Politics* (Princeton University Press, Princeton, 1970).

23 For a telling account of how, after all, scientific work in international relations remained deeply embedded in the Realist paradigm see Vasquez, J. 'Colouring It Morgenthau: New Evidence for an Old Thesis', *British Journal of International Studies* vol. 5 (1979), pp. 210-18.

24 For a collection of articles reflecting the traditionalist versus behaviouralist debate see Knorr, K. and Rosenau, J. (eds) *Contending Approaches to International Politics* (Princeton University Press, Princeton, 1969).

25 Easton, D. 'The Current Meaning of "Behavioralism"', in Charlesworth, J. *Contemporary Political Analysis* (The Free Press, New York, 1967) p. 30.

26 Ibid., p. 17.

27 Jonsson, C. (ed.) *Cognitive Dynamics and International Politics* (Frances Pinter, London, 1982).

28 Willetts, P. 'The Politics of Global Issues: Cognitive Actor Dependence and Issue Linkage', in Jones, B. and Willetts, P. *Interdependence on Trial* (Frances Pinter, London, 1984).

29 Festinger, L. *A Theory of Cognitive Dissonance* (Row Peterson, Evanston, 1957).

30 Mansbach and Vasquez (1981: 68).

31 Ibid., pp. xx and 87.

32 Cobb and Elder, *Participation in American Politics: The Dynamics of Agenda Building* (Allyn and Bacon, Boston, 1971).

33 Waltz (1979: 19).

34 Snyder, R., Bruck, H. and Sapin, B. (eds) (1962); Boulding, K. *The Image* (University of Michigan Press, Ann Arbor, 1956).

35 Snyder and *et al.* (eds) by introducing the 'internal' and 'external' settings undermined the Realist assumptions of the separation of domestic and international politics. Lind-blom, C. 'The Science of muddling through' *Public Administration Review* vol. 29

(1959), no.2; Lindblom, C. *The Policy Making Process* (Prentice Hall, New Jersey, 1968); Simon, H. *Models of Man: Social and Rational* (Wiley, New York, 1957) demonstrate the questionable nature of the assumption of 'rationality'. Allison (1971) not only demonstrated the weakness of the idea of assuming the state to be a rational actor but also the weakness of seeing the government as unified and monolithic.

36 Vasquez (1981: 154).
37 Alker, H. and Russett, B. *World Politics in the General Assembly* (Yale University Press, New Haven, 1967).
38 Vasquez (1981: 189–99).

3 The Analytical Framework

In the preceding chapter we tried to show how the Global Politics paradigm appears to be the most suitable one within which our research problem can be approached. This chapter offers an analytical/conceptual framework that will guide the examination of how the Palestinian Question became an important item on the global agenda. Mansbach and Vasquez in their book *In Search of Theory* have made a conscious effort to take their work beyond a criticism of the Realist paradigm and introduce an integrated theory that they hope will 'serve as a guide to research'.[1] The parts that apply to our research problem will be critically examined. Suitable elements from this theoretical framework will then be supplemented with concepts derived from mobilization theory to complete our analytical framework.

Agenda politics

Inspired by Cobb and Elder,[2] Cobb *et al.*,[3] and Easton,[4] Mansbach and Vasquez define global politics as the raising of and the authoritative resolution of issues. They stress the importance of developing a theory of agenda politics that takes into account the decentralized nature of world politics.[5] This theory, they suggest, should aim to explain 'how individual actors inject issues of concern to them into [an] agenda-building process and what happens to issues once they have been added'.[6] They identify the factors that play an important role in the agenda setting process as (i) the nature and variety of access routes and (ii) the salience of an issue to key actors.[7]

The analytical framework developed for this study relies heavily on Mansbach and Vasquez's theoretical work on agenda politics. This does not mean that the theory can be employed as it stands because there are certain general problems as well as problems particular to our research. These problems appear to arise from their definition of 'global agenda', 'high status actor' and 'critical issues', and the relationship between the three.

Mansbach and Vasquez offer a number of access routes that actors might follow in an effort to push an issue on to the global agenda[8] which are 'defined as those issues and associated proposals that attract serious attention from either a large number of actors or from those capable of resolving the claims'.[9] The most important access routes are those that lead to the particular agendas of 'high status actors', who will be equipped with the resources to put the issue on the global agenda. This they believe, occurs because a high status actor on its own or together with others can resolve issues in an authoritative manner and confer legitimacy to dispositions in the system.[10]

Besides direct access to the agendas of 'high status actors' Mansbach and Vasquez discuss two other access routes that may play an important role. These routes can also be seen as 'transmission belts' carrying a new issue from many actors to the agendas of 'high status actors'. These routes can be grouped into two.

International organizations that allow less-powerful member states to:

raise issues of importance to them (economic development, racism and colonialism), but of lesser importance to the mighty, in the General Assembly and other UN organs. The effects of ensuing rhetoric and resolutions upon the agendas of high status actors is far slower than direct access but can be cumulative if the existence of opportunities or the presence of threat to them is made clear.[11]

Similarly, certain liberation movements and functional non-govermental organizations also have the opportunity to influence the agenda of 'high status actors' through informal access to various parts of the UN and its specialized agencies. International organizations provide a forum within which new issues may be raised, but the process may not always be successful.

Familiarity and experience of participation in 'agenda politics', within a certain 'institutional framework' following the established rules and norms that govern it can help in mobilizing the attention of a 'high status actor'. Mansbach and Vasquez note that the skills and experience needed to participate effectively in agenda politics would not be unlike those associated with successful lobbyists in a domestic context.[12] The behaviour of the PLO since the mid-1970s at various General Assembly and Security Council sessions as well as in the diplomatic world is a typical example of an actor that has acquired the skill to promote its cause by working within the system.

A different access route is the use of violence and various forms of disruption. This strategy is employed by actors that have no direct or indirect access to 'high status actors'. The aim of such a strategy is to create publicity, as well as 'convince elites that ignoring the dissatisfied will be more costly than dealing with the issue they raise'.[13] This is most dramatically depicted in the use of international terrorism by certain Palestinian groups to change the world image of Palestinians as harmless refugees. The function of such a strategy was well summarized by G.Habbash when he noted that:

when we hijack a plane it has more effect than if we killed a hundred Israelis in battle. For decades world public opinion has been neither for nor against the Palestinians. It simply ignored us. At least the world is talking about us now.[14]

The first problem arises with the definition of high status actor. For Mansbach and Vasquez 'status refers to the relative worth or respect one is accorded by others',[15] yet their application of status to actors in global politics seems uncomfortably close to the Realist conception of major-powerful actors. This is evident when they note that the criteria for an actor's status is: 'related to overall political capability, which in turn seems to be based on such objective criteria as size (both demographic and territorial, including resource base), economic capability and military strength'.[16]

Such a definition, although difficult to reconcile with an attempt to develop a non-Realist paradigm, is not surprising considering that it draws heavily on the works of established Realist scholars.[17] This definition depends on an established set of indicators that enables a researcher to calculate the score that a country receives on each attribute and hence its rank in the overall hierarchy(ies). However, the problem arises when these attributes have to be aggregated into one single indicator. Is each attribute, i.e. military strength and size, to be given an equal weight? If not, what standards or guidelines can be employed to determine which resource yields more power?

This problem is further complicated if one wants to use a Realist-inspired definition of 'high status actor' for explaining world political behaviour that is not simply uni-dimensional but characterized by: 'multiple issues that are not arranged in a clear or consistent hierarchy. This absence of hierarchy among issues means, among other things, that military security does not consistently dominate the agenda'.[18] Does one use the same index for military security issues as for non-strategic issues?

Moreover, it is also central to the Global Politics paradigm that states are not the only important actors in world politics. According to Mansbach and Vasquez: 'Actors in global politics may consist of any individual or group that is able to contend for the disposition of a political stake.'[19] However, the above criteria that appear to equate 'high status actors' with 'major-powerful actors' would automatically preclude a large number of non-state actors who may command influence upon decisions on certain issues. As Willetts notes: 'IBFAN has had more impact than the US government upon the baby foods issue and the IPPF has had more impact upon the global politics of birth control than the Soviet government.'[20]

It seems it might be useful to take the definition of a 'high status actor' beyond one relying predominantly on Realist elements. A definition ought also to take into account resources other than economic and military ones. This would make it possible to consider actors that may have high levels of perceived legitimacy with low levels of 'economic capability and military strength'.[21]

However, an attempt to operationalize a 'high status actor' relying on legitimacy would be fraught with methodological and theoretical difficulties too. It would be difficult to find reliable practical indicators of legitimacy.

The manner in which a 'high status actor' is operationalized becomes important because Mansbach and Vasquez postulate a strong relationship between the prevailing status hierarchy in the system and the ranking of issues on the global agenda.[22] If the definition of a 'high status actor' remains synonymous to 'powerful actors' it would become difficult to account for a host of issues that find their way on to the global agenda in spite of such actors' opposition.[23] Historically, the Palestinian question as defined by the Palestinians is one such issue that was pressed on to the global agenda without any 'high status actor' taking the initiative and in spite of the opposition of at least one of the major 'high status actors'.

The United States' government for a long time remained reluctant to consider the Palestinian problem as an independent issue concerning the political rights of the Palestinians. Instead they maintained that the Palestinian problem was a refugee-humanitarian stake within the Arab–Israeli Conflict. But this, for any person familiar with world politics, has not kept the Palestinian Question from becoming an important item on the global agenda. Conversely, the United States in spite of being a 'high status actor' was able neither to impose its version of the Central American issue on the global agenda nor to allocate the stakes attached to the issue in a conclusive manner. It has also found its actions towards the imposition of a particular outcome on the problem increasingly difficult to support legally let alone to legitimize.

Although Mansbach and Vasquez offer highly useful theoretical insights to understand agenda building, their concept of a 'high status actor' poses some operational difficulties. We have also noted that the possibility of centering 'high status actor' around the concept of legitimacy has its own operational and practical difficulties. It would, however, be very unsatisfactory to drop completely the role that a 'high status actor' can play in helping issues reach the global agenda.

One practical way around this problem might be to relate the idea of 'high status actor' to highly active actors. There are three advantages of this formulation.

The first comes from the fact that such an 'active actor' can be a government as well as a non-governmental actor or an international organization. The second advantage is that it would be relatively easy to construct an index for ranking actors based on the number of acts they initiate or number of interactions they become involved in either on an issue or a selection of issues. In this way, the International Red Cross, for example, would, in the area of humanitarian law and the rights of prisoners of war, appear high up on the 'activity scale'. The other advantage would come in the resolution of the problem of determining what is a 'critical issue'. To appreciate this we will first have to look at the relationship between issue salience and the global agenda.

Issue salience, critical issues and 'high status actor' versus 'active actor'

Mansbach and Vasquez cite issue salience to key actors as the most crucial factor in determining whether an issue reaches the global agenda.[24] Without going into the details of factors that make an issue salient to an actor we shall examine the difficulties inherent in some of the more central elements in the scheme depicting the relationship between an issue and the global political agenda.

The difficulty in the scheme arises in the way in which a 'high status actor', conceived as a 'powerful actor', plays an important role in determining whether the salience of an issue is high enough to warrant it being on the global agenda.

Issues that have the highest salience in the political system can be referred to as *critical issues*. These are issues that are initially at the apex of the individual agendas of all or most of the high-status actors and that, in time tend to draw in or redefine other issues. Such issues dominate and shape the agendas of lesser actors and, consequently, the global agenda.'[25]

Such a formulation of a 'critical issue' has two limitations. First, it would be difficult to explain how a powerful actor or a group of actors, following the OPEC oil price increases in 1973, could not get the issue of the control of oil price increases and the question of energy supplies on the global agenda. Instead these attempts were frustrated by the convening, with an overwhelming support, of the Sixth Special Session of the General Assembly dedicated to questions of development. 'Lesser actors', 'had succeeded in carrying the discussions about the international economic system into to international arena' at the expense of economic issues of greater concern to 'major' actors.[26]

The second limitation is a result of the idea that a 'critical issue' draws in and redefines other issues. In certain cases, this is also rather difficult to substantiate. The re-emergence of the Cold War, in recent years, has become a central concern to the American administration. This development has, surely enough, led the United States government to redefine the predicaments of Central America from being problems associated with development and human rights to the realm of 'communist subversion' and global strategic considerations. However, the evidence so far does not suggest that many domestic and international actors have followed suit, in spite of considerable pressure to do so from the United States.

The idea of using 'active actors' rather than 'powerful-important actors' to determine a 'critical issue' is also supported by other scholars. Willetts notes that 'an issue can only be critical, with reference to salience, by dominating the attention of the actors which are most active on the issue'.[27] This should allow the global agenda to be made up of issues that would reflect the number of actors and the level of activity with each issue. In this way, there would not be a global agenda dominated by issues solely reflecting the concerns of only those actors occupying the higher echelons of a 'hierarchy' that heavily relies on indicators of economic and military strength.

The advantage of using levels of political activity and number of actors interacting on an issue is that they can be treated as rough measures of the degree of 'salience' being attached to an issue. It is those issues that generate high levels of activity and involve large numbers of actors which might best be seen as 'critical issues'. One such issue is the problem of apartheid in southern Africa. It is an issue that has been on the global agenda since the early 1950s. It has involved political activity eminating from a great variety of actors such as the ANC, the South African goverment, the International Olympic Committee, MNCs and the UN to name but a few.

So far, we have tried to show how the idea of an 'active actor' facilitates the process of determining the access routes available for an issue, the salience of that issue to various actors and the relationship between that issue and the global agenda. Before proceeding to introduce the analytical framework it should be pointed out that this formulation too suffers from two weaknesses for which we shall suggest local solutions.

The first weakness stems from the fact that an 'active actor' may not always be capable of allocating values authoritatively even though they may have an impact on the politics of raising an issue for the global agenda. It should become apparent, in the following section, that this does not constitute a major stumbling block with respect to our analytical framework since we are only interested in examining how an issue became an important item on the global agenda. It could be said that the Palestinian question is still going through the decision making stage of the issue cycle.[28] In other words the contention over the authoritative allocation of the values attached to the stakes that make up the issue still continues.

The second problem applies to both formulations. Neither Mansbach and Vasquez's formulation nor the above one provides any concrete description of what the global agenda actually is. Mansbach and Vasquez are aware of this problem and they see it as a result of the absence of explicit and authoritative decision makers who would have a 'formal agenda' the way Cobb and Elder visualize it.[29] The decentralized nature of world politics leads Mansbach and Vasquez to suggest that 'a global agenda can be seen as consisting of those elements of individual actors' agendas that overlap'[30] a kind of juxtapositioning of numerous agendas.

If each actor's agenda could be pictured as a matrix then the global agenda at any one point in time would be the aggregation of the individual matrices. The aggregation, however, would not be a simple straightforward additive process. Instead, it would take into account the amount of activity surrounding each issue. Only issues characterized with high activity would make it to the global agenda. Such an approach would pave the way to determining the agenda empirically. However, the collection and processing of the relevant data would call for resources beyond the ones available for this research. As a result of the determination to give the idea of a global agenda an empirical referent it was decided that the United Nations General Assembly and Security Council agendas would be used to represent the global agenda.

There are three advantages to using the United Nations' agendas supplemented by the agendas of regional organizations. First, these agendas in world politics are the nearest one can get to Cobb *et al.*'s 'formal agenda' used in studying agenda building in internal politics.[31] These agendas can be thought of as formal indicators of the kinds of issues that concern the majority of member states as well as various non-state actors. One word of caution: some states, with diminishing success, do keep certain issues off these agendas. Also, localized and short-duration issues tend not to reach United Nations' agendas. Thus, it would be futile to postulate one-to-one correspondence between United Nations agendas and the global agenda. However, such localized issues will appear on the agendas of regional organizations. The second advantage is that these agendas are easily obtainable and reliable. Moreover, the politics that is associated with the drawing-up of these agendas is extremely well documented. This documentation tends to provide interesting and often concrete insights into precisely the process that we are so interested in investigating. The third advantage is that from these records it is relatively straightforward to identify 'active actors' by examining participation in drafting resolutions, tabling resolutions, speech making and voting. The only disadvantage is that one can not easily gain information on either lobbying or activity that takes place without entering the official records.

The model

Our research problem will be examined within the context of agenda politics. In the preceding sections we tried to show and improve upon some of the weaknesses inherent in Mansbach and Vasquez's original formulation. This led us to conceive an agenda politics that is closer to Cobb *et al.*'s idea of 'agenda building'.[32] The stress in the study of this process is on the raising of an issue to public attention followed by entry to the formal agenda. Hence, the process to be explained is 'how individual actors inject issues of concern to them into this agenda-building process . . .'.[33]

Another way of stating this is to examine how actors appeal to other actors in the system in order to mobilize support to bring the issue on to the agenda. Such efforts can take two forms: either convincing other actors of the importance of one particular issue or getting them to change their perception of an issue in a way that will allow the accomodation of the interests of the actor promoting the new issue. In other words the issue could also be redefined along lines that would increase its potential of reaching the agenda. It should be noted that such a redefinition would be the product of an interactive process. The ultimate form that the issue takes may not always correspond to the original definition proposed by the initiators.[34]

As mentioned earlier, if one could assume that the global agenda is the aggregation of individual actor agendas, what we would like to examine is the process by which a global agenda which originally had the Palestinian Question as a stake subsumed within the Arab–Israeli Conflict evolved into an agenda with the Palestinian Question as an issue in its own right. How did world political actors change their perception of the Palestinian Question from being a refugee problem to being one of 'self-determination'? Needless to say this change did not occur overnight. Instead, it was a result of mobilizing support, over a certain period, in favour of redefining the Palestinian Question in such a way that it could reach the global agenda as a separate item.

The Model and its components

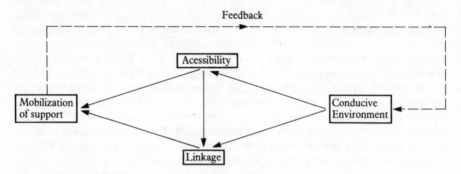

Figure 3.1. Model for studying the mobilization of support for the Palestinian cause

As figure 3.1 shows, the model is made up of four parts:

(i) The dependent variable conceived as the mobilization of support for putting an issue on the agenda;

(ii) Three sets of explanatory variables
  Conducive Environment
  Accessibility
  Linkage;

(iii) The relationship between the variables;

(iv) A feedback mechanism to capture the dynamic nature of the process.

The conducive environment variable is probably the most difficult one to operationalize in this model. It is a concept widely used in literature on mobilization theory. The nearest corresponding concept in international relations literature is the idea of a favourable 'international climate' or 'international environment'. Although widely used in both literatures this concept has not been defined in any clear and systematic way. Instead it often defines itself in the context of an analysis.

Obershall has this concept in mind when he points to 'the impact of outside events and the outside support that played an important role in loosening social control and providing the resources for black mobilization'.[35] He specifically notes:

...increased federal executive and judiciary activity in the 1940s [in the form of] ...the integration of the armed forces, the desegregation of Washington, D.C., fair employment in the federal government and, increasingly, in local and state governments outside the South, the requirement of nondiscrimnatory employment and hiring in private industry holding government contracts[36]

creating a favourable environment for efforts to expand the enforcement of black civil rights in the southern states.

Walsh, too, stresses the importance of the role of structural conduciveness in the mobilization of farm workers in the United Farm Workers' Union in the late 1960s in California. He notes that during the late 1960s:

The environment could hardly have been more favorable for the launching of the new mobilization effort. The Berkerley Free Speech Movement, the radicalization of the Black Civil Rights Movement, the first phase of the anti-Vietnam agitation, the post-Vatican II Catholic church era and signs of a revitalized labor movement in the search for new membership were all factors facilitating the growth of the UFW.'[37]

Both examples demonstrate the role that a favourable environment plays in the mobilization process. But this should not be taken to mean that it actually initiates a mobilization process. Instead, it simply either facilitates it or provides a basis for it. It might be referred to as a structural variable. In agenda politics the importance of such a variable would stem from the fact that it can point to the availability and nature of access routes to an agenda.[38] It would then depend on the actors who are trying to raise an issue to the agenda to decide what strategy to employ to convert a conducive environment into an active resource.

In the context of our research the conduciveness of the international environment can be determined by looking at the organizational set-up prevailing in the system. The composition and behaviour of various international and regional organizations can indicate whether they form a favourable basis for accommodating and promoting various issues. For example, the question of Algerian independence was prevented from reaching the UN agenda because the composition and concerns of the UN membership were still favourable for accepting the French argument that the issue was a matter of domestic jurisdiction, outside the organization's competence.

As mentioned earlier, a favourable environment is not sufficient to raise an issue on to an agenda. A conducive environment when conceptualized as organizational structures (in the form of formal international organizations such as the UN, the OAU) and informal political-diplomatic groupings provides 'would be mobilizors' with existing political and communication channels. It is the accessibility of this organizational set-up, to actors seeking support for their position, that constitutes the next variable.

Earlier in the chapter it was noted that the ability to exploit access routes to the global agenda is a crucial factor in raising an issue to the agenda. Three types of access routes were mentioned: (i) access to the agendas of 'active actors'; (ii) the ability to use an institutional framework effectively; (iii) the use of violence to force an item on the agenda for consideration.

Accessibility as a variable in this model will be defined, albeit not in a measurable form, in respect to the above types of access routes. The first two can be seen as complementary routes, while the third is mostly employed in situations where the initiators of an issue cannot have an impact on agenda politics in any other way. In that sense there is an inverse relationship between the use of the first two access routes and the last. Hence, it should be reasonable to assume that an actor will tend to resort less and less to violence as it perceives that it is gaining access to more established forms of participation in agenda politics.

The importance of having access to a network of existing channels of communication and political action within a favourable organizational fabric for mobilizing support is also stressed by mobilization literature. Oberschall notes that: 'The presence of numerous organizations ensures a preestablished communications network, resources already partially mobilized, the presence of individuals with leadership skills, and a tradition of participation among members of the collectivity.'[39]

Similar arguments are also put forward by Wilson, Orum and Cameron.[40] It should be noted that the 'existing organizational network of communication and influence' to which the mobilization literature refers, encompasses only the negatively privileged groups, 'challengers' in Tilly's terminology,[41] and not those dominated by the establishment. However, it relates to our model as far as it stresses the function of political networks and the accessibility of such networks. Naturally it is possible to think of groups which equate with 'challengers' in world politics. Some such groups are composed of governments and/or NGOs. Two such examples are the Casablanca Group in the early 1960s and the Arab Rejectionist Front after Camp David.

We have already noted the United Nations General Assembly and Security Council agendas together with the agendas of regional organizations form our global agenda. We shall, therefore, place our agenda politics around a quasi-centralized, institutional structure, whose major participants will be international organizations, delegations from member states and NGOs. The basis of this de-centralized international structure will be conceived of as the aggregation of the rules of procedures of various multi-lateral bodies, practices and decisions emerging from the interaction of the major participants and the body of law and customs as interpreted and implemented by these participants.

We shall conceive of two types of access to this institutional structure:

(i) A *direct,* formal access by which we mean the capacity for the initiators, in this case the PLO or an indigenous Palestinian representative organization, to raise the Palestinian issue with a government, a group of governments or an international organization. The PLO will be considered to have direct access to actors which recognize the PLO as a public body and as the representatives of the Palestinian people. The important effect of this recognition must be that the PLO acquires the right to raise the Palestinian cause through direct inter-action with the actors involved. In the case of an international organization this can take the form of granting observer status. On the other hand, with a state it can take the form of diplomatic recognition that entitles the PLO to have access to the government.

(ii) *Indirect* access occurs when an attempt is made to raise an issue with the assis-tance of sponsors who have direct access to the process of drawing up the global agenda.[42] These sponsors can be linked to Cobb *et al.*'s 'identification group'. They define such a group as:

> those people who feel strong ties to the originators of an issue and who see their own interest as tied to that of those raising the issue. The members of the identification group are not only the first to be mobilized but are also most likely to support the posi-tion of the originators.[43]

It is the role these identification groups play as an access route in raising the Palestinian issue on to the global agenda that will be examined.

Even though these access routes are postulated to play an important role in bringing the Palestinian issue to the attention of world political actors, there is one more explanatory factor that needs to be considered.

The third and final explanatory variable is the role that establishing linkages between separate issues plays in mobilizing support for an issue. Cobb *et al.* suggest that linking an issue with already existing ones and with 'emotionally laden symbols' is an important step towards 'expanding an issue to new groups'.[44] However, before introducing this variable it should be pointed out that the litera-ture appears to use the linkage concept in roughly three contexts.

The linkage concept is most commonly used in the context of bargaining and negotiations. Prutt notes that parties in a bargaining process may introduce a variety of linkages.[45] In this context the most familiar bargaining linkage in world politics is probably the one so often associated with H. Kissinger, reflected in Kissinger's belief that 'every problem between the United States and the Soviet Union was linked with every other problem; and progress on one would effect progress on all'.[46]

The concept of linkages is also encountered in efforts to break away from traditional Realist thinking in the study of world politics. According to Rosenau the need to develop the concept 'arose of a conviction that students of comparative and international politics were needlessly and harmfully ignoring each other's work'.[47] This conviction culminated in the articulation of the concept of 'linkage politics' that was defined as 'any recurrent sequence of behaviour that originates in one system and is reacted to in another'.[48] The purpose of the concept was to capture the way in which behaviour originating in one political system could influence behaviour in another one. Previously, the assumption that domestic and international politics were distinct and separate would not have allowed the possibility of taking into account the role of the 'Jewish lobby' or the 'Polish lobby' on American foreign policy behaviour towards the Middle East and the Soviet Union.

It is also possible to talk about linkage or rather cognitive linkage in the context of the perceptual world of political actors. Cognitive linkages acquire particular relevance in the context of the drive individuals feel towards perceptual consistency that induces them to bring harmony to the great diversity inherent in the empirical world surrounding them. These pressures to achieve cognitive consistency lead individuals to establish growing similarities between certain events or objects, enabling an individual to force these set of events or objects into pre-existing 'pigeon-holes'. Willetts argues that homologous processes can be assumed to operate at the group level: 'For the group, there is the need to hold the allegiance of its constituent members, to establish a coherent identity and to project a credible view of the world as the basis for appealing for wider support to achieve the group's goal'[49]

This opens the way for applying ideas from cognitive consistency theory to actors other than individuals.

Actors perceive the world around them on the basis of the belief-value system they have. It is with the help of this world image — *Weltanschauung*, ideology, meaning of values and expectations about the world and life in general[50] — that actors come to evaluate behaviour and interactions around them. Often central to this process are abstract values that can be represented as political symbols. It is via such abstract values that cognitive linkages (between an issue and a symbol) are formed and more support for an issue is generated. For example, symbols of equality have been stressed both in the growth of support for civil rights and women's liberation movements.[51] Similar processes are applicable to world politics too:

The Non-Aligned Movement has long been committed to the hyper-issue of non-use of force in international relations. This provided linkage between Yugoslav and Indian promotion of détente, African fears of South African military might and Arab hostility to Israeli expansionism.[52]

Actors by appealing to such symbols or abstract values will try to recruit more support for their position and try to raise the salience of the issue to other actors.

There is one other kind of cognitive linkage that could occur along the above lines. It happens when actors come to evaluate a new issue by establishing similarities between this new issue and an already recognized salient issue. A striking example of this process is 'when a "Declaration on the Struggle for National Liberation" defined Palestine as a colonial question "exactly the same as the situation in Southern Africa" '.[53] The consequence of such a 'cognitive linkage' is that it will tend to increase the legitimacy of the new issue and link it with an existing pool of support. Simultaneously, being linked to what is regarded as a 'high salience' issue will increase the salience of the new issue to the related actors and hence its potential of being supported for inclusion on the global agenda.

It has already been stated that the raising of an issue to an agenda will be conceived as a result of the mobilization of support and constitutes our depedent variable. The initiators' efforts to raise the issue of concern can be seen in the light of the interaction between the above three factors and a feedback mechanism. The relationship between these factors is of a positive nature, that is an increase in the 'conduciveness of the environment' is expected to effect the level of mobilization through the other two factors. As the model depicts, a 'conducive environment' on its own will not generate support. Instead initiators have to bring up the issue via 'accessibility'. 'Conducive environment' as a variable also affects the 'linkage' variable by making the actors more amenable to perceiving parallels between issues. 'Accessibility', in turn, interacts with the level of mobilized support directly by the initiators or sponsors raising the issue to the attention of would-be supporters or indirectly via the 'linkage' variable by arguing or promoting the similarity between their issue and already existing ones.

This interaction among the explanatory variables will lead to a level of mobilization that will be fed into the next round through a feedback mechanism. This attribute of a mobilization process appears to have first been suggested by Snyder and Kelly in their 'fully interrelated Model' for the analysis of mobilization processes.[54] The rationale behind this dynamic process is because:

> Social movements and their organizations do not necessarily, or even typically, move through a (nearly) linear sequence in which there is a single outcome (or at most a few). Instead, they are entities that persist through time, during which they continually mobilize resources, apply them in various forms of collective action or 'tactics' and experience the consequences of those strategies in a fully interrelated process that also affects subsequent 'rounds' of mobilization, action, and outcome.[55]

In other words, the purpose of the feedback mechanism is to capture the dynamic nature of the process whereby an issue is raised to the agenda as a consequence of 'rounds' of mobilization. Each 'positive' round leads (i) to the environment becoming more conducive (on top of what may be caused by exogenous factors); (ii) to an increase in accessiblity (e.g. one quantum increase would be the result of a shift from an indirect to a direct formal access route); (iii) to linkages growing stronger and culminating in realignments.

The increase in the level of mobilization at each round will be measured by a 'support' index constructed from data on UN General Assembly voting. Ideally, it would be preferable to think of rounds as a continuous process. However, the model and the accompanying analysis is based on discrete time frames, corresponding roughly to a UN General Assembly session. The construction of the index and the methodological and theoretical problems associated with this exercise are discussed in Appendix I. One major weakness of this index and hence the model is that the analysis is based on data about governmental behaviour. In consequence it takes the governmental position as given and representing a state's attitude on the matter, whereas the state is not a monolithic unit and particularly in the West there will be intra-state actors with conflicting attitudes towards lending support for raising the issue to the agenda. Where possible, such occurences will be pointed out. Elsewhere for all its disadvantages, we shall assume that the position of the government corresponds, roughly, to the aggregation of positions held by all actors within the society together with the government.[56]

Limitations of the model

The limitation of such a model is that although the conceptualization of it, in the sense of identfying the various variables and the relationships between these variables, is reasonably straightforward, to state and test the model in a formal way, in the 'hard science' sense of the word, was problematic. This was because the data concerning 'conducive environment' and 'accessiblity' is difficult to represent in a numeric form. This naturally excluded the possibility of using quantitative methods to examine the impact that these two variables have on the dependent variable, as well as their interaction with the feedback process. However, it was possible to operationalize and construct indices for the other two variables, making it possible to test the relationship between the 'linkage' variable and the dependent variable, the level of mobilized support. The discrepancy between these two sets of variables prevented us from offering a fully integrated formal model expressed in mathematical terms. As a consequence it became impractical to account for the variance in the dependent variable that could have be attributed to each independent variable and the feedback mechanism. It was equally not possible to account for the covariance resulting from the interaction between the independent variables that the model depicts.

These difficulties in many ways are not much different from the ones inherent in the study of social behaviour. The complexity of social behaviour coupled with the frequent lack of appropriate, reliable data and formal theories from which testable propositions can be derived, continue to leave a lot to be desired. Within the context of these broader limitations the aim of the model was to represent an analytical framework whose theoretical background, central assumptions, concepts and relationships were stated as clearly and as conspicuously as possible. Where possible some of the propositions emerging from the model were statistically tested. The relationships between the parts of the model that were not amenable to quantitative analysis and the empirical world were established by, hopefully, what still is a reproducable, qualitative analysis. The index associated with the dependent variable made it possible to observe the change in the level of support from one level to the other, hence opening the way for the model to account, albeit in an informal way, for the impact a previous level of mobilization had on the mobilization process leading to the next level.

Notes

1 Mansbach, R. and Vasquez, J. *In Search of Theory* (Colombia University Press, New York, 1981).

2 Cobb, R. and Elder, C. *Participation in American Politics; The Dynamics of Agenda Building* (Allyn and Bacon, Boston, 1972).

3 Cobb, R., Ross, J. and Ross, M. 'Agenda Building as a Comparative Political Process', *American Political Science Review*, vol.70 (1976), no. 1, pp. 126–38.

4 Easton, D. *A Framework for Political Analysis* (Prentice Hall, Englewood Cliffs, 1965).
5 Mansbach and Vasquez (1981: 87–8).
6 Ibid., p. 94.
7 Ibid., pp. 94–109.
8 Ibid., pp. 96–102.
9 Ibid., p. 94.
10 Ibid., p. 96.
11 Ibid., p. 99–100.
12 Ibid., p. 97.
13 Ibid., p. 101. The role of violence in raising the salience of the Palestinian problem is noted in Mansbach and Vasquez (1981) as well as in Mansbach, R., Ferguson, M. and Lampert, D. (eds) *The Web of Politics* (Prentice Hall, Englewood Cliffs, 1976) pp. 104–35.
14 Hirst, D. *The Gun and the Olive Branch* (Faber and Faber, London, 1977) p. 195.
15 Mansbach and Vasquez (1981: 58).
16 Ibid., p. 152.
17 See note at the bottom of ibid., p. 152.
18 Keohane, R. and Nye, J. *Power and Interdependence* (Little Brown and Company, Boston, 1977) p. 25.
19 Mansbach and Vasquez (1981: 68).
20 Willetts, P. in Jones, B. and Willetts, P. *Interdependence on Trial* (Frances Pinter, London, 1984) p. 97.
21 The role of resources other than economic and military ones can be particularly important if world politics is not seen as dominated by solely one single issue, the struggle for power. In this way one can talk of actors that have issue specific resources. Amnesty International and the Anti-Apatheid Movement are two such actors. On the issue of human rights and apartheid these two actors can rely on resources such as accurate information, high prestige and legitimacy. These resources will play a central role in their efforts to mobilize support for their cause and influence the behaviour of actors including 'economically and militarily strong' ones. For an analysis of a range of resources that enable NGOs to influence world politics see Willetts, P. 'The Impact of Promotional Groups on Global Politics', in Willetts (ed.) (1982).
22 Mansbach and Vasquez (1981: 114, 116) and Vasquez, J. and Mansbach, R. 'The issue cycle: conceptualizing long-term global political change', *International Organizations* vol. 37 (1983), no. 2, p. 264.
23 Mansbach and Vasquez note the tendency of such 'high status actors' to be 'prone to suppressing or ignoring issues that threaten to "rock the boat"' (1981: 97).
24 Mansbach and Vasquez (1981: 102).
25 p. 110.
26 Sauvant, K. *Changing Priorities on the International Agenda* (Pergamon Press, New York, 1981) p. 68 and see also Willetts, P. *The Non-Aligned in Havana* (Frances Pinter, London, 1981) pp. 29-30.
27 Willetts (1984: 97).
28 For a discussion of the issue cycle see Mansbach and Vasquez (1981: 113–24) and Vasquez and Mansbach (1983: 113–24).
29 Vasquez and Mansbach (1983: 260) and Cobb *et al.* (1976: 126–39).
30 Vasquez and Mansbach (1983: 260).
31 Cobb *et al.* distinguish between two kinds of agendas. A 'public agenda consists of issues which have achieved a high level of public interest and visibilty; the formal agenda is the list of items which decision makers have formally accepted for serious consideration' (1976: 126). In their article they do not make the meaning of 'serious consideration' adequately clear. Mansbach and Vasquez seem to interpret it as authoritative allocation of stakes over an issue (1981: 93).
32 Cobb *et al.* (1976: 126).
33 Mansbach and Vasquez (1981: 94).
34 Cobb *et al.* (1976: 127).

35 Oberschall, A. *Social Conflict and Social Movements* (Prentice Hall, Englewood Cliffs, 1973) p. 125.
36 Ibid., p. 215.
37 Walsh, E. 'Mobilization Theory vis-à-vis a Mobilization process: The Case of The United Farmers Workers Movement', in Kriesberg, L. (ed.) *Research in Social Movements, Conflicts and Change Vol. 1* (JAI Press, Greenwich, Conn., 1978) p. 165.
38 Mansbach and Vasquez (1981: 97).
39 Oberschall (1973: 125).
40 Wilson, K. and Orum, A. 'Mobilizing People for Collective Action', *Journal of Politics and Military Sociology* vol. 14 (1976), pp. 187-202 and Cameron, D. 'Toward a Theory of Mobilization', *Journal of Politics*, vol. 36 (February 1974), pp. 138–71.
41 Tilly, C. 'Revolutions and Collective Action', in Greenstein, F. and Polsby, N. (eds) *Handbook of Political Science* Vol.3 (Addison-Wesley, Reading, Mass, 1975).
42 Both Gamson, W. in *The Strategy of Social Protest* (The Dorsey Press, 1975) chs 5–6 and Walsh (1978: 174) stress the role of sponsorship by other organizations in a mobilization process.
43 Cobb *et al.* (1976: 128).
44 Ibid., pp. 128 and 131.
45 For a detailed discussion of linkage in bargaining and negotiations see Pruitt, D. *Negotiating Behavior* (Academic Press, New York, 1982) p. 158 and Druckman, D. (ed.) *Negotiations: Social-Psychological Perspectives* (Sage Publications, Beverly Hills, 1977); and Raiffa, H. *The Art and Science of Negotiation* (Harvard University Press, Cambridge, Mass., 1982).
46 Kalb, M. and Kalb, B. *Henry Kissinger* (Little Brown, Boston, 1974) p. 102.
47 Rosenau, J. *The Study of Global Interdependence* (Frances Pinter, London, 1980) p. 180.
48 Rosenau, J. (ed.) *Linkage Politics* (Free Press, New York, 1969) p. 44.
49 Willetts (1984: 88).
50 Deutch, K. *Nationalism and Social Communication* (The MIT Press, Cambridge, Mass., 1966).
51 For detailed studies of the role of symbols and abstract values in politics see Elder, C. and Cobb, R. *The Political Use of Symbols* (Longman, New York, 1983).
52 Willetts (1984: 98).
53 Ibid., p. 100.
54 Snyder, D. and Kelly, W. 'Strategies for Investigating Violence and Social Change: Illustrations from Analyses of Racial Disorders and Implications for Mobilization Research' in Zald, M. and McCharty, J. *The Dynamics of Social Movements* (Winthrop Publishers, Cambridge, Mass., 1979) p. 220.
55 Ibid., p. 219.
56 For a discussion of the aggregation concept see Rosenau (1980: 129–94).

4 Mobilization of Support at the Palestinian Level

Introduction

This chapter is concerned with the emergence and consolidation of modern Palestinian nationalism. This does not mean, however, that the Arab inhabitants of Palestine had not previously experienced some sense of a national identity. Ovendale notes that as early as the 1890s Palestinian Arabs were aware of an Arab awakening set against both Ottoman rule and the threat caused by the 'increasing flow of Jewish settlers' into Palestine.[1] During the period between the defeat of the Ottomans and the establishment of the new post-World War I order in the Middle East the Arabs in Palestine, had looked towards the short-lived rule of Faysal in Syria for their political future:

But Faysal's fall in July 1920 resulted in a swift reorientation of Palestinian political attention and aspirations. A Palestinian nationalism emerged which was concerned with problems caused by Zionist aspirations, problems that were not faced by the other Arab countries.[2]

The early Palestinian Arab calls for independence failed and Palestine became a British Mandate with provisions for the establishment of a Jewish homeland. The inability of the Arab and Muslim world to respond, in an effective manner, to Palestinian Arab calls for support culminated in an increase in resistance activities against the Mandate. This resistance became particularly fierce when Jewish immigration into Palestine grew after Hitler's accession to power.

Palestinian national identity found expression in resistance against Jewish immigration and against the British rule that facilitated it while denying them independence. This resistance attained the level of a rebellion in the mid-1930s. The rebellion was suppressed by Britain in a heavy-handed manner which destroyed the local Palestinian political structure.

In the aftermath of World War II, the Palestinian Arabs were unable to meet the Zionist challenge. As Israel emerged the Palestinian Arabs turned completely to the Arab world for help. The failure of Arab governments to prevent the establishment of Israel and the demographic as well as political dislocation caused by the 1948 war left the Palestinian Arabs in a situation even worse than when their rebellion collapsed just before World War II.

Nevertheless, from then on the Palestinian Arabs came to look to the independent Arab world as their means of achieving independence. The growth of the idea of 'Arab unity' and pan-Arabism in the 1950s strengthened the belief that: 'Palestine was not merely a Palestinian problem: since it was an integral part of the Arab nation, they expected Arabs everywhere to assist in its liberation.'[3]

The purpose of this chapter is to examine how, against this background, support for a separate Palestinian national identity was mobilized. We shall refer to the emergence of this new identity as modern Palestinian nationalism. The period of study will be limited to the 1960s and 1970s. The Palestinian Arab identity that developed during the Mandate period will be assumed to be one belonging to a different historical period and hence of no direct interest to the study of the growth of a separate modern Palestinian Arab consciousness.

With respect to studying how the Palestinians were mobilized to assert and struggle for their independent political identity, the Palestinian community constitutes a unique problem. As a result of the 1948 and 1967 Arab–Israeli wars the Palestinian community was to a certain degree dispersed. This dispersion for 1977 can be seen in Table 4.1. Structurally it is possible to talk of a Palestinian community divided into four groups.

(i) Palestinians living within Israel and often referred to as Israeli Arabs;
(ii) Palestinians of the territories occupied since 1967:
    (a) in the West Bank;
    (b) in the Gaza Strip;
(iii) Palestinians in the numerous refugee camps in the countries neighbouring Palestine;
(iv) Palestinians of the diaspora:
    (a) those living in the Arab world;
    (b) those living beyond the Arab world.

It is important to make these distinctions when studying the mobilization process among the Palestinians because these four groups have been exposed to the process in different ways and at different times. While the initiators, in the form of the elite as well as the rank and file of the resistance movement, tended to come mostly from Palestinians in the refugee camps and those living in the Arab world, the Palestinians living within Israel and outside the Arab world had a more passive role. Similarly, Palestinians living in the refugee camps were more easily accessible to the Palestinian resistance movement than the Palestinians living in Israel. Hence the Palestinians in the refugee camps were the first to lend their support to the resistance movement and later recognize and support the PLO as their representative.

Table 4.1. Estimated distribution of
Palestinians for 1977[4]

West Bank	750,000
Gaza Strip	410,000
Israel	380,000
Jordan	1,100,000
Lebanon	260,000
Syria	180,000
Kuwait	170,000
Egypt	37,000
Iraq	16,000
Gulf States	18,000
Saudi Arabia	25,000
Libya	7,000
USA	25,000
West Germany	17,000
Latin America	6,000
Total	3,401,000

The emergence of the Palestinian resistance movements: the initiators

In studying the emergence of the Palestinian national identity a distinction should be made between the initiators of the mobilization process and the targets. The initiators constituted the sections of the society that were not content with the prevailing status-quo and were prepared to take measures to bring about change. In this case the initiators were the various groups that made up what is referred to as the Palestinian resistance movement and the early PLO, as sponsored by the Arab League.

The target, at this level of analysis, is the Palestinian community. After the traumatic experience of the 1948 war and the establishment of Israel the Palestinian community had become dispersed. The indigenous political infrastructure of the Palestinians had been destroyed. They found themselves either under the political rule of Israel or Arab states, or in refugee camps administered by the United Nations Relief Works Agency.

Although a very small group of Palestinians remained committed to their national identity as Palestinian Arabs and to the liberation of Palestine, the large majority allowed their struggle and identity to be submerged within the broader concept of Arab unity. The immediate concern of displaced persons was the struggle to return to their homes.[5] The larger problem of liberating Palestine from foreign occupation was left to the Arab states.[6] In the aftermath of the 1967 war the general feeling among many Palestinians was one of helplessness and despair.

Al-Fatah

The situation among the initiators was different. The first and most important of the initiators was Al-Fatah. The origins of Al-Fatah can be traced back to the mid-1950s to a group of Palestinians that had neither relinquished their national identity nor their belief in the necessity of liberating Palestine via Palestinian means rather than relying on Arab states.[7] Yet, throughout the 1950s the attitude of the Palestinians remained largely sceptical if not uncommitted to Al-Fatah's ideology.[8] It was in the early 1960s that the situation began to change enabling Al-Fatah to expand its organizational structure and base. These developments reached a particularly critical point in December 1964 when Al-Fatah's military arm mounted its first operation against Israel.

Under the leadership of Arafat, Al-Fatah pursued an ideology which simply stressed the nationalist struggle to liberate Palestine without dwelling too deeply on any theoretical speculations about the nature and form of the future Palestinian society.[9] The nationalist and uncontroversial nature of Al-Fatah's ideology enabled it to relate to various parts of the Palestinian community as well as some Arab governments. This manifested itself in the growing support that Al-Fatah mobilized both among the Palestinians and Arab governments, and culminated in its eventual domination of the PLO after 1969.

The PFLP and the PDFLP

The first of the two radical Palestinian resistance groups emerged in late 1967 as a direct result of the June war. Before the 1967 war, G.Habbash, the founder of the Popular Front for the Liberation Palestine (PFLP), had been the leader of the radical Arab Nationalist Movement (ANM). This organization had existed for almost two decades within the framework of pan-Arabism and had conceived the liberation of Palestine within the context of an Arab struggle against Zionism and imperialism. However, it was the decisive failure of Arab armies against Israel that forced Habbash to reconsider his position. The ANM was then transformed into a 'Palestinian organisation with its "nationalist" goals recast in a Marxist–Leninist ideological framework'.[10]

The PFLP, unlike Al-Fatah, became a group which articulated its ideology to its limits. The liberation of Palestine was envisaged as part and parcel of a larger revolutionary struggle to transform Arab society along Marxist–Leninist lines. The radical and narrow nature of its ideology limited its base of support mostly to students and intellectuals. However, its readiness to embark on spectacular acts of international terrorism played a crucial role in bringing the Palestinian problem to the world public agenda. Similarly the impact of this type of violence is noted by Rodinson to have had its share in mobilizing not only the Palestinians but also Arab masses.[11]

The Popular Democratic Front for the Liberation of Palestine (PDFLP) is a smaller group that came into existence as a result of a split from the PFLP in February 1969.[12] Just like Habbash, the background of Hawatmeh, the leader of this group, lies with the ANM. However, the more radical and pro-Soviet position of Hawatmeh culminated in an eventual ideological confrontation between the supporters of Hawatmeh and what they perceived to be the less-revolutionary and moderate section of the PFLP, led by Habbash. It was as a result of this conflict that PDFLP became separated from the PFLP.

Although its ideological arguments have mostly appealed to radical circles among Palestinian students abroad[13] in practice it has followed policies more in line with Al-Fatah and the PLO. After the mid-1970s this alliance collapsed when Arafat became increasingly willing to enter into a dialogue with Arab governments, in particular Jordan. In the late 1960s the PDFLP played a leading role in placing on the Palestinian political agenda the idea of a 'democratic Palestinian state' with Jews and Arabs living along side each other followed by the idea of a 'mini state' in the early 1970s.

Arab government sponsored resistance groups

The PFLP, PDFLP and Al-Fatah were purely Palestinian in the sense that they were established and run by Palestinians without any direct political dependence on any Arab government. After it became quite evident that the Arab states were unable to liberate Palestine and the Palestinian resistance movement began to emerge and consolidate itself, some Arab governments felt the need to continue to have some direct influence in Palestinian politics. Syria and Iraq were two such governments.

Traditionally, Syria always had an interest in the politics of Palestine and Lebanon which for Syrians forms an entity known as Greater Syria. Furthermore, the loss of actual Syrian territory during the 1967 war brought the problem of liberating Palestine closer to home. Hence the Baathist regime, in 1968, established Al-Saiqa which became the second largest guerrilla organization after Fatah. It follows a strict Syrian line and reflects the Baathist thinking that dominates the Syrian political scene. This has led Al-Saiqa to envisage a struggle for the liberation of Palestine fought within a pan-Arab movement led by Syria.[14]

The Iraqi equivalent of Al-Saiqa is the Arab Liberation Front (ALF). The growing rivalry between Iraq and Syria led the new Iraqi Baathist regime to establish ALF in April 1969 in order to have its own means of influence on the

Palestinian resistance movement. Although the ideology of the ALF was very similar to Al-Saiqa in stressing the primacy of Arab unity it never achieved the size of its Syrian rival. Its membership remained mostly Arab rather than Palestinian.[15]

It is interesting to note that as a result of Al-Saiqa's and ALF's Baathist backgrounds, which uphold pan-Arabism, they remained reluctant to talk about an independent separate Palestinian entity; the absence of the word 'Palestine' in their names is conspicous.[16]

The PLO

The PLO, among all the initiators that have been mentioned so far, is without any doubt the most important. However, it is important to make a distinction between the PLO from 1964 to 1969 and the PLO thereafter.

The PLO was set up in 1964 by an Arab League decision in response to growing signs of Palestinian unrest. The position of the Arab governments was that a PLO under Arab League supervision would be the best way of satisfying the demands made by an emerging Palestinian national consciousness. Also, it was felt that through such an organization Arab governments could control Palestinian political activities. Hence, it is generally accepted that during Shuikary's leadership the PLO did not attain a great degree of independence in developing and pursuing policies towards the liberation of Palestine. In spite of this weakness the PLO between 1964 and 1969 did build the basis of what gradually became a complex political-economic-social organizational entity.

In the aftermath of the 1967 war the situation changed drastically. The resistance activities of various guerrilla organizations, in particular Al-Fatah and the PFLP, gained the increasing support of the Palestinians. The activities of the Palestinian resistance movement reached a turning point when Fatah and to a lesser extent PFLP emerged politically triumphant from a military engagement with Israeli forces near Karameh in March 1968.

This oft-cited battle led to a significant increase in support and membership for guerrilla groups. It was in the immediate aftermath of this battle that the agreement to re-allocate the seats at the next Palestine National Council was reached at a meeting between the PLO, Al-Fatah and the PFLP in Beirut. This decision was then formally endorsed by the PLO Executive Committee. This represented a rather formal recognition on the part of the PLO's traditional moderate leadership of the prestige and support that guerrilla groups had come to enjoy among Palestinians.[17] However it was not until the Fifth National Council in Cairo, in February 1969, that the PLO came under the control of a resistance-orientated new leadership, with Arafat as the Chairman.

This new political composition enabled the PLO to have a more effective and central role in mobilizing the Palestinians and in expanding its basis of support both at the local and the international level. The PLO became an umbrella organization for the various guerrilla groups. These groups had direct access to decision making as members of the Executive Committee. The legislative arm, the Palestine National Council, provided a wide range of Palestinian groups from various sections of the Palestinian community with the ability to participate in the decision making process. In turn, these various local Palestinian groups represented at the Palestine National Council enabled the PLO to reach parts of the Palestinian community not otherwise directly accessible.

In respect to mobilizing the Palestinian community the role of the various economic and social-welfare institutions run by the PLO must also be noted.

These institutions enabled the PLO to bring day-to-day services including education and health services to the Palestinian community, in particular to those living in refugee camps. Here it might be possible to draw an analogy to the way in which most modern governments retain their citizens' loyalty by, *inter alia*, providing a variety of public services. However, this analogy has its limits as the PLO does not actually have full mandate over a definite piece of territory; instead it has varying degrees of access to parts of the Palestinian community.[18]

So far, the main initiators have been identified in the belief that an awareness of the more central actors will facilitate the application of the model to understand the mobilization process. It should be noted that the initiators that make up the Palestinian resistance movement are not necessarily the actual agents of the overall mobilization process itself. Instead it might be more appropriate to think of the resistance movement as performing the function of a catalyst in a chemical reaction.

The fluid, interactive and dynamic nature of the mobilization process makes it rather difficult to pinpoint with any exactitude where this stage actually begins. Yet, intuitively, it can be said that once protest groups emerge as a response to demands for change, these groups will articulate their objectives and policies to bring about the desired change. It is in their attempt to achieve their objectives that the need to acquire the support of outside or identification groups will become important. In the case of this study the primary identification group or target for the Palestinian resistance movement was the Palestinian community.

The mobilization process

In the coming sections the model depicting the mobilization process will be applied to the emergence of the Palestinian national identity. The first set of outcomes from the mobilization process will be the formation of the various groups that make up the Palestinian resistance movement. The second set of outcomes of interest to this study will be the growing support for the Palestinian national identity received from various parts of the Palestinian community. This will be seen mostly as a result of the Palestinian resistance movement's efforts to aggregate support for the expression of the Palestinian national identity through the liberation of Palestine and the establishment of a Palestinian state.

Although the emergence of initiators is relatively easy to follow, the same cannot be said about the mobilization of Palestinian support for the Palestinian resistance movement and the PLO. This is mainly the result of a measurement problem caused by the absence of suitable data to construct reliable and valid indices to measure growth in Palestinian support. The lack of data such as regular and systematically taken public opinion polls, election results, membership and financial contributions to guerrilla groups makes it difficult to develop measurable indicators of support.

Therefore, the growth or change in the levels of support for the Palestinian cause, as represented by the Palestinian resistance movement and the PLO, will be established mostly by indirect indicators such as speeches made by public persons and written documentation. A disadvantage of this is that analysis based on such indirect indicators cannot achieve the thoroughness and reliablity of an analysis based on reproducible indices constructed from systematically and exhaustively collected hard data. Furthermore, such analysis will only point towards trends in change and will provide neither the rate nor the amount of change.

Conducive environment

This part of the mobilization process accounts for certain external and structural changes central to the emergence of the modern Palestinian identity. It has already been noted that throughout the 1950s the Palestinian community remained in a state of passivity. The political structure of the community had collapsed and most Palestinians had come, in one way or another, under the rule of other states. Furthermore, to this must be added the disruption caused by the displacement of a large number of Palestinians.

This state of affairs within the Palestinian community produced a situation receptive to Nasser's newly revitalized idea of Arab unity. Nasser had become successful in articulating the ideology of Arab nationalism that was to be expressed in Arab unity. His success in nationalizing the Suez Canal followed by the declaration of Union in 1958 between Egypt and Syria were seen as the tangible fruits of his struggle for Arab unity. Naturally, in such an environment dominated by pan-Arabism and the charismatic leadership of Nasser, the Palestinians strongly identified themselves with the Arab world: 'In the eyes of the Palestinian masses Nasser was the only horizon.'[19] The Palestinians came to accept and even stress their Arab identity. It was through this identity that they saw the liberation of their land, symbolically demonstrated, for example, in the request of Haji Hussein, the head of the Arab Higher Committee, to join the United Arab Republic.

In the early 1960s, a series of events appears to have created a situation favourable for a sustained mobilization process to begin within the Palestinian community. One of the first events to have significant consequences for the emergence of Palestinian nationalism was the break-up of the union between Egypt and Syria. Nasser had spent a good part of the 1950s promoting his revitalized ideology of pan-Arab nationalism. In the 1950s this ideology found a wide range of followers from all corners of the Arab world.

It played a central role in bringing about significant political changes in many Arab countries. However, it was not until 1958 that pan-Arabism, as a transnational force, achieved something tangible in the struggle towards Arab unity. Hence, when in February 1958, Egypt and Syria announced the establishment of the United Arab Republic, this was hailed as a major step towards Arab unity. In Palestine it carried particular significance as the liberation of Palestine had always been envisaged within the context of the struggle for Arab unity. Yet when the union came to an end, in September 1961, the particular symbolic importance that the Palestinians had given to the union led them to begin to question their belief in the liberation of Palestine through Arab unity.

The collapse of the union was soon followed by the independence of Algeria in July 1962. The significance of this event for the Palestinians stemmed from the fact that the liberation of Algeria was seen as the product of a revolutionary-nationalist armed struggle. The Algerians had achieved their independence as a result of a purely nationalist struggle outside the context of pan-Arabism. The Algerian example, in some ways, gave the Palestinians the possibility of countering the disappointment caused by the breakdown of the only tangible evidence of the successful struggle for Arab unity, and in its place offered an example for an alternative but successful liberation ideology.

Historically a less spectacular but nevertheless significant event, at least from the Palestinian point of view, occured in January 1964 at the very same Arab summit that led the way to the eventual establishment of the PLO. Arab states had either been unable or unwilling to take any effective counter-measures against Israeli efforts to divert the Jordan river, in spite of their repeated promises and their announcement that 'the battle of the Jordan river is a part of the Battle of Palestine'.[20] Their hesistancy was conspicuous when the first Arab summit voted not to engage in a war with Israel over the Jordan river diversion scheme.[21] The diversion programme itself was perceived by the Palestinians as an act of aggression committed against their homeland.[22] It is, to some extent, in defiance of the Arab leaders inability to respond to the diversion scheme that Al-Fatah mounted its first operation against an Israeli irrigation installation.[23]

The last, but in its implications the most significant, event to contribute to an environment favourable to the mobilization of the Palestinians was the defeat of the Arab armies in 1967 and the consequent acceptance by Egypt and Jordan of the United Nations Security Council Resolution 242, which referred to the Palestinians simply as refugees. During the period preceding the 1967 war, Arab leaders, in particular Nasser, had repeatedly stressed the preparations being made to liberate Palestine. However, after the defeat of the Arab armies in June 1967 a growing number of Palestinians joined ranks with those who had already been, for some time, arguing the need for a national armed struggle to liberate Palestine. As a PLO official notes: 'By the defeat of 1967, the Arab governments had forfeited all claims to speak or negotiate on behalf of the Palestinian people'.[24]

Egypt and Jordan's acceptance of Resolution 242 and in July 1970 their willingness to participate in negotiations around the Rogers' Plan (this plan was first announced by the American Secretary of State William Rogers in December 1969 in an attempt to bring about a diplomatic solution to the Middle Eastern Conflict) was more than enough to convince even the sceptics that there should be an alternative to relying on Arab governments for the liberation of Palestine. It had become quite evident that these governments were not going to put Palestine before national considerations. This belief was once more reinforced when Jordan mounted an operation to eradicate the Palestinian resistance movement from Jordan while Arab governments remained relatively passive.

In the literature concerning this subject these events are widely referred to as factors that appear to have brought about the emergence of the Palestinian national identity.[25] There seems to be one major problem inherent in such an analysis of the relationship between these events and the growth in Palestinian consciousness. Such an analysis tends to assume that these events had a direct and uniform impact in getting the Palestinian Arab community, as a whole, to raise its Palestinian consciousness. The relationship between the occurrence of these events and the emergence of a widely felt Palestinian national identity is not necessarily direct and uniform. Such an analysis remains rather static and unable to account for the fact that the interaction between these events and the growth of Palestinian consciousness was dynamic and an indirect

The analytical model presented in chapter three provides the means for conceptualizing the emergence of the Palestinian national identity as a result of a dynamic and complex mobilization process. It is within the context of the first element of this model, the 'conducive environment', that the impact of these events on the mobilization process should be seen. They were events that took place at different times and signalled a growing need among Palestinians to reconsider the prevailing attitudes towards the question of the liberation of Palestine.

One point to bear in mind is that as a result of the dynamic nature of the relationship between the two phenomena, the form of the response to these signals differed depending on when and where it came from. At the very early stages of the mobilization process the initial response was in the form of the emergence of indigenous Palestinian political organizations that were earlier introduced as initiators. However, these organizations did not emerge all at the same time and also did not have the same kind of response to the mobilization support for the liberation of Palestine.

Al-Fatah and the early PLO entered the Palestinian scene in the early 1960s. It was the collapse of the Union between Egypt and Syria and the success of the Algerian revolution that began to lend credibility to Al-Fatah's argument for the need to liberate Palestine through a Palestinian led armed struggle. Until then these ideas had only been received with suspicion.[26] On the other hand, while Al-Fatah was led by a radical-nationalist Palestinian leadership the early PLO was founded and led by a conservative Palestinian elite, closely associated with the Arab governments. As a result of this conservative leadership coupled with Arab governments' control, the PLO at this time could not envisage the liberation of Palestine by means that would be unwelcome to the Arab governments.

The other major Palestinian political organizations emerged only later on, as a result of the final blow inflicted by the 1967 war on pan-Arab thinking in the liberation of Palestine. The guerrilla organizations that came into existence in the aftermath of the war developed a different approach to the problem of Palestine. PFLP, PDFLP and Al-Saiqa were such organizations. While the PFLP and later the PDFLP professed strongly Marxist-revolutionary ideologies in respect of the liberation of Palestine, they were different from Al-Saiqa because of their independent Palestinian basis. Compared to the Al-Fatah and the PLO these groups had a relatively different response to the Palestinian problem.

The 1967 war had its own impact on the already existing Palestinian organizations. Al-Fatah was able to expand its resistance operation as it gained access to growing numbers of volunteers from refugee camps freshly swollen with a new wave of refugees. On the other hand the inability of the PLO's conservative leadership to promote any effective resistance operations culminated in the eventual transfer of power to the armed-struggle orientated guerrilla organizations. The PLO under its new leadership was then able to develop and consolidate an organizational framework that in itself could be utilized for the mobilization process.

As has been pointed out this series of events generated a response from within the Palestinian community that culminated in the emergence and growth of the Palestinian resistance movement, loosely organized under the umbrella of the PLO. The picture, however, would not be complete without mentioning a number of other contributory factors that made possible the emergence of an environment successful for starting and perpetuating a mobilization process.

The Palestinian community during the 1950s was characterized by socio-political attributes associated with traditional societies. The leadership remained split usually along the lines of two prominent families. This made the development of a unified approach to the Palestinian problem difficult.[27] At least in practice this leadership remained status-quo orientated and was strongly aligned with the Egyptians in Gaza and with the Jordanians in the West Bank. However, a process of modernization, largely attributable to UNRWA's educational programmes and to Israel's direct influence, precipitated changes in the social-political structure of the Palestinian community both inside and outside Israel.[28] Most influenced by this modernization process was a new generation of young people in whose eyes the authority and legitimacy of the traditional leadership became gradually eroded. Hence, the modernization process not only planted the seeds of a new leadership independent of traditional social-political ties but it also caused at least a section of the Palestinian community to become more receptive to modern nationalist approaches.[29]

Finally the 1967 war affected the Palestinian community in two further ways which did have some implications for the mobilization process. The war created another wave of refugees, most of them suffering the frustration of having been displaced twice in a lifetime. This did generate, especially among the young, a mood of defiance, ready to question the credibility of the idea of relying on Arab governments to liberate Palestine. Furthermore, as a consequence of the war a large proportion of the Palestinian community became territorially re-united. This brought the possibility of direct interaction between the various sections of the Palestinian community that previously had remained isolated from each other.

These last set of factors must be seen in the context of the earlier series of events and the emergence of the Palestinian resistance movement. The 'conducive environment' should then be seen as the end result of the dynamic interaction between these three sets of factors: the weakening of pan-Arabism as a means of liberating Palestine, the changes within the Palestinian community; the defeat of Arab armies, in 1967. The interaction constitutes the 'conducive environment'. The 'conducive environment' is a part of the mobilization process that itself mobilized a certain level of support for the Palestinian cause represented by the emergence of various guerrilla groups and their supporters.

Although difficult to capture in any tangible form, the role of the feedback mechanism must also be kept in mind. Once the 'conducive environment' generated a certain level of support for the Palestinian cause, the feedback mechanism performed a positive loop and made the 'conducive environment' even more favourable, leading to the emergence of other participants. For the further expansion of this support to cover growing sections of the Palestinian community one must examine the role of the two other elements in the mobilization process.

Cognitive linkages

In chapter three while introducing the mobilization process model it was argued that initiators (protest groups), in an effort to mobilize support, try to establish linkages or similarities between their movement and already existing prestigious movements and ideas. Such linkages or efforts appear to perform two functions.

First, cognitive linkages are useful in assisting the development and articulation of a group ideology. The role of ideologies is central to any actor who has to mobilize support. It helps the actor to interpret one particular situation, determine its goals and develop policies in an attempt to achieve these goals.[30] The nature and level of articulation inherent in an ideology with which an actor works will to a certain degree influence the mobilization of support within and outside the group.[31]

Second, cognitive linkages also provide an effective way of expanding a movement's basis of support. One of the primary ways of expanding one's basis of support is to persuade potential supporters of the just nature of one's cause. The likelihood of receiving such support is enhanced if the applicability of certain symbols (values) and the existence of similarities between one's own cause and widely supported other causes can be demonstrated. Once a successful linkage has been established the initiator can benefit from an already existing pool of support mobilized by an established movement or accruing to a prestigious symbol.

Literature on cognitive dissonance points out the need that individuals feel to bring some form of structure and harmony to their perceived world. This structure and harmony is achieved by maintaining and working within the realm of cognitive structures or world views. An individual confronted with a situation demanding a change in his attitude towards a certain issue is more likely to make this change if he can establish a degree of congruence between the cognitive structure that he works with and the new demand being made on his assessment of a situation. It is at this point that cognitive linkages can play an important role by enabling the individual to establish relationships between various concepts which previously had been ignored or not seen as being related to more central concepts. Although this is a process that takes place at the individual level, it has been argued that homologous processes at group level are also possible. This opens up the possibility of suggesting a similar mechanism for the role of cognitive linkages affecting actors other than individuals.

Among the Palestinians, one can observe the role of cognitive consistency in two closely related areas. The first, in some ways the more interesting, is the attempt to decouple the role of pan-Arabism from the liberation of Palestine; the second area was in developing a new approach for the liberation of Palestine.

It was pointed out previously that during the 1950s the majority of the Palestinians looked to Arab capitals, in particular to Cairo, for their liberation. The liberation of Palestine was then tightly bound with the struggle for Arab unity. With the exception of the early supporters of Al-Fatah, the attitude of the remaining Palestinians towards their homeland was determined by pan-Arabism. The Palestinians participated in the politics of Arab nationalism with enthusiasm. The consequence of the strength of this pan-Arabist hold on Palestinians was that it created a situation whereby Palestinian efforts and energies were drawn away from their Palestinian identity towards the enhancement of Arab unity.[32]

The first changes in this state of affairs began to occur in the early 1960s and were reflected in an interesting way during the adoption of the PLO Covenant. The draft constitution of the PLO, as prepared by Shukairy, referred throughout the text to 'Palestinians' or the 'Palestinian people'.[33] The use of the label 'Palestinian people' instead of 'Palestinian Arabs' or the more distant 'Arabs of Palestine' can be regarded as the expression of an independent Palestinian identity. This argument is clearly supported by the manner in which the final text differed from the first draft.

The text, when it was finally adopted as the National Covenant of the PLO, saw a number of changes that may well reflect the conflict between a Palestinian identity and pan-Arabism; it referred to the 'Palestinian Arab people', suggesting a possible compromise between the latter label and 'Arabs of Palestine' or 'Palestinian Arabs'; it also included clear references to Arab unity and its role in the liberation of Palestine.[34]

Al-Fatah had always stressed the primacy of Palestinian interests and the role of a national armed struggle. The influence of Al-Fatah's thinking together with the mood created after the 1967 defeat of the Arab armies was reflected in the adoption of the new Palestinian National Covenant at the 4th PNC in July 1968.[35] Although the new Covenant continued to refer to the 'Palestinian Arab people' it included a series of new articles that stressed the importance of the Palestinian 'national' liberation struggle.[36] A much stronger Palestinian identity was expressed in Al-Fatah's seven-point policy outline adopted by its Central Committee in January 1969[37] which referred to the 'Palestinian people' and its liberation struggle although some lip service was also paid to the distant objective of a 'progressive and united Arab society'.

The idea of Palestinian nationalism did not receive instant support among Palestinians. This is quite evident in West Bank demonstrations that continued to stress an Arab rather than a Palestinian identity by continuing to use slogans supportive of Nasser and Arab unity.[38] It is at this point that another set of cognitive linkages played an important role in mobilizing support for an indigenous Palestinian identity and struggle. Al-Fatah as well as radical groups such as the PFLP and the PDFLP used the Algerian and Vietnamese national liberation struggles as examples to improve their own arguments; that is, parallels were drawn to gain support for a Palestinian national struggle.

These Palestinian groups also came to stress the anti-colonial and anti-imperialist nature of the Palestinian struggle in an attempt to increase the prestige of an argument favouring a Palestinian national struggle. This is evident in the 1969 Al-Fatah programme stating: 'The struggle of the Palestinian people, like that of the Vietnamese people and other peoples of Asia, Africa and Latin America, is part of the historic process of the liberation of the oppressed peoples from colonialism and imperialism.'[39]

Al-Fatah was not the only group to exploit the concept of anti-imperialism. The PFLP and the PDFLP also employed this concept to articulate their ideology which was heavily influenced by Marxist and Leninist thinking. In both cases the Algerian and Vietnamese struggles were portrayed as anti-imperialist struggles and similarities were drawn between these struggles and the need for a revolutionary struggle for the liberation of Palestine.

Prior to 1967 most Palestinians considered themselves Arab. In the minds of these Palestinians, equating a Palestinian identity with an Arab one and stressing Arab nationalism and unity as a source of strength for liberating Palestine formed a cognitively consistent whole. However, a series of events, in particular the 1967 war, steadily increased the stress on this cognitive structure and eroded its consistency to the point where the liberation of Palestine could be visualized by stressing a separate Palestinian identity.

Hence, the de-linking of the Palestinian identity and the liberation of Palestine from Arab nationalism and the struggle for Arab unity was a crucial step in bringing about the necessary conceptual modifications in Palestinian cognitive structures. These conceptual modifications helped to bring about the change in Palestinian attitudes towards their own identity and towards the way to express this identity. The arguments that precipitated this process of cognitive change were aided by references to successful liberation struggles such as Algeria and to concepts such as anti-imperialism and anti-colonialism. The last two concepts helped the Palestinians place an indigenous struggle to liberate Palestine into a broader world view.

Accessibility

During the building of the mobilization process model it was argued that access to the political decision making processes and agendas of actors plays an important role in drawing attention to an issue and in aggregating support for it. It was argued that initiators, in their efforts to raise an issue, try to gain access to the public and/or formal agendas of political actors. Initiators achieve this by means of either direct or indirect access to the actors and by employing methods ranging from lobbying to terrorism.

Earlier in this chapter, the various members of the Palestinian resistance move-ment and the PLO were presented as the initiators. Their aim, *inter alia*, was to raise the national consciousness of the Palestinians and mobilize, among the Palestinian community, support for their struggle to liberate Palestine. The Palestinian community at large constituted the major target for the initiators.

Table 4.2 depicts the various access routes employed by the Palestinian resis-tance movement and the PLO in their efforts to reach and mobilize support from the Palestinian community. Although in the late 1970s Palestinian violence directed towards other Palestinian groups or individuals did occur, there were no reported attempts to intimidate the Palestinian community to support the Palestinian cause. The role of violence in mobilizing the Palestinian community

Table 4.2. Matrix of access routes to the Palestinians

	Violent means	Non-violent means
Direct access	local coercion	organizational access
Indirect access	attacks on Israel international terrorism	access via proxy organizations

was of an indirect nature. In the sense that once the Palestinian guerrilla groups emerged with the intention of liberating Palestine by fighting a popular war, the armed struggle directed towards Israel had a spillover effect in bringing about a change in Palestinian attitudes. This particular role of violence in the mobilization of the Palestinians is noted by Frangi, a PLO official, in his description of the posi-tion of the leadership of Al-Fatah on armed struggle.[40]

The lack of publicly available, systematically collected data on armed guerrilla operations and the growth of Palestinian national consciousness precludes the possibility of establishing a statistically supported relationship. Hence, most of the analysis on this relationship relies on partially available data and impressions derived from interviews and news reports.

Nevertheless, Hudson does demonstrate in a relatively tangible manner the impact of armed operations on the growth of guerrilla membership: 'Before the June war, according to a reliable Palestinian source, Fatah numbered no more than 200–300 men; by the time of the Karamah battle it had increased to around 2000; but in three months following the Karamah battle it had burgeoned to 15000.'[41]

Other scholars have also noted the impact of armed struggle, particularly of the Karameh battle of March 1968, on enrolments of Palestinians to guerrilla organizations.[42] The growth in membership of guerrilla groups reflects the grow-ing support enjoyed by the Palestinian resistance movement, at least among young Palestinians. Whether the Palestinian resistance movement's armed struggle against Israel also brought the new line of thinking for the liberation of Palestine closer to the Palestinian community at large, is more difficult to establish.

The same literature also notes the impact that international terrorism appears to have had on Palestinian attitudes towards their national identity. Although Al-

Fatah limited its operations to Palestine, the PFLP, as a result of its more radical and revolutionary ideology, took its armed violence to the international arena. The purpose was not simply to weaken Israel and attract world attention but also to mobilize Arab support for the Palestinian cause.[43] The spectacular PFLP terrorist operations in the late 1960s and early 1970s did bring the Palestinian problem to the world public agenda, even at the cost of Western outrage, but more importantly it caught the imagination of the Arab masses.[44]

Violence was not the only way that the Palestinian resistance movement gained access to the Palestinian community and mobilized their support. Al-Fatah, soon after the 1967 war began to develop an infra-structure to cater for the health, education and welfare needs of the Palestinians, particularly those in refugee camps. Once the PLO came under the control of the Palestinian guerrilla groups, and despite the damage inflicted by the Jordanian civil war in 1970–1, the organizational structure providing these services continued to grow. The PLO, through these facilities influenced the education programmes run by United Nations Relief Works Agency, ensured the physical security of Palestinian refugee camps, ran commercial ventures providing jobs for Palestinians and provided funds for its welfare programmes. This complex organizational structure gave the PLO growing access to the Palestinian community in the refugee camps and other areas not under the control of Israel.

These activities did not remain restricted to the Palestinian community to which the PLO had direct access. The 10th PNC in April 1972 stressed the importance of organizational assistance to education, welfare and cultural institutions in the occupied territories in increasing the Palestinian awareness of their identity. The PLO, particularly after its 13th PNC in March 1977, also channelled funds to various municipalities in an attempt to decrease their dependence on Israel. A variety of social bodies, such as women's associations and the Palestinian Red Crescent, have also received PLO funds. Their role is seen in the light of nation building, 'strengthening, deepening, and solidifying the identification of the Palestinian people with the Palestinian nation as a whole and with the goals of the Palestinian nationalist movement'.[45]

Probably the most important institution within the PLO that enables it to gain access to the Palestinian community at large is the PNC. Recognized as the supreme legislative body of the PLO, PNC meetings are held at approximately annual intervals.[46] They bring together usually more than 200 Palestinians in their capacity as representatives of various parts of the Palestinian community as well as various organizations ranging from guerrilla groups to student associations. The meetings allow Palestinians representing all sections of the Palestinian community, including those from outside the Middle East, to deliberate over wide-ranging issues and adopt binding decisions. Through the PNC members the PLO achieves political access to various parts of the Palestinian community and ensures the implementation of decisions adopted by the PNC.

Palestinians in the West Bank, the Gaza Strip and Israel are not directly accessible to the PLO. Although groups from the Palestinian resistance movement have mounted armed operations, the PLO cannot maintain direct organizational existence in these areas. Instead, during the 1970s, a variety of organizations came to represent the views of the PLO, allowing the PLO to reach these communities indirectly.

Throughout the 1950s and the 1960s both the West Bank and the Gaza Strip remained under the administrative control of a traditional leadership strongly attached to the Jordanian and Egyptian regimes.[47] It was not until early 1973 that the PLO made a formal attempt to build a political network to reach the Palestinian community in the occupied territories. In August 1973, the Palestine National Front (PNF) was formed to act as an organizational framework to co-ordinate nationalist forces in the occupied territories with full allegiance to the PLO.[48] The unwillingnes of Jordan to enter the 1973 war strengthened the hand of the PNF. The support that the PNF enjoyed was demonstrated by the readiness of Palestinians from the occupied territories to join strikes and demonstrations to disrupt Israel's war efforts.

The PNF activists who were expelled from the occupied territories after the war were incorporated into the PLO, facilitating the maintenance of close ties between the PLO and the PNF supporters in the West Bank and the Gaza Strip. The growth in the PLO's influence in the occupied territories was consolidated when candidates affiliated with the PNF won a substantial majority during the local elections in April 1976.[49] These results conspicuously confirmed the end of the conservative and traditional rule by a few families.[50] Although not in a direct manner, both the West Bank and the Gaza Strip had become reasonably accessible to the PLO.

The Palestinians in Israel had remained politically passive with strong pressures for assimilation. The limited political participation that did take place was in an environment that lacked institutions encouraging Israeli-Arabs to join in politics in any effective way.[51] The sole exception was the Israeli Communist Party (Maqi), which was founded after the 1948 war by Palestinian Arabs and anti-Zionist Jews. It had recognized the Palestinians' right to self-determination as early as October 1949, opening the way for some Arab participation.[52] In 1965, the New Communist List, Rakah, split from Maqi which became an all-Jewish Communist Party. After this development Israeli-Arabs began to participate in political party politics in a more active manner.[53]

Rakah, notes Gilmour, 'is the only political party which represents the Arabs in Israel at a national level and which is prepared to fight for their rights.'[54] It has received increasing support from the Arabs at the cost of the Israeli Labour Party, which has usually been associated with local traditional leadership.[55] Rakah is also an active participant in the Democratic Front for Peace and Equality which recognizes the Palestinian people's right to self-determination and the PLO as their representative.[56] The relationship between the PLO and Rakah, since 1977, has probably enabled the PLO to gain some degree of accessibility to the Palestinians in Israel.[57]

As the above analysis points out, during the early stages of the mobilization period the use of violence appears to have played an indirect but important role in bringing the Palestinian cause to the attention of the Palestinian community. This period was one when actions spoke louder than words in raising the political consciousness of the community. It was only in the aftermath of this period that non-violent politics began to play an increasing role in expanding and strengthening the Palestinian national identity. However, it would be wrong to think that these two stages were completely separate from each other. It is better to conceptualize two stages that significantly overlapped, with each stage being dominated by one or the other form of access routes.

The output: growth of support

Four points need to be stressed in respect to the growth of Palestinian support for the Palestinian cause. First, the growth of support was not uniform throughout the

Palestinian community. Second, the three set of factors that have just been discussed influenced parts of the Palestinian community at different rates. Third, the role of the feedback mechanism must be kept in mind. Finally, the mobilization process within the Palestinian community is treated in isolation from similar processes outside it. The role of the interactions between the mobilization processes at different levels will be introduced at a later stage.

It was pointed out that with the exception of the founders of Al-Fatah and a number of student groups in Egypt the rest of the Palestinian community did not stress their national identity. It is not surprising therefore that as the Arab environment became to favourable to the mobilization process, it was Al-Fatah who first responded to it. Although a growing number of smaller guerrilla groups, mostly supported by Arab states, joined Al-Fatah and Palestinian workers and student organizations, particularly in Europe, lent their support to Al-Fatah, its views continued to raise suspicion until after the June war.[58] Al-Fatah's difficulty in making some headway can be attributed to the formation of the PLO in 1964 by the Arab League. By this move, the Arab governments although recognizing the Palestinian identity, were able to perpetuate the role of Arab unity in the struggle to liberate Palestine.

Prior to the 1967 war, it would have been very difficult to talk about a broad basis of national awareness among Palestinians, let alone support for the Palestinian cause, but in the immediate aftermath of the war the situation began to change significantly. The impact of the Arab armies' defeat on pan-Arabism showed itself in the emergence of a new guerrilla leadership with radical ideologies. The growth in the number of refugees on the other hand provided a pool of recruits for these guerrilla groups. The battle of Karameh, in March 1968, became a landmark as violence directed towards Israel increased the awareness of the Palestinian national identity.

In the late 1960s, the emergence of a Palestinian identity remained limited to the formation and consolidation of the Palestinian resistance movement. Even though the size and activities of the Palestinian resistance movement grew, as the PLO came under the control of Palestinian guerrilla groups and began to consolidate itself in refugee camps in Jordan and Lebanon, the mobilization of support for the Palestinian cause had not yet made any substantial progress in the occupied territories and among the Palestinians in Israel. The West Bank and the Gaza Strip were still under the influence of pan-Arabism as a number of pro-Nasser demonstrations in 1968 and 1969 seem to indicate.[59] Furthermore, the traditional Palestinian leadership in the West Bank not only remained intact but also tended to take an apologetic stand on Palestinian resistance activities and favoured deals with Israel. As late as 1972, the strength of the traditional leadership's grip on the West Bank is epitomized by the very high turnout of the Palestinian electorate at the mayoral elections in March, despite the call for a boycott by the PLO.[60]

Nevertheless, it was in the early 1970s that the signs of support for the Palestinian cause, in the occupied territories, began to surface. The early 1970s was a period marked by dramatic events such as the death of Nasser, the spectacular Palestinian violence at the international level, the Jordanian civil war, and the Israeli and Lebanese attacks on the Palestinian resistance movement in South Lebanon. In the aftermath of these events the mood of the West Bank and the Gaza Strip residents towards their Palestinian national identity is best demonstrated in the way they reacted to the assassination of three PLO leaders by Israel in April 1973:

There were manifestations of grief and condemnations in all towns and areas of the West Bank and the Gaza Strip, while nearly a quarter of a million Palestinians and Arabs marched behind the coffins of the three leaders in Beirut. The Palestinian people, both inside and outside the occupied homeland, seemed moved by the same feelings of unity, suffering and aspirations to a common future.[61]

This event was not the only one to point towards a strong Palestinian national identity in the occupied territories. The establishment of the pro-PLO PNF, its role in organizing the Palestinians against Israel's efforts during the October war and the pro-PLO demonstrations the day Arafat addressed the UN General Assembly, in November 1974, are all indicative of the same phenomenon. The Israeli media too recognized these developments even before the October war. The Israeli daily, *Maariv*, after the October war noted and commented on the political developments in support of the PLO in the occupied territories.[62] The pro-PLO mood surfaced again when Sadat made his peace initiative with Israel. This move triggered student demonstrations in the West Bank against Sadat and led the West Bank mayors to support the PLO's criticisms of Sadat.[63] Sadat's attempts to lobby support for his initiative in the occuppied territories met little success. The only people to respond were some notables which the Israeli daily, *Haretz*, chose to refer to as 'third rate personalities'.[64]

The most decisive indicator of this strong Palestinian national consciousness and pro-PLO sentiment in the occupied territories came in April 1976 at the West Bank local elections. The results of these elections were generally recognized as a referendum giving the PLO the mandate to represent the political aspirations of the Palestinians to express their national identity in a Palestinian state.

The Palestinians in Israel were probably the last to become mobilized. In this the traditional nature of the dominant leadership played an important role. It was a leadership that showed a readiness to work with Israeli political parties not necessarily receptive to the idea of a separate Palestinian identity. The lack of Arab political institutions, until the late 1960s, was another factor that contributed to their passive mood. By the late 1960s this began to change and Rakah appears to have played a significant role in this. It is generally assumed that the gradual shift in the Arab vote in favour of a political party supportive of Palestinian political rights and the PLO following the early 1970s is a reasonable indication of growing Palestinian consciousness and support for the PLO among Israeli Arabs.

The Palestinian national identity became completely consolidated by the mid-1970s as a result of a decade-long mobilization process. It was the emergence of a Palestinian resistance movement that constituted the first signs of a Palestinian national consciousness that had remained dormant for more than a decade. The first to be mobilized were young recruits to the guerrilla groups from the many refugee camps. Soon, the PLO began to consolidate its authority and legitimacy within refugee camps in the Lebanon and Jordan. From the early 1970s the Palestinians of the West Bank and the Gaza Strip became aware of their Palestinian national identity and supported the Palestinian cause in great numbers. By 1976, it was generally accepted that the Palestinians, at large, regarded the PLO as their representative and supported the PLO's efforts to express the Palestinian national identity in the establishment of a Palestinian state.

So far the mobilization process among the Palestinians has been studied in isolation from its Arab and larger environment. The following chapter will examine the gradual recognition of a separate Palestinian national identity by Arab governments and the PLO's efforts to consolidate itself as 'the sole and legitimate representative of the Palestinian people.' The study of the mobilization process at the Arab governmental level should also pave the way for a concluding analysis of the interactive nature of the mobilization process as it influenced the growth of support at different levels of analysis.

Notes

1 Ovendale, R. *The Origins of the Arab–Israeli Wars* (Longman, London, 1984) p. 10.
2 Quandt, W., Jabber, F. and Lesch, A. *The Politics of Palestinian Nationalism* (University of California Press, Berkeley, 1973) p. 14. The Palestinian Arab efforts to achieve self-determination taking into account their desire to be separated from Arab neighbouring states is forcefully argued in a Palestinian delegation's letter addressed to the League of Nations in September 1921. See League of Nations' document no. (1/15437/4213).
3 Gilmour, D. *Dispossessed: The Ordeal of the Palestinians* (Sphere Books, London, 1982) p. 143.
4 Amos, J. *Palestinian Resistance: Organization of a Nationalist Movement* (Pergamon Press, New York, 1980) p. 9. The slight difference in our grand total from the one in Amos arises from the inclusion of the Palestinians living outside the Middle East in the Table.
5 Shuaibi, I. 'The development of Palestinian Entity-Consciousness: Part I', *Journal of Palestine Studies* vol. 9 (Autumn 1979), no. 1, p. 79.
6 Ibid., p. 78.
7 For an analysis of the origins of Al-Fatah see Frangi, A. *The PLO and Palestine* (Zed Books, London, 1983) pp. 94–6; Shuaibi (1979-I: 79–82) and Cobban, H. *The Palestinian Liberation Organization* (Cambridge University Press, Cambridge, 1984) pp. 21–7.
8 Shuaibi (1979-I: 84).
9 For a discussion of Al-Fatah's ideological background see Quandt *et al.* (1973: 55–6) and Amos (1980: 43–67).
10 Metz, R. 'Why George Habash turned Marxist', *Mideast*, August 1970, p. 31.
11 Rodinson, M. *Israel and the Arabs* (Penguin Books, London, 1982) p. 259.
12 A number of other splits occurred from the PFLP. PFLP-General Command split from the PFLP in 1968 with a pro-Syrian leadership advocating the primacy of military struggle over ideological concerns. In April 1977 another group known as the Palestine Liberation Front broke away from the PFLP–GC to follow a pro-Iraqi stance. The Popular Revolutionary Front for the Liberation of Palestine on the other hand split from PFLP in 1972 when it decided that hijackings had become counterproductive.
13 Metz (1970: 36).
14 Yodfat, A. and Arnon-Ohanna, Y. *PLO Strategy and Tactics* (Croom Helm, London, 1981) p. 27.
15 Amos (1980: 107–10).
16 Yodfat and Arnon-Ohanna (1981: 27–8).
17 Quandt *et al.* (1973: 68–70) and Hamid, R. 'What is the PLO?' *Journal of Palestine Studies*, vol. 4 (Summer 1975), no. 4, p. 99.
18 For a study of the PLO's institutional structure including the function and role of various welfare societies see Rubenberg, C. *The Palestine Liberation Organization: Its Institutional Infrastructure* (Institute of Arab Studies, Belmont, Mass., 1983).
19 Shuaibi (1979-I: 78).
20 Quoted in Kadi, L. *Arab Summit Conferences and The Palestine Problem* (Research Centre, PLO, Beirut, 1966) p. 93.
21 Ibid., p. 109.
22 Frangi (1983: 98).
23 Schleifer, A. *Search for Peace in the Middle East* (Fawlett Publications, Greenwich, Conn., 1970) p. 16.
24 Frangi (1983: 107).
25 Gilmour (1982: Ch. 7); Hamid (1975: 92–3) and Shuaibi, I. 'The Development of Palestinian Entity-Consciousness: Part II' *Journal of Palestine Studies* vol. IX (Winter

1980), no. 2, pp. 50–70, are three representative sources of the line of argument that explains the rise of Palestinian national consciousness by referring to the break-up of the Egyptian-Syrian Union, the successful Algerian national struggle for independence and the Arab defeat in the 1967 war.

26 Nakhleh (1971: 192).

27 Quandt *et al.* (1973: 75).

28 Hudson, M. 'The Palestinian Arab Resistance Movement: Its Significance in the Middle East Crisis', in Moore, J. (ed.) *The Arab–Israeli Conflict Volume II* (Princeton University Press, New Jersey, 1974) p. 494.

29 Hudson notes the modern rather than traditional orientation of the resistance elite who were largely Western educated; Hudson, M. 'Developments and setbacks in the Palestinian resistance movement', *Journal of Palestine Studies* vol. I (Spring 1972), no. 3, p. 70.

30 See Hudson (1972: 77-80) on the role of ideology within the Palestinian movement.

31 In the case of the Palestinian resistance movement Sharabi notes the strong relationship between the PFLP's success among the Arab masses and its well developed and articulated ideology. Sharabi, H. *Palestine Guerrillas, their Credibility and Effectiveness* (Georgetown University, Washington D.C., 1970) p. 28.

32 Shuaibi (1979-I: 78).

33 For the text of the Draft Constitution see Laquer, W. *The Israeli–Arab Reader: A documentary history of the Middle East conflict* (Penguin Books, Harmondsworth, 1970) pp. 165–9.

34 Becker, J. *The PLO: The Rise and Fall of the Palestine Liberation Organization* (Weidenfeld and Nicolson, London, 1984) p. 39, notes the influence of Nasser on the PNC and the Charter.

35 See Yodfat and Arnon-Ohanna (1981: 147–53) for an article by article comparison of the two Covenants.

36 See articles 21, 28, 29 in ibid..

37 Laquer (1970: 444).

38 *Arab Report and Record* (1968: 338).

39 Laquer (1970: 445).

40 Frangi (1983: 97). For Fatah's arguments in 1968 on the role of armed struggle to awaken mass consciousness and for the redefinition of the Arab–Israeli conflict as one between the Palestinians and Zionism see Sharabi, H. *Palestine and Israel: The Lethal Dilemma* (Pegasus, New York, 1969) p. 198-9.

41 Moore in Hudson (1974: 498).

42 Frangi (1983: 111); Schiff, Z. and Rothstein, R. *Fedayeen, The Story of the Palestinian Guerrillas* (Vallentine Mitchell, London, 1972) pp. 81–5.

43 Rodinson (1982: 259).

44 Ibid. pp. 236–7, Frangi (1983: 119).

45 Rubenberg (1983: 18).

46 See Appendix III for a comprehensive list of PNC meetings.

47 Quandt *et al.* (1973: 88).

48 It was at the 11th PNC that the PLO decided on the need to set up the PNF. The task of the PNF was to be the mobilization of 'Palestinians in the occupied territories' *ARR*, (1973: 47).

49 *ARR* (1976: 329).

50 Gilmour (1982: 123).

51 Landau, J. *The Arabs in Israel* (Oxford University Press, London, 1969) pp. 71–2.

52 Ibid., p. 84.

53 Landau (1969: 73).

54 Gilmour (1982: 115).

55 For an analysis of Israeli Arab voting behaviour see Zureik, E. *The Palestinians in Israel: A Study in Internal Colonialism* (Routledge and Kegan Paul, London, 1979) pp. 167–72).

56 Frangi (1983: 196).

57 For details of the first PLO–Rakah meeting in Prague see *ARR* (1977: 376).

58 Frangi (1983: 97–103).
59 *Keesing's Contemporary Archives* November 1968, pp. 23029 and 23327 and *ARR* (1968: 338).
60 The high turn out of 84 per cent in spite of the boycott calls led Dayan to claim that the residents had responded to 'the Israeli administration rather than to the Arab countries and terrorist organization' *ARR* (1972: 157).
61 Shuaibi, I. 'The Development of Palestinian Entity-Consciousness, Part-III', *Journal of Palestine Studies* vol. IX (Spring 1980), no. 3, p. 102.
62 Shuaibi (1980-III: 102, 116).
63 *ARR* (1977: 960); *ARR* (1977: 1023).
64 Ibid.

5 The Arab Governmental Level

Introduction

In this study, the Arab governmental level is constituted by membership of the Arab League through which a country asserts its Arab identity. At its inception the Arab League had six members and it has since expanded to twenty-two.[1]

The study of the mobilization process in support of the Palestinian cause at the Arab level concentrates mostly on Arab governments that have had a direct involvement with the Palestine Question. These are the countries neighbouring Palestine (Egypt, the Lebanon, Jordan and Syria) together with Algeria and Iraq. Most of the other Arab governments have tended to follow the lead of the core group.[2] The group has not, however, been uniform and coherent. The idiosyncracies of each regime and its leadership, together with the primacy of each individual Arab government's immediate concerns and goals over the interests of Palestine has culminated often in individual and conflicting approaches to the problem. The resulting rivalries that seem to characterize Arab politics in the region have, even at the height of pan-Arabism, prevented the development of a coordinated and unified approach towards Palestine; the only point of agreement has been Israel's illegality.[3]

The purpose of this chapter is not to chart the development, changes and nature of each Arab government's policy towards Palestine, but to study how Arab governments, as a group, interacted with the mobilization process and came to revise their attitudes towards the Palestinian Problem.

The established Arab governmental attitude of the 1950s was one which defined Palestine as an Arab problem. On the one hand, Egyptian, Syrian and Iraqi governments saw the liberation of Palestine within the context of Arab unity. On the other, King Hussein, who represented part of the royalist and traditional trend in Arab politics, remained concerned with the consolidation and recognition of Jordan's rule over the West Bank. This attitude began to change during the 1960s. The emergence of Palestinian groups stressing an independent and separate Palestinian national identity together with the inability of Arab governments to put pan-Arab rhetoric into effect and their defeat, in the June 1967 war, were developments that contributed towards these changes.

These changes were examined from a Palestinian perspective. That is these changes were seen as the product of a Palestinian initiated mobilization process to bring the redefined Palestinian cause to the attention of Arab governments and to mobilize support for it. It should be noted that Palestinian efforts to gain the support of Arab governments were an interactive process whose net effect was that Arab governments changed their attitudes towards Palestine and the Palestinian cause and the Palestinian resistance movement found it necessary to reconsider and revise its goals and policies.

The mobilization process

The analysis focuses on Arab governmental responses to demands put forward by the Palestinian resistance movement and the PLO to gain Arab recognition and support for the Palestinian cause.

Conducive environment

In the Arab world the 1950s, as in Palestine, was a period of optimism caused by a series of achievements attributed to the growing strength of Arab nationalism. The conservative regimes in Egypt and Iraq had been swept away by Arab nationalist forces. Nasser's challenge against colonial powers over Suez had culminated in a political victory. The independent Arab world was expanding as more and more areas under colonial rule achieved independence. Furthermore, this period of struggle for Arab unity bore its first fruit with the establishment of the United Arab Republic.

All these events made the Arab world confident of the eventual liberation of Palestine. It was a matter of time before the Arab armies would move on to liberate Arab Palestine. According to Nasser this was predicted to happen:

once we are fully emancipated from the shackles of colonialism and intrigues of colonialist agents, we shall take a further step forward towards liberation of Palestine. When we have brought our armed forces to full strength and made our own armaments we will take another step forward towards the liberation of Palestine ..., and when we have manufactured jet aircraft and tanks we will embark upon the final stage of this liberation.[4]

Such an environment was far from receptive to a mobilization process in support of a Palestinian cause stressing the indigenous nature of the Palestinian national identity and the need to mount an independent armed struggle to achieve it. It is, as was pointed out earlier, this lack of a conducive environment that kept Al-Fatah from surfacing until 1964. This does not mean that the idea of an independent Palestinian struggle was not on the public agenda at all. Al-Fatah together with some smaller Palestinian groups had been talking about an independent Palestine throughout the 1950s.[5] By the early 1960s the issue was taken up by Arab governments too. Iraq, for example, became the first country to commit itself to an independent Palestinian enity and expressed a willingness to assist a Palestinian armed struggle as early as 1961. Algeria followed suit.

The event that probably had the most significant impact in changing the environment towards one more conducive for a Palestinian initiated mobilization process, was precipitated by Israel. Israel had been working on a project to divert the waters of the Jordan river since 1953. This irrigation project was perceived by the Arab world as an aggression committed against Arab land precipitating promises of preventive Arab governmental action. However, as sections of this project reached its completion, Arab governments began to criticize each other for not doing something concrete about it. In the face of growing criticism directed towards Egypt's reluctance to engage Israel and pressure from 'revolutionary elements in the Arab World ... accusing Nasser of having neglected the Palestine problem', Nasser called for a summit meeting of all Arab governments in January 1964 to discuss the situation.[6] It was during the summit deliberations that 'Bourguiba and Ben Bella put forward a proposal to the Summit Conference for the formation of a "FLN-style" organisation (i.e National Liberation Front) to push forward the campaign for the restoration of the rights of the Arabs of Palestine'.[7]

This proposal was then endorsed by the summit and it was agreed that an organization of the Palestinian people should be set up to enable them to liberate their homeland and determine their future. The summit authorized an ex-Saudi Arabian diplomat of Palestinian origin, Shukairy, to take necessary measures to establish a Palestinian organization to represent Palestinian Arab aspirations. Even though the Arab governments decided not to go to war with Israel over the Jordan river, they set in motion the process that brought about the establishment of the PLO. As a result of Shukairy's consultations with the Palestinians and Arab governments, the PLO was formed by the first Palestinian National Council in May 1964 and endorsed by the Alexandria summit conference of the Arab League in September 1964.

Although in a letter to U Thant, 25 May 1964, Shukairy claimed the right to be regarded as the 'only legitimate spokesman for all matters concerning the Palestine people'[8] this was a long way from reality. Instead, the PLO remained under the tutelage of Arab governments, particularly in military affairs. The Palestine Liberation Army, which was set up as the PLO's military arm, was never allowed to mount any military action in spite of Shukairy's urgings, and his attempts[9] to make the PLA an effective military unit remained frustrated.[9] It was quite evident from the decisions of the Third Arab Summit in September 1965 that the liberation of Palestine was still envisaged through Arab unity and conventional military action. This was also reflected in the reluctance of the summit to endorse Boumedienne's suggestion that the PLA adopt a strategy of guerrilla warfare.[10] Nevertheless, the establishment of the PLO was, to some extent, an acknowledgement by Arab states of a growing Palestinian political awareness.

The outcome of the 1967 war had an impact on the Arab governments in two ways. First, Nasser's resignation after Egypt's defeat demonstrated the difficulty Arab armies would have in liberating Palestine.[11] The growth of the Palestinian resistance movement in the aftermath of the war, and the Karameh battle in particular, increasingly convinced Nasser that a Palestinian armed struggle could have a role to play in the liberation of Palestine.[12] Syria and Iraq too came to support the idea of guerrilla warfare and sponsored guerrilla groups. In addition, Jordan, in the face of growing support, was induced to change its negative attitude towards the Palestinian resistance movement.[13]

Secondly, the war left Israel occupying territories belonging to Arab countries, dramatically increasing the salience of the conflict with Israel.

Israel now occupied in addition to all of Palestine, significant portions of Syria, ... and Egypt. This condition made it impossible for Arab leaders to put the question of Israel 'on the back burner' as President Nasser did between the wars of 1956 and 1967.[14]

It brought Egypt and Jordan together in their concern to ensure the return of the occupied areas.[15]

This development, however, was rather like a double-edged sword. On the one hand, the Israeli occupation was increasing the salience of the Palestinian issue to the Arab governments and on the other, the narrower territorial considerations were making a political settlement along the lines of Security Council Resolution 242 and the Rogers' Plan more tempting. Hence, King Hussein and, more importantly Nasser, were drawn away from the position held by the Palestinian resistance movement which stressed the role of armed struggle in liberating Palestine.

The damage inflicted to the prospects of Arab unity with the collapse of the Egyptian-Syrian Union, the establishment of the Arab-League-sponsored PLO, the defeat in the 1967 war, the growth in size and effectiveness of the Palestinian resistance movement were major events that brought about an environment more receptive to the demands of the Palestinians. This occurred as a result of the impact that these events had both on the structure of the regional political system and on the dominant political processes.

The entry into the Middle Eastern political system of new elements in the form of the PLO and the Palestinian resistance movement brought about structural changes which enabled these elements to gain access to the Arab governments. The role of accessibility in mobilizing Arab governmental support will be examined more closely when the 'accessibility' variable of the mobilization model is introduced. Events such as the collapse of the union between Egypt and Syria and the 1967 defeat of the Arab armies weakened the dominance of pan-Arabism in the political system, allowing the possibility of new political processes to emerge. These stressed a separate Palestinian national identity and recognized the role of an independent Palestinian struggle in liberating Palestine. The following section will examine how these processes altered Arab governmental attitudes towards the Palestinian problem.

Cognitive linkages

In the preceding chapter the inhibiting role of pan-Arab thinking on the mobilization of support among Palestinians was pointed out. Arab nationalism and the struggle for Arab unity had a similar effect on the approach of the major Arab governments to the Palestinian problem.

As new leaders, motivated by Arab nationalism, began to replace royalists and conservatives they introduced changes in their foreign policies. The revolutionary nature of Arab nationalism under the leadership of Nasser began to challenge the status quo in the region. An early manifestation of the revolutionary nature of the struggle for Arab unity was evidenced in Nasser's determination to challenge Britain over the status of Suez. A similar challenge was also directed towards Israel. Soon after Nasser came to power he closed the straits of Tiran to Israeli shipping, the first major belligerent move of any significance directed towards Israel since 1949. Suez and the problem of Palestine were perceived in the context of Arab nationalism and Arab unity.

Arab nationalism constituted a major input into Egypt's foreign policy behaviour. Accordingly the liberation of Palestine was part and parcel of a struggle against colonialism and imperialism to bring about Arab unity. The ultimate goal was Arab unity, and the liberation of Palestine constituted a major task within that.

This cognitive linkage between Arab nationalism and the liberation of Palestine denied any role to an indigenous Palestinian armed struggle for a long time. When the idea that Palestine was a problem for the Palestinians was first brought up by Syria and Iraq at the Arab League meeting in September 1963 it was more as a result of the rivalry between Egypt and Syria in alliance with Iraq, rather than a break away from a pan-Arab attitude towards Palestine. Even then the role of the Palestinians in the liberation of Palestine was never envisaged as superceding Arab governmental efforts.

This stance is well demonstrated by the attitude that Syria and Egypt took towards Al-Fatah's public pronouncement on the question of Palestine. Both Syria[16] and Egypt regarded Al-Fatah's activities with suspicion and did not hesitate to arrest and imprison its members.[17] This attitude was also shared by the Arab media which in the aftermath of Al-Fatah's first military operation regarded the activities of Al-Fatah as one that would undermine Arab unity.[18] In early 1965 this culminated in the adoption of a resolution by the Arab League defence ministers which called on all Arab governments to supress Al-Fatah operations.[19]

As an Algerian observer noted most Arab states were suspicious of Fatah before 1967 because 'for the first time a Palestinian organisation presented itself as exclusively Palestinian, with exclusively Palestinian objectives. A revolutionary attitude because it was totally unorthodox'.[20]

The situation with Algeria was very different. Algeria had just achieved its independence after a long national liberation war, a war that was after all fought by the Algerians alone. Even though Arab states did lend their political support, at the international level, and, after the establishment of its provisional government, gave Algeria financial support,[21] at no point did the Arab governments contemplate liberating Algeria for the Algerians. The nearest the Arab governments came to commiting themselves to military action was in an Arab League decision in March 1960 calling for volunteers to fight for Algeria.[22] The Algerian struggle for independence was a national one that did not rely on Arab unity or pan-Arabism. Hence, it is not surprising that soon after its independence Ben Bella expressed support for Al-Fatah, allowing them to open an office in Algiers and argued among Arab governments the need for guerrilla warfare led by an FLN-style Palestinian national organization.[23] Boumedienne for his part during the deliberations at the Third Arab Summit, in September 1965, supported guerrilla warfare rather than conventional military action.[24]

Pan-Arabism and the struggle for Arab unity influenced perceptions of who the Palestinians were and whether they could achieve a state of their own. From the early days of the Arab League, the Palestinians were referred to as 'Arabs of Palestine'. When revolutionary Arab regimes came to power in the 1950s this terminology gained particular strength; Arab League Council decisions appear to reflect this in their regular reference to the Palestinians and Palestinian refugees as 'Arabs of Palestine' and 'Arab refugees of Palestine'.[25] Evidence is also provided in a speech made by Nasser in 1960 where the Palestinians were referred to as 'Arabs of Palestine' and Palestine was treated as an Arab land.[26]

While the Arab nationalist regimes saw Palestine within the framework of a unified Arab world, King Hussein's monarchy had a different approach particularly to the West Bank. The residents of Palestine were seen as Jordanians and any debate over the liberation of Palestine including the West Bank was seen as undermining the sovereignty of Jordan. This remained as a particular tension between Egypt and Jordan during the late 1950s and was only resolved during the establishment of the PLO in the early 1960s with a clear understanding of respect for Jordanian sovereignty.[27]

The hold of Arab nationalism on most Arab governmental attitudes towards the Palestinians and their perception of the role of an indigenous Palestinian struggle continued until after the 1967 war. The changing environment brought about particularly by the defeat of the Arab armies and the growing success and popularity of Palestinian resistance movement began to weaken the influence of pan-Arabism. Both changes occurred at roughly the same time.

The first signs of change began to take a concrete form in 1969. Nasser, who had started to reconsider his attitude towards the Palestinian resistance movement after the 1967 war, decided to attend the Fifth Palestine National Council. The symbolic importance of Nasser's attendance stemmed from the fact that this PNC session elected Arafat as its chairman. Arafat, as the leader of Al-Fatah, had urged

Palestinian armed struggle to liberate Palestine since the early 1960s. He had also challenged the Arab sponsored Palestinian leadership of the PLO to adopt this policy. It was at this PNC meeting that the transfer of the PLO leadership to the Palestinian resistance movement was completed, with the blessing of the most important Arab government and its leader. This attitude did not, however, gain broad, instant and continuous support.

Arab governmental perceptions of who exactly the Palestinians were and whether they were to be a part of a unified Arab nation began to change soon after the goal of Arab unity had experienced its first set-back with the break-up of the UAR. Arab governmental decisions and speeches that used to refer to the Palestinians as 'Arabs of Palestine' introduced the term 'Palestine Arabs', suggesting a certain degree of change in their perception of the Palestinians.[28] This change occurred when Arab governments became increasingly aware of the difficulties of achieving 'Arab Unity'. Nasser's policies stressing Arab unity were seen as interference in their domestic affairs particularly by the conservative regimes. It is as a direct result of these developments that the concept of 'Arab solidarity' developed to replace the idea of 'Arab unity'. 'Arab solidarity' stressed the, 'right of every Arab state to determine its own internal and external policies.'[29]

A second set of changes in Arab governmental perceptions occurred after the 1967 war and during a period when the Palestinian resistance movement began to have an impact on both Palestinians and Arab governments. References to 'Arabs of Palestine' disappeared. Arab governments used the term 'Palestinian Arabs' together with 'Arab Palestinians'. Until the Algiers summit in 1973 it is difficult to substantiate a clear and unambiguous pattern. It was here that reference to the 'national rights' of the Palestinian people was first used, suggesting the recognition of a separate Palestinian national identity. This took an even clearer form at the Rabat summit of October 1974 when Arab governments supported the right of the Palestinian people to establish an independent national authority. The Palestinians were now perceived as a distinct nation, entitled to exercise their right to self-determination in the form of their own state.

The Palestinian resistance movement's and later the PLO's accessibility to the Arab governments played an important part in influencing this conceptual-perceptual change in Arab thinking, giving them the chance to raise and argue their case and try to change Arab perceptions of themselves and the Palestinian problem.

Accessibility

From its early days, the PLO enjoyed direct access to the Arab governments through the Arab League. However, during Shukairy's leadership it did not mobilize support for armed struggle. In the case of the Palestinian resistance movement in the mid-1960s violence appeared to be the only means by which it could have its voice heard. It was only after the Palestinian resistance movement received recognition for its role in the liberation of Palestine that it began to acquire the means for direct though informal access to the Arab governments. This accessibility increased when the Palestinian resistance movement, in the late 1960s, took over the leadership of the PLO. As the prestige and status of the PLO, both inside and outside the Palestinian community, became evident and the PLO was recognized by the Arab governments as the representative of the Palestinian people, the PLO's direct access to these governments was formalized by the opening of PLO offices.

Table 5.1. Access routes to Arab governments

	Violent means	Non-violent means
Indirect access	against Israel	early PLO participation in the Arab League
Direct access	against Arab states	informal, 1973 formal, 1974

As Table 5.1 depicts there were a number of different ways of reaching the Arab governments. Al-Fatah, all along, had recognized the importance of having access to the Arab public and the Arab governments in launching an armed struggle to liberate Palestine.[30] Al-Fatah's first military operation, even though not well received by the Arab governments and the public, put the Palestinian armed struggle on Arab governments' agendas. In the light of Al-Fatah's unsuccessful early attempts to establish links with the Egyptian government and gain its co-operation,[31] the only remaining option left to it was to continue to use violence against Israel so as to increase the tension between Israel and its Arab neighbours. This was at least a successful way of drawing attention to what they had to say, violence against Israel was a way of keeping the Palestinian cause on the agendas of Arab governments.

Simultaneously, the PLO, led by Shukairy, also constituted a channel through which the Palestinian cause was raised. Although there remained a gap between the PLO's and Al-Fatah's approach to the liberation of Palestine, at least the PLO had some direct access to the Arab governments. It was able to participate in the Arab League deliberations on Palestine[32] and raise the need for support for the Palestinian cause including military action. The effectiveness of this access route is questionable, however, as Shukairy appears to have had little impact on Arab governments' attitudes towards making the Palestine Liberation Army an effective fighting force.[33]

Al-Fatah and the Palestinian resistance movement's access to Arab governments and the public improved significantly after the 1967 war and Arab nationalism began to lose its hold. Violence continued to play its role as an access route. The guerrilla fighter won the support of the Arab people as 'an individual who has taken his future into his own hands, who sacrifices personal advantages, who works as part of a team for a noble purpose.'[34] It was in such an atmosphere that the Palestinian resistance movement's violence against Israel began to make Arab governments reconsider their earlier position. The first evidence of a change in attitude came from Nasser as he developed direct relations with Al-Fatah. Throughout 1967 and 1968 Arafat met with Nasser on numerous occasions. As early as 1968 Arafat was included in Nasser's delegation to Moscow. Similarly, the takeover of the PLO by the Palestinian resistance movement at the Fifth PNC opened the way for their participation in Arab League meetings. This, naturally, enabled the PLO to argue its case directly with the Arab delegations during such meetings.

The Palestinian resistance movement found itself in a situation where it resorted to violence against Arab states, too. The presence of the PLO in the Lebanon and Jordan became increasingly unacceptable to both countries' governments. These governments saw the presence and activities of the PLO as under-mining their sovereignty. The tension between the PLO and these two governments errupted into violence in 1969, 1970–1 and early 1973. The armed confrontations had three results.

First, these confrontations attracted the attention of the public in Arab countries. During the civil war in Jordan the public appears to have expressed support for the Palestinians.[35] Second, it resulted in the Arab governments' inter-vention to try to bring the violence to an end in a manner favourable to the PLO. Third, this violence forced the Arab governments to face up to the problems created by the Palestinian armed struggle against Israel. At the end of these events it was quite evident that the role of the Palestinian armed struggle had been accepted. But there were naturally deep disagreements over the distributions of the costs of the consequences of Israeli retaliation that this armed struggle attracted.

After the June 1967 war Arafat, first as head of Al-Fatah and then as the chair-man of the PLO, was received by Arab leaders particularly those in Egypt, Syria and North Africa. This situation came to a crucial turning point in November 1973, at Algiers. As the possibility of an international conference to resolve the Middle East conflict, in accordance with Security Council Resolution 338 emerged, an Arab summit was called to discuss the matter.

The summit decided to support the idea of a Geneva Conference but simul-taneously declared the PLO to be the sole representative of the Palestinian people with Jordan entering a reservation concerning the Palestinians living in the West Bank.[36] Although Jordan's position was briefly supported by Sadat[37] the problem, after extensive lobbying,[38] was resolved by the next Arab summit meeting in October 1974, at Rabat. The summit recognized the PLO not only as the sole but also as the legitimate representative of the Palestinian people.

A reference to the PLO's 'legitimacy' to represent all Palestinians was specially included to stress the PLO's right to represent the Palestinians in the West Bank. As Frangi notes: 'At last, the Palestinians were equal with other states and the Palestinian leadership had to be accepted as equal as others.'[39] Subsequent to the Rabat decision the PLO acquired direct formal access to Arab governments and opened offices in all Arab League member countries except Oman. These offices, most of which had diplomatic status, gave the PLO the opportunity of raising any matter with the Arab governments. Furthermore, the Rabat decision on the PLO opened the way for the PLO to become a full member of the Arab League. Egypt, as a direct result of a series of talks between Arafat and the Egyptian premier, aimed at redressing the rift caused by the Sinai disengagement agreements called on the Arab League to grant the PLO full membership. This was then granted by a unanimous decision at the Council session in December 1976.[40]

Output: the growth of Arab governmental support

The growth of Arab governmental support for the Palestinian cause as a result of the mobilization process can best be summarized by breaking it down to three stages. The first stage, covering the period prior to the 1967 war, is characterized by little change in governmental perceptions of the Palestinian problem. The second, between 1967 and 1973, is a period of transition and of fluctuating atti-tudes. The last covers the period from 1974 onwards when the Arab governments recognized the PLO and the Palestinian cause as defined by it.

It was during the early 1960s that the Arab governments began to encounter the first open signs of a Palestinian awareness. They sought to respond to this within the context of the Arab League. By this means, the PLO was established. The PLO did represent and to some extent mobilized Palestinian aspirations, but the fact that it had to operate within an Arab governmental framework limited its scope of action. This limitation was reflected in numerous complaints by Shukairy and in his willingness to support, at least verbally, the Palestinian resistance movement.[41]

The establishment of the PLO itself was a recognition of the urgency of responding to the Palestinian problem and to a growing Palestinian national awareness. This development must be assessed with caution as it was also an attempt to control and channel emerging Palestinian nationalism, amply demonstrated by the negative attitude most governments took towards the guerrilla groups that constituted the Palestinian resistance movement of the same period. These governments were reluctant to deal with the Palestinian resistance movement but also saw them as a threat to their security and to the eventual liberation of Palestine.

This rather unfavourable attitude to the Palestinian resistance movement and to Al-Fatah, in particular, was evident in Arab governmental responses to Palestinian resistance movement positions on the role of a Palestinian armed struggle against Israel. The first Al-Fatah operation triggered a very unfavourable response from the Arab governments. A string of Palestinians associated with Al-Fatah were arrested across the Middle East.[42] This clampdown and the subsequent Arab League decision on January 1965 calling for the supression of military operations by Palestinian groups reflected the attitude that Arab governments held towards a Palestinian identity expressed outside the framework of the PLO. The only exception to this rather negative attitude of an independent Palestinian resistance was Algeria. Algeria supported Al-Fatah's principle of 'guerrilla warfare' in the liberation of Palestine.

This negative stance towards indigenous Palestinian military capabilities was also evident in the Arab governments' reluctance to cooperate with Shukairy's attempts to build an effective military arm for the PLO. The PLO had been allowed to develop as a political and administrative organization to preserve the Palestinian entity with little muscle. Arab governments neighbouring Palestine were particularly reluctant to see a Palestinian organization with military capabilities. Although Egypt, Iraq and Syria did eventually allow the PLO to set up the PLA, the units from this conventional army were kept under the control of the respective host countries. Jordan remained completely opposed to the idea.[43]

The second period was one characterized by changing attitudes. It was not a period where governmental attitudes changed uniformly and simultaneously. Nevertheless the changes that did take place were of great significance to the Palestinian cause. The defeat of the Arab armies, in the 1967 war, led to the growth of the Palestinian resistance movement and support for it among Palestinians. Similarly, in the aftermath of this defeat coupled with growing support for the Palestinian resistance movement, Arab governments began to reconsider their position *vis-à-vis* the role of a Palestinian national armed struggle. This did not, however, happen at once and when it did, the change was rather erratic.

The decision adopted by the Arab summit, held after the June 1967 war, fell short of Shukairy's request to have no dealings, even indirect, with Israel that might affect the Palestinian cause.[44] The Arab governments did not just stop at refusing to take into consideration the wishes of the PLO's chairman, their own appointee. Instead most Arab governments, including Egypt and Jordan, found it expedient to accept Resolution 242, in spite of the Khartoum Arab summit decision of 'no negotiations with Israel'.[45]

Yet it should be noted that in face of the Arab armies' defeat coupled with the Karameh action in March 1968, Nasser did begin to take a favourable position towards the arguments of the Palestinian resistance movement. He began direct contacts with Arafat. This was generally regarded as a symbolic acceptance of the centrality of the Palestinian resistance movement's arguments for the liberation of Palestine. This acceptance of the guerrilla groups' role was also reflected in an Arab League council meeting in March 1969 that promised aid to the new PLO and confirmed, 'the right of the Palestinian people to liberate their fatherland and achieve their right to self-determination'.[46] The ability of the PLO to gain the support of a high status actor in the Arab world improved its position both among the Palestinians and Arab governments.

These developments, favourable to the Palestinian resistance movement, did not continue unabated. As Quandt et al. note, the honeymoon was short lived.[47] There were three setbacks. The rather unclear position of most governments towards the PLO became evident during 1969 and 1970. After the initial enthusiasm over the role of Palestinian armed struggle in liberating Palestine some Arab circles became sceptical. Gaddafi, at the cost of undermining his early role as the champion of the Palestinian cause, 'dismissed the idea of popular war against Israel as fanciful and told the fedayeen to join with the Arab armies to fight Israel'.[48] A similar position was taken by Nasser in the aftermath of his and Jordan's acceptance of the Rogers' Plan in July 1970. Heikal, Al-Ahram's editor often quoted as Nasser's spokesman, in an article underplayed the role of Palestinian armed struggle in the conflict with Israel.[49]

The acceptance of the Rogers' Plan also constituted a setback and reflected the inherent ambiguity in Arab governmental attitudes towards the problem of Palestine during this period. Even though Resolution 242 had initially been endorsed, it had fallen into some disrepute as a result of Israeli intransigence. Hence after a period of rapprochement between the Palestinian resistance movement and Nasser during 1968 and 1969 the acceptance of the Rogers' Plan came as another source of ambiguity. The implied recognition of Israel through negotiations inherent in the peace-making process suggested by the Rogers' Plan undermined the Palestinian resistance movement in two ways. First, it went against the official position taken by the PLO and the individual member guerrilla groups, not to mention the Arab summit decision of August 1967. Second, the negotiations, in the context of the Rogers' Plan, were clearly intended to exclude the Palestinian who were referred to as 'refugees'.

These developments were received with growing anxiety among the Palestinians. The resistance movement promoted protests against the Rogers' Plan especially in Jordan and the PNC, and at its emergency session in August 1970 rejected the Plan and proclaimed the independence of the Palestinian resistance movement and its armed struggle.[50] This situation exacerbated tension between the Jordanian authorities and the Palestinian resistance movement. In September it finally erupted into violence when King Hussein felt the need to respond to what he perceived as a challenge to his authority.

The third setback was embedded in the Arab governments' response to the brutal manner in which Jordan was suppressing the PLO. Although Iraq and Syria showed early signs of military support and Nasser threatened to intervene, militarily, to stop the Jordanian suppression of the Palestinian resistance movement, no Arab government made a decisive move.[51] Nevertheless, to reflect the deep disapproval of Jordan's behaviour, the Arab governments did take certain relatively mild but concrete measures. Libya and Kuwait stopped financial aid to Jordan. Algeria, Iraq, Libya and Syria either broke or severed diplomatic relations and announced a series of boycotts. These measures, according to Quandt, 'doubtless increased Hussein's receptiveness to the Egyptian Saudi mediation efforts'.[52]

However, by then most of the Palestinian resistance had been eradicated. The feeling among Palestinians was one of having been let down. While Arafat talked about an Arab plot against the Palestinians, the PDFLP accused the Arab governments of collusion with Jordan.[53] At first, it looked as though the damage inflicted on the Palestinian resistance movement was not going to stop at this point. King Hussein, in an attempt to reassert his challenged role as the representative of the Palestinians in the West Bank, got the Jordanian parliament, in February 1971, to reject any idea of a Palestinian state and affirmed that the Jordanians constituted a single integrated people.[54] This happened at a time when the PLO declared its intention to liberate all of its usurped homeland, including the West Bank.[55]

The following year, King Hussein announced his plan for a United Arab Kingdom. The plan, which envisaged a federal Kingdom set up through negotiations with Israel, was not however well received by the Arab governments.[56] Its unequivocal rejection indicated the beginnings of a gradual process of convergence between the Arab governments and the PLO, pointing the way towards the end of the setbacks in the mobilization of support for the Palestinian cause.

After the death of Nasser, it had become quite evident that Sadat did not intend to follow the radical policies of his predecessor. Sadat seemed to be primarily concerned with obtaining Israel's withdrawal from the occupied territories even if that meant guaranteeing the existence of Israel.[57] Most Arab governments, including Syria, appeared to support this position. The Syrian government in March 1972 after a change in leadership supported a negotiated solution along the lines of Resolution 242, providing the rights of the Palestinians were recognized.[58] The Central Committee of the PLO dominated by Al-Fatah, too, seemed to accept Egypt's position. As early as January 1971, it was prepared to accept Arab efforts for a negotiated settlement with Israel provided Arab governments did not compromise the rights of the Palestinian people.[59]

This convergence of positions between the PLO and Arab governments, although at first opposed by radical guerrilla movements, did consolidate itself. This was evident in the Arab governments' rejection of King Hussein's plan for a United Arab Kingdom. To King Hussein's dismay, the decisive turning point came roughly a year after the announcement of his plan. An Israeli raid into Beirut killed three leading PLO personalities and changed the atmosphere in the West Bank and the Gaza Strip significantly.[60] The funeral of these three PLO personalities turned into an impressive show of support for the PLO, coupled by demonstrations during which the Palestinian flag was flown.

The raising of the Palestinian flag on a nationalist occasion was certainly the expression of a consciousness that gathered momentum from then on; the flag has since been raised on many occasions, whereas throughout the period following the June War it was the Jordanian flag that headed demonstrations and flew over the graves of the soldiers and civilians who had fallen during the war.[61]

This major breakthrough in the Palestinian expression of support for their national identity and the PLO did not go unnoticed among Arab governments. After the October War, Sadat spoke of the legitimate rights of the Palestinian people together with the liberation of 'our territories occupied by Israel' as his primary task.[62] However, the most decisive and complete affirmation of support, at the Arab level, for the Palestinian rights came at the Algiers Arab summit in November 1973. The decisions taken at Algiers stressed 'the restoration to the Palestinian people of their established national rights'.[63] The Algiers Arab summit decided also to confer upon the PLO the right to be sole representative of the Palestinian people with Jordan entering reservations. The Algiers decision was the first of its kind at this level to refer, without any ambiguity, to the 'national rights' of the Palestinians as a 'people'.[64]

By 1974, the PLO had won the crucial part of the battle for recognition. Apart from Sadat's brief flirtation with Hussein, in respect to the PLO's representative status, other Arab governments held their position. At the Rabat summit Jordan too was convinced to join ranks with the other Arab governments. Hence, at Rabat, the Arab governments were able to adopt unanimously a resolution that *inter alia* asserted the: 'Palestinian people's right to return to their homeland and determine their own fate'. It also stressed 'that any Palestinian territory liberated through struggle in any form shall revert to its legitimate Palestinian ownership under the leadership of the PLO; ... the Palestinian people's right to establish their own indepedent authority in all liberated territories.'[65]

Since the Rabat summit, Arab governmental support for the role of the PLO and the political rights of the Palestinians has been reaffirmed at the Tripoli, Algiers and Baghdad Arab League summit meetings. The Baghdad summit, in March 1979, marked the occasion when Egypt became isolated and ejected from Arab ranks for having violated the letter and the spirit of the Rabat decision by implementing the Camp David peace process.[66] This process, which began informally with Sadat's visit to Jerusalem in November 1977, culminated in the signing of a peace treaty in March 1979 between Egypt and Israel. The peace treaty made no references to the Palestinian problem but had instead an adjoining commitment to proceed with the implementation of the 'Framework for Peace in the Middle East' agreed at Camp David in September 1978.

This framework stated that:

Egypt, Israel and Jordan will agree on the modalities for establishing the elected self-governing authority in the West Bank and Gaza or other Palestinians as mutually agreed. The parties will negotiate an Agreement which will define the powers and responsibilities of the self-governing authority to be exercised in the West Bank and Gaza.[67]

The provisions of this framework were far from meeting earlier Arab governmental decisions recognizing the PLO as representing the Palestinians in their aspirations to achieve statehood.

The reactions in the Arab world to the announcement of the peace treaty between Egypt and Israel are indicative of the extent to which the PLO had mobilized support for the Palestinian cause. The day after the treaty was formally signed, an Arab summit was held in Baghdad that suspended Egypt's membership of the Arab League, decided to move the League's headquarters from Cairo to Tunis and announced economic boycotts. The PLO had already, in September 1978, formed the Steadfastness Front with Algeria, Libya, Syria and Yemen.

The Front had rejected the Camp David agreements because, they argued, it renounced the principle of a just peace in the Middle East; they stressed this could only be achieved by the recognition and realization of the inalienable rights of the Palestinian people.[68] The negative reactions were not limited to the PLO and Arab governments but extended to the Palestinians and Arabs at large, as well. The visit of Sadat to Jerusalem had triggered protest demonstrations in the occupied territories.[69]

An overwhelming majority of the Arab governments continued to support the official PLO position during the post-Rabat period. However, two points need to be made. First, the official PLO line did not always reflect the position of the Palestinian resistance movement as a whole. The PFLP, PFLP–GC and ALF, as a result of the PLO's acceptance of the idea of a 'mini-state' and the possibility of comprehensive peace talks, formed the 'rejection front'. They asserted the continuation of the armed struggle for the total liberation of Palestine. Particularly, the PFLP's involvement in hijackings during 1974 and 1975 brought this guerrilla group into direct conflict with the PLO leaders, which had by then banned hijackings. The consequence of this division was that Arab governments such as Libya and in particular Iraq supported positions *plus royaliste que le roi*.

Second, although the PLO at the 12th PNC in June 1974 opened the way to negotiations, its position on this matter was at times unclear. In the immediate aftermath of the Sinai disengagement agreements and Sadat's visit to Jerusalem, it hardened its position and moved to one closer to that held by the rejection front. This was particularly evident in the Palestinian declaration of unity signed in Tripoli in 1977 by leaders of guerrilla groups, including those of the rejection front. The declaration reasserted the right of the Palestinian people 'to self-determination within the framework of an independent state set up on any part of Palestinian soil that may be liberated.'[70] The declaration appears to have left the issue of 'peace talks' unclear. However, the consequence of the PLO's change in its position *vis-à-vis* peace talks has been such that it has strained and complicated its relationship with conservative Arab governments that have favoured the resolution of the problem through negotiations. Nevertheless, the essential point to bear in mind is the fact that the PLO remained recognized as the sole representative of the Palestinian people.

Two concluding points need to be made. First, the above analysis shows how, as a result of the mobilization process, the PLO found itself reconsidering the definition as well as the means of realizing the Palestinian cause. The PLO, during its efforts to gain support among the Arab governments, modified its goals as well as the means of achieving them.

The second point relates to the interaction between the mobilization process at different levels. In chapter 4, it was noted briefly that the PLO's improved status in the Arab governmental world and the international community did generate support for the PLO among Palestinians. This is quite evident from the strong pro-PLO demonstrations in the West Bank and the Gaza Strip both after the Rabat summit and after Arafat's speech to the United Nations General Assembly. A similar process exists at the Arab level too. The growing support for the PLO among the Palestinians, as well as at the international level, did pressure the Arab governments to come out in support of the PLO. It is probably not a coincidence that the Algiers Arab summit decision, in 1973, was closely preceded by the Non-Aligned recognition of the PLO as the legitimate representative of the Palestinian people and by the announcement of the establishment of the pro-PLO PNF in the West Bank.

Notes

1 A list of the members of the Arab League can be found in Appendix II.
2 With the exception of Morocco who suggested the recognition of Israel in April 1965.

Kadi, L. *Arab Summit Conferences and The Palestine Problem 1936–1950, 1964–1966* (PLO Research Centre, Beirut, 1966) pp. 162–3; Rodinson, M. *Israel and the Arabs* (Penguin Books, London, 1982) p. 203.

3 MacDonald notes the integrative impact that relations with Israel has on Arab countries compared to the disintegrative impact of the Palestine problem. MacDonald , R. *The League of Arab States; A Study in the Dynamics of Regional Organization* (Princeton University Press, Princeton, 1965) pp. 85–94.

4 Laquer, W. *The Israeli–Arab Reader; A Documentary History of the Middle East Conflict* (Penguin Books, London, 1970) p. 175.

5 Information on these smaller groups is scarce and ambiguous. Hamid refers to 40 such groups without mentioning names, Hamid, R. 'What is the PLO?', *Journal of Palestine Studies*, vol. IV (Summer 1975), no. 4, p. 93. Kadi (1966: 105) on the other hand mentions and names six such groups.

6 Kadi (1966: 93–4).

7 Kadi (1966: 99).

8 Ibid., p. 106.

9 For Shukairy complaints see Kadi (1966: 176–7), see also Quandt *et al.* for Shukairy's problems with Jordan: Quandt, W., Jabber, F. and Lesch, A. *The Politics of Palestinian Nationalism* (University of California, Berkeley, 1973) p. 164.

10 Kadi (1966: 179).

11 Frangi, A. *The PLO and Palestine* (Zed Books, London, 1983) p. 107.

12 Hudson, M. 'The Palestinian Arab Resistance Movement: Its Significance in the Middle East Crisis', in Moore, J. (ed.) *The Arab–Israeli Conflict, Volume II* (Princeton University Press, Princeton, 1974) p. 499.

13 Quandt *et al.* (1973: 195). See Quandt *et al.* (1973: 163–5) for Jordan's hostility to Fatah and reserved attitude towards the PLO.

14 Hudson, M. 'Developments and Setbacks in the Palestinian Resistance Movement', *Journal of Palestine Studies* vol. 1 (Spring 1973), no. 3, p. 67. As Israel did not occupy any part of TransJordan, 'Jordan' was left out from the original text.

15 Quandt *et al.* (1973: 180–1).

16 In the wake of the June war, as a result of a change in leadership, the Syrian government reversed its policy and became supportive of the resistance. However, in 1968–9 Syria followed policies that hindered the movement of guerrillas: Quandt *et al.* (1973: 166–7, 194).

17 Gilmour, D. *Dispossessed: The Ordeal of the Palestinians* (Sphere Books, London, 1982) p. 144; and Frangi (1983: 102–3).

18 Frangi (1983: 102).

19 Ibid., p. 102.

20 Quoted in Quandt *et al.* (1973: 51 footnote 8).

21 MacDonald (1965: 362).

22 Ibid., p. 365.

23 Becker, J. *The PLO; The Rise and Fall of The Palestine Liberation Organization* (Weidenfeld and Nicolson, London, 1984) p. 43; Kadi (1966: 99).

24 Ibid., p. 176.

25 MacDonald (1965: Appendix G).

26 Laquer (1970: 174).

27 Kadi (1966: 99–102, 139).

28 For parts of Nasser's speech in May 67, see Laquer (1970: 228–9).

29 Kadi (1966: 183).

30 Laquer (1970: 467).

31 Frangi (1983: 103).

32 See MacDonald (1965: 372, 326) for Arab League decisions to select a Palestinian representative to participate in debates.

33 Kadi (1966: 109) notes that the PLA was only approved because Arab governments believed it would remain ineffective.

34 Hudson (1973: 79).

35 Rodinson (1982: 238).
36 Yodfat, A. and Arnon-Ohana, Y. *PLO Strategy and Tactics* (Croom Helm, London, 1981) p. 166.
37 Ibid., pp. 40–1, p. 175.
38 *Arab Report and Record* (1974: 363, 411–12).
39 Frangi (1983: 142).
40 *ARR* (1976: 554).
41 Quandt *et al.* (1973: 171).
42 Ibid., p. 165 footnote 18.
43 *ARR* (1970: 301).
44 Rodinson (1982: 203); Quandt *et al.* (1973: 185).
45 For the full text of the Khartoum resolution, see Fraser, T. *The Middle East 1914–1979* (Edward Arnold, London, 1980) p. 115.
46 *ARR* (1969: 111).
47 Quandt *et al.* (1973: 195–6).
48 Ibid., p. 116.
49 Rodinson (1982: 235).
50 *ARR* (1970: 488).
51 Quandt *et al.* (1973: 202–4, 203).
52 Quandt *et al.* (1973: 202, 210).
53 Ibid., p. 210.
54 *ARR* (1971: 129).
55 *ARR* (1971: 129–30).
56 *ARR* (1972: 157).
57 Quandt *et al.* (1973: 207, footnote 16).
58 *ARR* (1972: 27).
59 Quandt *et al.* (1973: 207).
60 Shuaibi, I. 'The Development of Palestinian Entity-Consciousness-Party II' *Journal of Palestine Studies* vol. 9 (Winter 1980), no. 2, pp. 101–2.
61 Shuaibi, I. 'The Development of Palestinian Entity-Consciousness: Part I', *Journal of Palestine Studies*, vol. 9 (Autumn 1979) no. 2, 103.
62 Fraser (1980: 130).
63 Ibid., p. 134; Yodfat *et al.* (1981: 166).
64 Yodfat *et al.* (1981: 40, 57). This was in marked departure from previous practice, which tended to stress the Arab nature of the problem and referred to Arab Palestinians or Palestinian Arabs rather than the Palestinian people.
65 Yodfat *et al.* (1981: 180).
66 Frangi (1983: 167).
67 Fraser (1980: 173–4).
68 Frangi (1983: 167).
69 Ibid.
70 *ARR* (1977: 1013).

6 Mobilization of Support among Third World Regional and Political Groupings

In this chapter we shall look at the mobilization process among major Third World regional-political groupings, focusing on five such groupings, three regional and two political. The regional groupings are African, Latin American and Asian whose membership is similar to those of the United Nations' regional groupings. The politically based groupings are composed of Non-Aligned and Islamic countries respectively. Although the first groups have mutually exclusive membership, the composition of the latter two overlap significantly with each other. [1]

The analysis will focus on the responses to various demands put forward by Arab governments and the PLO in their efforts to mobilize support for the Palestinian cause in the Third World. It concentrates on group behaviour as reflected in the decisions adopted by the political institutions of these Third World groupings, with the exception of the Asian group which does not have an institutional structure of its own. The data on which the application of the mobilization model rests is based on various speeches made during the debates and the decisions adopted at the formal gatherings of these Third World groups.

Two limitations in respect to these speeches and decisions must be noted. First, the speeches were made by governmental delegations and reflect the position of the governments involved. Although, more often than not, it can be assumed that the position of the government reflected the general attitude of the country this may not necessarily be valid in all cases. Second, the decisions adopted by the political institutions associated with these groupings may not always have reflected the position of all its members. The tendency of these groupings to reach their final decisions through consensus building rather than by taking votes makes it difficult to establish with certainty the unity and support these decisions enjoyed.

The actual change in attitudes and support for the Palestinian cause is established in two ways. First, Third World decisions and statements on the Palestinian cause are examined for changes in their content and emphasis. Second, member states' voting behaviour at the United Nations General Assembly on the Palestinian Question have been quantitatively studied. This has enabled the construction of an index of political support for the Palestinian cause derived from the agreement scores of each delegation with Israel on roll calls concerning the Palestinian issue at the UN.[2]

Conducive environment

The first variable in the mobilization process is the 'conducive environment'. This part of the mobilization process consists of certain structural changes and events in the Third World that brought about an environment suitable for raising the Palestinian issue and aggregating support for it.

The very first structural changes began to take place as Third World forums and political institutions emerged, enabling participants in such forums to raise and discuss problems of salience to their respective regions. These multilateral interactions gave Third World statesmen the opportunity for exchanging views, for discussions and for trying to formulate a unified approach to problems in an attempt to find solutions. Such interactions had the cumulative effect of paving the way toward the gradual articulation of a broadly supported world view that can be likened to an ideology. This ideology then came to perform the role of a yardstick for determining whether issues raised by participants warranted their inclusion on the agenda for discussion and eventual support.

The first Third World political institutions to appear in world politics were the Arab League in 1945, and the Organization of American States (OAS) in 1948. The role of the former, in respect to our model, has already been considered in the previous chapter. The case of the OAS is rather different from the Arab League and the other Third World political institutions.

Throughout the 1950s and 1960s the Cold War was an issue of much concern to the OAS. Its members tended to follow policies closely associated with the United States and in general the Latin Americans were seen as close allies of the Western Bloc. The influence of the United States and Cold War politics, for example, was reflected in the way in which Cuba, after Castro's accession to power, was promptly excluded from the Organization's activities. This American influence on Latin Americans did not remain restricted to East–West relations but also conditioned their attitude towards colonial issues. At the 16th session of the United Nations General Assembly the Latin Americans were closely aligned to the West in their voting behaviour. It was not until a decade later that the agreement between 'the Western Bloc and the Latin Americans dropped to less than half of its original value' set during the 16th Session.[3] This rather strong pro-Western position of the Latin Americans throughout the 1950s and for most of the 1960s makes it rather difficult to consider the OAS as an institution to be included as a contributor towards the emergence of a conducive environment.

As a force independent from the West, the rest of the Third World first appeared in the world political scene in a significant way in the late 1950s. It was the entrance of an increasing number of newly independent states into the world political arena that generated the need for these countries to meet and discuss problems of interest to them. The agenda of world politics in the immediate aftermath of the Second World War remained dominated by the Cold War. The issues and problems deemed significant by the participants in the Cold War did not necessarily include problems of greater salience to the newly emerging states. The decolonization of peoples still under colonial rule, the racial policies of South Africa and economic development were such problems.

It was during the late 1950s and early 1960s that development towards the emergence of a Third World approach to world problems evolved. The Bandung Conference, in 1955, was the first ever major gathering of Afro-Asian countries. Here, even though the influence of Cold War attitudes was reflected in the debates, racialism and decolonization emerged as matters of importance to particular Afro-Arab participants.[4] The Bandung Conference was then followed by a series of African meetings that paved the way to the establishment of the OAU in May 1963.[5] The OAU provided African states with a formal institutional structure and a common denominator.[6] This denominator was reflected in the OAU's determination to eradicate both colonialism and racialism from Africa, supplemented by the realization of the need to pool efforts in that direction.

The Non-Aligned gatherings provided another possibility, this time for a wider geographical area, to discuss problems and develop common approaches. As these meetings became institutionalized into the Non-Aligned Movement in the early 1970s, an ideology of particular importance to concerted action emerged. In the early 1960s, the Cold War, the achievement of a stable world peace together with anti-colonialism were the major issues of concern to the Non-Aligned.[7] In the following decade, as the Cold War lost its salience to the Non-Aligned, anti-colonialism continued as a very central element of the Non-Aligned ideology and gradually came to cover the Palestinian question too. At the same time, the Non-Aligned began to direct greater attention towards the establishment of a New International Economic Order; the Non-Aligned ideology came to condition the foreign policies of an ever growing membership.

The Islamic Conference Organization (ICO) established in March 1971 is another forum that has contributed to the emergence of a conducive environment. Although the first Islamic Conference was called in response to a perceived threat to Islam caused by the fire at Al-Aqsa mosque in Jerusalem, it quickly expanded to include the Palestinian problem in general. Hence, the Islamic Conference Organization became a forum for the promotion of Islamic solidarity on the Palestinian Question and the coordination of a common Islamic stand on this question in other Third World and international forums.

The conduciveness of this environment arises as a result of three factors. First, these forums and gatherings constituted a place where problems of concern to the Third World could be raised and demands formulated. Second, these meetings enabled members to articulate an ideology that guides them in determining which issues and demands warrant their support. Third, access to these forums, with the exception of the OAS, gave Arab governments the chance to raise the Palestinian problem.[8]

In chapter four, it was noted how a series of events, such as the Algerian liberation war, the break-up of the United Arab Republic and the 1967 war played an important role in generating a situation favorable for mobilization. There are a number of events with similar consequences that have helped to bring about an environment more receptive to Arab initiatives on the Palestinian problem at the level of Third World groupings.

One such event was the role that Israel played in the 1956 Suez War. During the Bandung Conference Nasser had described Israel as a tool of Western imperialism. In the aftermath of this conference Israel's alliance with Britain and France during the Suez crisis played a central role in increasing the credibility of such Egyptian arguments and undermining Israel's image in the Asian world.[9] Decalo, too, notes the loss of considerable Asian goodwill toward Israel as a result of the latter's role in the Suez war.[10]

Not being independent at this time, a large part of Africa was not influenced by Suez. Instead, another event within the African context did, later, have some adverse effect on African perceptions of Israel. Israel had not hesitated to lend her support to Biafra during the Nigerian Civil war. Israel's readiness to support a seccessionist movement, particularly in a country with which it had good relations, alienated several African governments.[11] For most Africans it was difficult to reconcile such behaviour with one of the major tenets of the OAU Charter which stresses the integrity of each African state.

The two Arab–Israeli wars of 1967 and 1973, in particular the latter, raised questions about the nature of Israel. The wars provided hard evidence for Arab arguments about the expansionist nature of Israel. Although the African response to the 1967 war was relatively muted and reflected a desire not to get embroiled in someone else's conflict, by the early 1970s African attitudes began to change in a way that prepared the ground for a stronger reaction to the 1973 war. A number of factors played a role in this.

First, and probably most importantly, in the 1973 war it was not just the territory of an OAU member that had been invaded. As a consequence of the Israeli thrust across the Suez Canal, the African continent itself had been violated. The African governments felt they could not remain indifferent to this development. Second, the gravity of this development was accentuated by the failure of their earlier mediation attempt in the Middle East. The OAU summit in 1971 had sent a mediation mission to the Middle East.[12] The failure of the OAU mission became attributed to a perceived Israeli intransigence towards negotiating about withdrawal from captured Arab territories.[13] Hence, Israel was seen to be undermining another central African principle: rejection of the acquisition of territory by the use of force.

The failure of the OAU mission on its own had 'brought Africa a few degrees closer to the Arab position',[14] generating a conducive environment for the Palestinian cause in two ways. The Africans became more receptive to Arab demands for the withdrawal of support from Israel by severing diplomatic relations. They also began to respond to Arab arguments on the similarities between the Southern African problem and the Palestinian Question.

The 'conducive environment' as constituted by these structural changes and the key events is dynamic in nature and continuously interacts with the other parts of the mobilization process model. The Bandung Conference gave the Arabs the chance to gain access to a large audience and raise the Palestine Question. When the Bandung Conference was seen together with the Suez war which lent credence to Arab arguments about Israel, it enabled an early consolidation of a reasonably broad base of Asian support and solidarity. The Non-Aligned, on the other hand, provided the Arabs with another forum with growing membership where problems of direct concern to the Third World were discussed. This, together with the gradual development of an ideology reflecting Third World thinking and attitudes towards a wide range of issues, provided the Arab governments the raw material with which to commence the mobilization of support.

The initial accessibility and the possibility of linkages to existing legitimized concepts allowed by this conducive environment brought about a degree of support for the Palestinian Question that gradually enabled the PLO itself to enter the process. The PLO now had access to Third World forums where it could put forward its own arguments. Thus, it not only benefited from but contributed to an ideology providing legitimacy and support for the Palestinian cause.

Cognitive and bargain linkages

In the introductory chapter it was pointed out that the Zionist success, in linking the solution of the problem of Jewish displaced persons to the establishment of Palestine, played an important role in mobilizing support for the Zionist cause. Similarly, when Israel embarked on a policy to expand its basis of international support it made use of various cognitive and bargain linkages.

Israel's brand of socialism and her access to the Socialist International played an important role in gaining legitimacy in the eyes of the ruling political parties of countries such as Burma, Ghana, Nepal and Tanzania.[15] During the 1960s the Israeli government followed policies aiming to project the image of an anti-colonial and anti-apartheid country, alienating both the South African government with whom it had had good relations in the 1950s and sections of the Jewish community there.[16] Israel's ability to draw similarities between historical Jewish persecution and the sufferings of black peoples appears to have contributed to her strong image in Africa. This is reflected in the Congolese (Kinshasa) Premier Mulamba's June 1966 statement that: 'The African people like Israel because we are all victims of racial discrimination and we have had to fight for our liberty.'[17]

To these cognitive linkages upon which Israel relied to improve her standing in the Third World one can also include bargain linkages. In the late 1950s, as newly independent African and Asian countries discovered the problems of economic development, Israel became interested in lending her expertise to the Third World in terms of technical and development aid. Her offers of aid were made conditional upon the recipient government extending diplomatic recognition to Israel.[18] This was done, primarily, in the belief that African support cultivated at the bilateral level would either counter or neutralize Arab pressure on African countries to revise their attitude towards Israel.[19] This relationship which remained a major objective for Israel in Africa can be said to constitute a bargain linkage. It brought highly sought after Israeli developmental aid for Africa in return for African denial of support for the Palestinian cause. The Arab governments and the PLO, too, in their efforts to gain support for the Palestinian cause among Third World regional groupings, made wide use of similar linkages.

The Arab efforts to establish cognitive linkages were directed towards achieving two aims. One was to weaken the status and legitimacy of Israel in the eyes of the Third World. This was done in two ways: first, by stressing Israel's reluctance to respect a number of principles embodied in the OAU Charter , and second, by pointing out the growing relations between Israel and South Africa. The latter was intended to undermine Israel's legitimacy by associating her with South Africa, a state with low standing in the eyes of Africans and the Non-Aligned. The second aim was to get the Palestinian cause integrated into the anti-colonial thinking of the Non-Aligned Movement. In this way the Palestinian problem would be perceived and treated as an issue falling within the domain of the anti-colonial dimension of the Non-Aligned ideology, benefiting from the same support accruing to other issues covered by anti-colonialism.

It was pointed out above that overt Israeli support for one secessionist movement together with the 1967 and 1973 wars created a conducive environment for the mobilization process to begin: these events by their nature undermined principles central to African thinking as reflected in the OAU Charter.[20] Arab governments, in particular Egypt, played an important role in exploiting these principles to weaken the position of Israel in Africa. At the OAU summit in September 1967 Arab members argued[21] that Israel had violated the integrity of an African state and Israeli occupation of 'their territory was an affront to the OAU'.[22] For the African states 'to fail to support Egypt was to question the letters on which the OAU Charter was written'.[23]

Although at the 1967 OAU meeting the Arabs had to restrain themselves, this was not the case at the UN. Particularly with the adoption of the Security Council resolution which declared the acquisition of territory by force as illegal, Arab arguments began to gain strength and influence African thinking. This is quite evident in the Tanzanian delegate's observation of the similarity between the situation in the Middle East and the vulnerability of African states to potential aggression from racist governments of Portugal, Rhodesia and South Africa.[24]

The gradual change of mood among African states was quickened by Israeli preparedness to support the Biafran secession. The growing national liberation struggle, particularly in Guinea-Bissau, brought the problem of aggression home.

The Portugese regularly undermined the territorial integrity of neighbouring countries. African countries came to appreciate the need to support the Arab cause in order to strengthen the principle of territorial integrity.

The African recognition of Arab, particularly Egyptian, arguments on the need for African support for the Arab cause was reflected in the growing strength of the decisions of the 1971 and 1972 OAU summits. These decisions supported the Egyptian position in the Middle East conflict and called for total Israeli withdrawal from 'all' Arab territories occupied since 5 June 1967. The June 1972 decision was particularly strong as it reaffirmed, 'in the name of African solidarity ... its effective support for Egypt in its legitimate struggle to restore the integrity of its full territory by all means'.[25] Establishing the applicability of a highly regarded African principle to the Middle East undermined Israel's legitimacy and mobilized support for the Arab cause. Although this process did not contribute directly to the Palestinian cause it did bring the Africans nearer to lending their support to it. The legitimization of Arab demands for the return of the occupied territories was crucial in mobilizing support for the political rights of the Palestinians.

Anti-colonialism and the struggle against racism have been central to both the Non-Aligned Movement and the OAU. The anti-colonial dimension of the Non-Aligned ideology has played a leading role in determining the attitudes of the majority of Third World countries towards the colonial and racial problems of Africa. In Table 6.1 the average level of support for a standard anti-colonial position on all the relevant roll-calls is shown for various political groupings.[26] The results, which are for the years preceding and following the 1967 and 1973 wars, point towards the very high level of support that anti-colonialism enjoyed in the Third World, throughout the 1960s and 1970s. The Arab governments, since as early as the Bandung Conference,[27] have tried to draw similarities between apartheid, imperialism and Israel in the hope of gaining support from Afro-Asians.[28] This was not, however, immediately accepted.

The OAU and the Non-Aligned Movement did not share the Arab perception of an ideological linkage between the Palestinian issue and colonial-racial problems until the late 1960s. In the late 1950s and early 1960s, the only occasion when Arab efforts to establish a link took a concrete form was at the meeting of the Casablanca Group in 1961. This meeting 'linking the problem of Palestine with the general theme of the defence of independence and security on the African

Table 6.1. Level of average anti-colonial voting scores* for groups of countries

Assembly sessions	Political and regional groupings (per cent)				
	Latin Americans	Non-Aligned	Africans	Asians	Islamic
1966	72	89	84	82	88
1969	90	99	96	98	96
1974	94	99	98	98	100

* Percentages are based upon countries meeting the minimum attendance levels.

continent' denounced Israel as an instrument in the service of imperialism and neocolonialism.[29] The reluctance of Africans to discuss the question of Palestine, let alone its similarities with African colonial problems, forced Egypt to keep the Middle East away from the first and subsequent OAU summits during most of the 1960s.[30] However, during the 1964 summit, this did not prevent the Algerian President, Ben Bella, from making a direct comparision between the apartheid policy of South Africa and the racial discrimination that the Arab minority in Israel faced.[31] Other Arab members drew similarities between the roles of the newly formed Palestine Liberation Army and that of African liberation movements.[32]

At the 1973 OAU summit the Arab governments, in particular the Algerian President, strongly argued that the Palestinian problem was a part of the African struggle against colonialism, imperialism and Zionism. One of the immediate consequences of the debate was the adoption of a unanimously supported OAU resolution, 'calling on African nations to consider taking collective and individual steps, both political and economic, against Israel should that country persist in its refusal to evacuate occupied Arab territories'.[33]

This led the OAU, for the first time, to express their support for Palestinian rights. Although this OAU decision on the Middle East was not as far reaching as the Algerian call for the outright suspension of relations[34] with Israel, it still signified a change in African perceptions of the Palestinian problem.

In respect to the Non-Aligned Movement, the developments on the question of cognitive similarities between the problem of South Africa and Palestine were quite different from the OAU. Primarily, as a result of a greater Arab presence and a more radical composition, the Palestinian issue had not only received early recognition but had also been defined as a 'struggle for liberation from colonialism and racism'.[35] This remained the position held by the Non-Aligned Movement without any significant change during the period between the Cairo and Algiers summits. It was the adoption of the 'Declaration on the Struggle for National Liberation' at the Algiers summit in September 1973 that signified a major change in Non-Aligned thinking towards the Palestinian problem. In this, Arab governments, in particular the Algerians, and the PLO played an important role.

In this Declaration the Non-Aligned recognized that, 'the case of Palestine is completely identical with the situation in South Africa, where racist and segregationist minorities have resorted to the same methods of colonial domination and exploitation . . .'[36] This unambiguous formulation of a cognitive linkage between the Palestinian and South African problems influenced Non-Aligned attitudes towards Israel and the Palestinian cause. First, Israel lost considerable status and legitimacy when the Pretoria–Salisbury–Lisbon military-political alliance against national liberation was extended to include Tel-Aviv.[37] Second, the Non-Aligned reaffirmed 'the legitimacy of the struggle of the Palestinian people against colonialism, Zionism and racism' and recognized the PLO as 'the legitimate representative of the Palestine people and their legitimate struggle'.[38]

This change in the attitude of the Non-Aligned extended beyond the realm of verbal political support. The decisions adopted at Algiers called on its members to extend a wide range of measures, including the severance of diplomatic relations, initially introduced to isolate Portugal, Rhodesia and South Africa, to cover Israel too. Furthermore, the summit called on member states who still maintained relations with Israel, 'to work for a boycott of Israel in the diplomatic, economic, military and cultural fields and in the sphere of maritime and air traffic in accordance with the provisions of Chapter VII of the United Nations Charter'.[39]

These developments within the Non-Aligned Movement, the October War and the alleged collaboration between South Africa and Israel during the war hardened the position of the OAU. At the emergency meeting of its Council of Ministers, held in November 1973, in Addis Ababa, the OAU responded to the linkage between southern Africa and the Palestinian problem in a much more strongly worded manner than at its summit in May of the same year. The meeting declared that the

open military collusion between the United States, Portugal, South Africa, Rhodesia and Israel during the recent Middle East War further confirms the justification of the pre-occupation of the African and Arab countries and has further strengthened their conviction in the need for a common struggle'.[40]

The OAU's new found belief in the perceived similarities between the imperialist and racist threats facing the Africans and the Arabs culminated in a call on all member states and friendly countries to impose a total economic embargo and in particular an oil embargo against Israel, Portugal, South Africa and Southern Rhodesia.[41] At the ideological level it led to the description of the Palestinian problem as a struggle for self-determination against colonial and racial discrimination.

This change in the ideological outlook of the Non-Aligned was also reflected in their voting behaviour. A comparative analysis of Third World voting behaviour gives an indication of the way in which attitudes towards the two issues converged.

The anti-colonial dimension of non-alignment had always upheld support for the struggles being waged against colonialism and racialism in Southern Africa. This continuous support for anti-colonialism as it relates to matters concerning Southern Africa was depicted in Table 6.1. A large proportion of the Third World political and regional groupings under study have on the whole supported anti-colonialism, whereas this had not been the case in respect to the Palestinian Problem especially prior to the 28th Session of the General Assembly.

However, as the Palestinian problem became integrated into anti-colonial thinking, the voting behaviour of the Afro-Asian countries began to change too. These countries began to extend their anti-colonial support for the Palestinian cause. Table 6.2 shows the number and percentage of countries which were adopting both a highly anti-colonial and a highly pro-Palestinian position. A growing proportion of Third World countries came to vote in a manner suggesting an integration of the two dimensions at the United Nations General Assembly.

Table 6.2. Distribution of highly anti-colonial and pro-Palestinian votes* across three sessions

Assembly sessions	Political and regional groupings									
	Latin Americans		Africans		Asians		Non-Aligned		Islamic	
	n.	%	n.	%	n.	%	n.	%	n.	%
1969	(2)	18	(8)	35	(9)	69	(29)	69	(24)	83
1973	(6)	50	(22)	100	(12)	86	(55)	98	(32)	97
1974	(20)	95	(34)	97	(21)	96	(81)	99	(31)	100

* Percentages and figures are based upon countries meeting the minimum attendance levels.

If Arab arguments on a successful exploitation of the principle of territorial integrity played an important role in raising questions about Israel's behaviour, the ideological linking of the Palestinian problem to colonialism, imperialism and racism faciliated the extension of political support for the Palestinian cause.

Earlier on it was noted that one of the factors that contributed to Israel's high status in the Third World was her ability to make developmental and technical skill available to Third World countries. It is possible to identify a number of similar cases in respect to Arab efforts to mobilize support. It may be necessary, however, to treat these bargain linkages with some caution. Although, these cases, when studied individually, may look like straightforward trade-offs, they could also be seen as the natural manifestations of a political solidarity maintained by a common world outlook.

One such bargain linkage is the striking deal reached between the Arab and African governments at the extraordinary meeting of the OAU Council of Ministers in November 1973. During this meeting the OAU called on its members to take 'measures to put an end to Israel's defiance of the International Community'[42] and invited its members and Arab states to impose an oil boycott of Portugal, Rhodesia and South Africa as well as Israel. Within days, the Arab governments at their own summit in Algiers reciprocated by adopting the OAU recommendations.

In isolation from its wider context this event may well appear to be the result of a conscious bargaining process whereby the Africans and Arabs have simply exchanged logistical support to weaken their respective enemies. Yet, such an approach would be insufficient. In the immediate aftermath of the African severance of relations with Israel, many have argued that this occurred as a result of Arab pressure resulting from their oil-based economic and financial power. Such arguments hold the view that Africans broke diplomatic relations and came to support the Arabs because of expected and promised Arab economic rewards and not as a result of a legitimization process. However, as Legum argues

It cannot be convincingly argued that the reason for this breach was ... fear of the Arabs' 'oil weapon' since the movement to break diplomatic relations first began to assume some significance in 1972, it escalated in September 1973, after the Summit of Non-Aligned Countries in Algiers and reached its high tide on 5 November when no fewer than 17 countries broke with Israel. Therefore the decision to break came before the punitive nature of oil sanctions had become manifest. ... the reasons must be sought in other explanations.[43]

Without necessarily discounting the role of trade-offs motivated by narrowly defined governmental considerations, the picture would not be complete without taking into account the influence of a broader ideology on the perceptions and behaviour of its adherents.

Accessibility

In the introductory chapter it was noted that the ability of the Zionists to gain access to the domestic political systems of first Britain and then the United States played an important role in mobilizing support for the Zionist cause. Similarly, the conscious and rigorous efforts on the part of Israel to establish strong diplomatic and economic links enabled her to gain direct access to a great number of governments in the Third World. In early 1970 Israel had cooperation treaties with 33 Third World countries and had 70 diplomatic representatives including non-resident ones.[44] The Israeli presence in certain countries, particularly in the early

1960s, was of such quality that Israeli ambassadors were reputed to have enjoyed immediate access to some African heads of state including the influencial leader, Nkrumah.[45]

No doubt Israel's strong diplomatic presence in Africa played a major role in frustrating Egyptian efforts to mobilize African support. A vivid example of the consequences of Israeli advantages, arising from the access to African governments she enjoyed, was evident in African reluctance to discuss and adopt decisions on the Middle East favourable to the Arabs at the 1958 Accra Conference and at the first OAU summit, in 1963. According to Sawant, the exclusion of the Palestine question from the debates and decisions of these two conferences can be linked to the Israeli Foreign Minister's visit to Ghana in early 1958 and 'the great deal of [Israeli] diplomatic spade-work' prior to the OAU summit cautioning African leaders against possible Egyptian moves against Israel.[46]

As Table 6.3 depicts, the Palestinians enjoyed a number of access routes through which they could reach the agendas of Third World governments and forums. Until the early 1970s when the PLO was first invited to the Islamic Conference Organization, the Non-Aligned and the OAU meetings, and opened offices in various Non-Aligned capitals, the Palestinian issue was brought up by Arab governments. In respect to violent access routes, the Palestinians did not stage any violent acts that involved the Third World in any direct way. The two Palestinian hijackings that involved two African airports, Entebbe and Mogadishu, occurred well after African support for the Palestinian cause had been consolidated. However, the guerrilla warfare waged in Palestine did have an indirect impact as it helped the Non-Aligned countries to see similarities with national liberation struggles elsewhere.

Table 6.3. Access routes to Third World agendas

	Non-violent means	Violent means
Indirect access	Arab governments i.e. Egypt, Algeria	M.E. wars, armed struggle
Direct access	PLO participation, PLO offices	not used

Indirect access through Arab governments

From the very early days of the emergence of independent Afro-Asian countries, Arab governments enjoyed certain advantages over Israel. Arab countries by their uncontroversial geographical and cultural location in Africa and Asia were readily accepted within the newly emerging Afro-Asian forums. The preparatory meeting for the Bandung Conference chose to invite Arab states rather than Israel at the end of a long debate over whether Israel could be regarded as an Asian country. The Bandung Conference set the trend for Arab participation in Afro-Asian forums at Israel's expense.

This gave the Arab governments the chance to bring the Palestinian question to the attention of an international forum outside the UN. In respect to the significance of accessibility, it is interesting to note that during the Bandung Conference a future leader of the PLO, Shukairy, also had the opportunity to raise the Palestinian problem with the other delegates as a member of the Syrian delegation.[47] Even though the final wording of the Bandung resolution on Palestine did not satisfy the Arab governments, at least the other Afro-Asian countries had been exposed to the Palestinian problem and the issue of the rights of the Palestinians. This early exposure to the Palestinian question and the impact of the Suez War doubtlessly played a role in Israel's failure to set up extensive diplomatic relations with Asian countries.

Israel's swift response to exclusion from the Bandung Conference culminated in the establishment of an impressive Israeli diplomatic network, particularly in Africa. This diplomatic network, coupled with the striking of a successful linkage, undermined the Arab advantage based on access to Afro-Asian forums. Throughout most of the 1960s, Egypt found its membership of the OAU of little use, as the OAU remained unwilling to discuss the Middle East in any way. Nevertheless, Egypt, later joined by Algeria, continued in raising the Question of Palestine and describing Israel as a colonialist and racist state. This was done in Nasser's belief that Africa would eventually discover what he saw to be the truth.[48] The Arabs had to wait for this to happen until the failure of the OAU mediation mission to the Middle East which created a favourable environment for the cumulative efforts of Arab governments during the 1960s to take effect.

Direct access to multilateral forums

The larger Arab membership and the more radical nature of the Non-Aligned Movement permitted the Arab governments to be more forceful. One of the consequences of this approach was that the PLO, at an early stage, gained access to the Non-Aligned meetings. The PLO was able to address the Non-Aligned for the first time during the Consultative Meeting of the Non-Aligned in Belgrade in July 1969.[49] This meeting set a precedent and the PLO, together with other liberation movements, was invited to the Lusaka summit in 1970 as a guest. From then on the status of the PLO gradually increased. As a result of a strong Algerian initiative the PLO was granted observer status at the Algiers summit in 1973 and full membership at the Lima Ministerial Meeting in 1975.[50]

The PLO's access to Non-Aligned delegates played an important role in mobilizing full support for the Palestinian cause. It was at the Havana Coordinating Bureau meeting, in 1974, that the Non-Aligned expressed their full and unambiguous support for the Palestinian cause.

The establishment of the first bilateral relationship came in 1965 soon after the PLO was actually founded. That year the People's Republic of China granted the PLO the right to open an office with a quasi-diplomatic status.[51] The relative ease with which the Chinese government had made itself accessible was reflected in her position that saw the Palestinian Question 'no longer as merely an international dispute over refugees, but as a manifestation of the national liberation struggle of a distinct Palestinian people'.[52] This early achievement in Asia was followed by North Korea and North Vietnam's preparedness to have relations with the PLO. Various PLO representatives including Arafat made frequent visits to China and North Korea throughout the early 1970s. These visits played an important role in the PLO expansion of its own basis of Asian support particularly among radical governments. However, it was only from the early 1970s that the PLO began to open offices abroad and gain access to host governments in any significant way.

The first two black African countries to allow the opening of PLO offices were Chad and Uganda. Uganda, soon after it severed its relations with Israel, invited the PLO to take over the premises of the Israeli embassy.[53] Similarly, Chad, the third African country to break diplomatic relations with Israel in December 1972, welcomed the PLO.[54] These were followed by invitations to open offices from the Congo, Guinea and Senegal during 1973. Doubtlessly, at a time when Israel's influence in Africa began to diminish, the ability of the PLO to gain access to some African governments contributed to the PLO's efforts to mobilize support for the Palestinian cause. It gave the PLO the opportunity to discuss the Palestinian Problem with these host governments and seek their support in lobbying others. Furthermore, the PLO's presence in these countries gave the PLO representatives the opportunity to lobby among the diplomatic corps, particularly in those capitals where it was accorded full diplomatic status.

The number of PLO offices rapidly expanded following the Non-Aligned, OAU and ICO decisions calling for the severance of relations with Israel and was also helped by the ICO decision in Lahore in February 1974 calling on its members to allow the PLO to open offices in their countries.[55] A similar decision was adopted at the Non-Aligned Coordinating Bureau Ministerial Meeting at Havana in March 1975.[56] The combined effect of these decisions, coupled with the Non-Aligned (August 1975) and Arab League (December 1975) decisions to accord full membership to the PLO, contributed to the expansion of the PLO offices abroad. As Table 6.4 depicts, by 1984 the PLO had 45 offices in the various Third World countries.

Although the opening of these offices was an indication of a certain level of support for the Palestinian cause it should not be treated simply as the end product of a mobilization process. Instead, by allowing the PLO direct access to these governments and regional forums, it gave the PLO a basis from which to continue and expand the mobilization of support. The presence of PLO representatives in a country gave the PLO the possibility of both keeping the Palestinian Problem on the public agendas of those countries and also of continuing to strengthen the legitimacy of their cause.

There were limits on how far governments were prepared to go along with the demands of the PLO. At the July 1975 OAU summit in Kampala, the PLO together with Libya lobbied for a decision to work towards Israel's expulsion from the United Nations. However, the majority of members, supported by Egypt, refused to endorse it.[58] Instead the summit adopted a much milder decision that called on member states 'to take the most appropriate measures to intensify pressures exercised against Israel at the UN and other institutions including the possibility of eventually depriving it of its status as a member of these institutions.'[59]

Table 6.4. PLO offices by Third World regional and political groupings[57]

Africa	21	Non-Aligned	41
Asia	16	Islamic Group	16
Latin America	8	Arab League	20
Total	45		77

Similarly the PLO initiative to persuade the Non-Aligned Movement to call for sanctions against Israel faced difficulties. The August 1976 Non-Aligned summit in Colombo, noting the obstacle caused by American vetoes in the Security Council, declined to go any further than the earlier position taken by the OAU summit.[60]

These developments in many ways established the parameters within which the PLO could expect support. More interestingly, the consequences of these developments for the PLO's behaviour reflect the dynamic and interactive nature of the mobilization process. The accessibility enjoyed by the PLO contributed to the mobilization of support for the Palestinian cause but this same accessibility put systemic pressure on the PLO to moderate its policies. As its international standing increased the PLO found itself revising some of its more radical attitudes and policies towards the solution of the Palestinian problem.

One last way in which the PLO gained access to the Third World countries was as a result of its armed struggle. The use of violence by the PLO had two consequences. The spectacular hijackings mounted by the Palestinians attracted attention to the Palestinian problem. It put this problem on the public agenda. Second, and more importantly, violence against Israel had a different impact particularly on African countries and those countries that achieved independence through armed struggle. The violence in Palestine made them aware of 'another' armed struggle to which they could relate and with which they could sympathize. Establishment of the cognitive linkage between the problems of South Africa and Palestine aided this process. The Africans perceived growing similarities between the Israeli raids into refugee camps and on alleged guerrilla hide-outs and Portuguese/South African raids into neighbouring African countries.

Growth of support among Third World groupings

Support for the Palestinian cause did not grow in a uniform manner across different Third World groupings. While the Non-Aligned and the ICO were more forthcoming, the OAU support came slowly and only in two stages. First, with great reluctance the OAU changed its attitudes towards the Middle East conflict and the Arab cause. Only after it began to support the Arab cause in the Middle East conflict did the OAU begin to express separate support for the rights of the Palestinians. Least forthcoming among Third World groups were the Latin Americans. The regional forum for Latin America, the Organization of American States, never adopted any decision on the Palestinian problem. It was, only after 1973 that the Latin Americans, too, began to lend their support to the Palestinian cause.

The growth of support for the Palestinian cause has been established in two ways. First, the formal decisions and, where possible, the debates of the regional forums have been studied. This was done in the belief that the change in the content and the wording of the decisions would reflect the changing position of these forums in respect to the Palestinian problem. Second, given the practical difficulties of examining the attitude and position of every individual government towards the Palestinian cause, an index of political support has been constructed.

This index is based on a modified Lijphart formula and gives agreement scores between Israel and every member of the Assembly on a set of selected roll-calls concerning the Palestinian problem. The scores range from 0.0 to 100.0 where 0.0 indicates complete disagreement with Israel while, at the other end of the scale, a score of 100.0 suggests full agreement with Israel. In view of the large number of scores generated for approximately 140 countries per session and the need to differentiate between levels of support, the results obtained from the index were grouped into five different bands of support:

$$\geqslant\ \ 0.0 \text{ and } <\ \ 20.0 = \text{highly pro-Palestinian}$$
$$\geqslant 20.0 \text{ and } <\ \ 40.0 = \text{medium pro-Palestinian}$$
$$\geqslant 40.0 \text{ and } \leqslant\ \ 60.0 = \text{intermediate}$$
$$>\ 60.0 \text{ and } \leqslant\ \ 80.0 = \text{medium pro-Israel}$$
$$>\ 80.0 \text{ and } \leqslant 100.0 = \text{pro-Israel.}$$

Non-Aligned Movement

The first Non-Aligned summit in September 1961 in Belgrade did express some support for the 'full restoration of all the rights of the Arab people of Palestine'.[61] Yet this brief reference to the relatively ambiguous term of 'all the rights' of the Palestinians fell short of what Nasser would have liked to see. In his address to the summit he strongly argued for the need to recognize the colonialist and imperialist nature of Israel.[62] He had probably expected the adoption of a decision not very different from the relatively clearer and more elaborate Casablanca resolution. This resolution had condemned Israel's imperialism and had called for the restoration of 'all the legitimate rights' of the Arabs of Palestine.

This lack of commitment to the Palestinian cause was also evident in the way in which out of 16 non-Arab delegations only one, Guinea (a member of the Casablanca group), referred to the problem of Palestine in their speech.[63] Nehru, one of the founding fathers of the Non-Aligned movement also confirmed the trend. In his speech he did not include Palestine among the list of urgent 'ills' awaiting immediate attention.[64] Under these circumstances it would be difficult to say that the Palestinian problem held much salience for a sizeable proportion of the participants. The second summit in Cairo, in 1964, brought the Non-Aligned nearer to Nasser's position when in two short paragraphs the summit expressed support for the inalienable right of the Palestinians to self-determination in their struggle against colonialism and racism.[65]

When the Non-Aligned Movement was reactivated, after a lull of five years, a conspicuous increase in Non-Aligned support for the Palestinian cause occurred. In the intervening years since the previous summit in 1964, the 1967 war created a cognitive environment favourable to Arab mobilization efforts. The war raised questions about Israel in the minds of increasing numbers of Non-Aligned countries. It enabled the Arab delegations gradually to develop the argument for the need to respect and express support for the principle of 'territorial integrity' and the 'inadmissability of the acquisition of land by force'. The violation of these principles by Israel gave the Arab states the opportunity to substantiate their arguments about the imperialistic nature of Israel and lay the ground for the eventual establishment of the cognitive linkages between the Palestinian Problem and the problems of southern Africa. Furthermore, in this period the Non-Aligned began, for the first time, to hear about the Palestine Problem directly from the Palestinian themselves.

The beginning of a significant change in the attitude of the Non-Aligned towards the Middle East and the Palestinian Problem was reflected in the decisions of the Lusaka summit in September 1970. In the first full resolution on the Middle East, the Non-Aligned condemned Israel for its occupation of Arab territories and called on it to withdraw from these territories. Simultaneously they declared that 'respect for the inalienable rights of the Arab people of Palestine is a prerequisite to peace in the Middle East'.[66] These developments brought the Non-Aligned relatively nearer to the positions held by the Arabs and the PLO.

Throughout the early 1970s, the position of the Non-Aligned continued to harden. The failure of the OAU mission played a crucial role in mobilizing solid Non-Aligned support for the Arab cause. This became quite evident in the decisions of the Algiers summit in September 1973 which expressed unequivocal support for Egypt, Syria and Jordan's, 'lawful struggle to regain by all means their occupied territories' and recommended hardening measures against Israel, including the severance of diplomatic relations.

The decisive breakthrough in Non-Aligned support for the Palestinian cause came during the Algiers summit. A number of factors played a crucial role. First, by then the prestige of Arab countries had increased at the expense of Israel, with whom increasing numbers of Non-Aligned countries were breaking relations. This development naturally began to lend increasing credibility to Arab arguments. This is reflected in the readiness of the Non-Aligned delegations to concur with the Algerian arguments on the similarities between the problems of southern Africa and the Palestinian Problem. As a direct consequence the Palestinian struggle was included among other national liberation struggles.[68]

Second, the PLO as an observer was able to participate in the formal as well as informal deliberations of the summit and argue her own case. The impact of the PLO presence in the deliberations is reflected in the adoption in the final declaration of a reference of solidarity with the three PLO officals killed by the Israelis in Beirut.[69] Thirdly, the growing support for the PLO, particularly in the occupied territories, increased its status in the eyes of the Non-Aligned Movement. This was vividly reflected in the summit's recognition of the PLO as 'the legitimate representative of the Palestine people and their legitimate struggle'.

This breakthrough in Non-Aligned support for the Palestinian cause is also supported by their voting behaviour at the United Nations. As it can be seen from Table 6.5 the Non-Aligned attitude towards the Palestinian cause changed significantly. At the 24th Session the Non-Aligned Movement had been divided, particularly as a result of some Afro-Asian members' reluctance to support the Palestinian cause. There was a significant minority of almost 10 per cent which

Table 6.5. Distribution of Non-Aligned support

	General Assembly Sessions					
	24th 1969		28th 1973		29th 1974	
	n	%	n	%	n	%
Highly pro-Palest.	(31)	67	(57)	93	(54)	98
Medium pro-Palest.	(2)	4	(4)	7	(1)	2
Intermediate	(6)	13	—		—	
Medium pro-Isr.	(3)	7	—		—	
Highly pro-Isr.	(4)	9	—		—	
Total*	46		61		55	

* Percentages and figures are based upon those countries meeting the minimum attendance levels.

was fully supportive of the Israeli position.[70] This situation changed during the early 1970s and by the General Assembly's 28th Session, held just after the Non-Aligned Algiers summit, an overwhelming majority were strongly supportive of the Palestinian cause. This support reached saturation point at the following Assembly session with only Nepal expressing less than full support.

This strongly pro-Palestinian position at the UN found further expression at the Ministerial Meeting in March 1975 in Havana. Until then the Non-Aligned had expressed its support for the 'restoration of the Palestinian people's national rights ... and its right to self-determination.' At Havana, this support became quite elaborate and much clearer. In its first separate resolution on Palestine, the Non-Aligned Movement having reiterated that the Palestinian struggle was an integral part of the world liberation movement, reaffirmed

its full and active support for the PLO in its struggle to restore the national rights of the Palestinian people, particularly their right to return to their homeland, the right to self-determination, sovereignty, independence and the creation of a national authority, by all means'.[71]

The wording of this paragraph suggests two changes in emphasis from previous Non-Aligned decisions. First, the meaning of the right to self-determination is clearly spelled out to mean 'sovereignty, independence and the creation of a national authority'. Second, throughout this resolution the Palestinians are referred to as 'the Palestinian people' rather than the 'Arabs of Palestine'. This doubtlessly signifies a complete change in Non-Aligned perception of Palestinians from displaced Arabs with ambiguous political rights to a distinct nation struggling for independence, a position argued and defended by the PLO since the late 1960s.

OAU support

OAU support for the Palestinian cause did not come until the Addis Ababa summit in May 1973. The OAU, for a long time, remained extremely reluctant to get involved in the Middle East conflict in any manner. Although the Arab members tried to inject the Palestinian problem into the debates no formal decision was adopted until after the 1967 war. Even then the Africans faced the problem with some reluctance. This was quite evident in their refusal to take up a Somalia–Guinea proposal to call an emergency OAU meeting. Ambivalance was also reflected in some African countries readiness to support a Latin American draft resolution during the 5th Emergency Session of the General Assembly, in 1967.[72] This draft resolution, which had stressed negotiations without prior Israeli withdrawal, was strongly opposed by the Arabs. Nevertheless, the first signs of change did begin to surface at the fourth OAU summit in Kinshasa in 1967. The Africans without expressing any particular position decided to work together within the United Nations to assist Egypt to secure the withdrawal of the Israeli forces.

This development brought the Africans nearer to Egypt and culminated in their lending support for Security Council Resolution 242. From then onwards Arab arguments based on the need to respect the basic OAU principles and the growing African recognition of the implications of the violation of these principles of African security began to gain ground over those who argued the need to keep the Middle East conflict outside African politics. The breakthrough in the African stand towards the Middle East occurred at the 8th Summit in Addis Ababa in 1971. Here, the OAU not only decided to intervene directly in the dispute but also, departing from previous practice, called on Israel to withdraw from all three Arab states and not just Egypt.

The failure of the OAU mission created a situation whereby Arab arguments began to undermine Israel's grip on Africa maintained through bilateral relations. Arab arguments that had previously gone unnoticed began to have an impact. During the 1973 Summit, the Algerian speech calling on Africa to establish some harmony in its attitudes towards the Middle East and southern Africa was particularly influential in swaying African opinion. Africa was finally behind the Arabs in full force. It was only in such an atmosphere that the OAU expressed its support for the 'inalienable rights of the Palestinian people'.

This African slowness in expressing support for the Palestinian cause is also reflected in their voting behaviour at the United Nations General Assembly. As Table 6.6 suggests, until as late as the 27th Session the Africans had been divided over the Palestinian question. At the 24th Session they appeared to be evenly split between those who were prepared to support the Palestinian cause and those aligning with Israel. During the 27th Session although a large minority preferred to take a intermediate stand the rest of the Africans moved towards a distinctly pro-Palestinian position. This growth in support for the Palestinian cause quickly reached a saturation point when at the following session all Africans included in the statistical analysis (except Lesotho) became highly pro-Palestinian.

Table 6.6. Distribution of African support for the Palestinian cause

	General Assembly Sessions							
	24th 1969		26th 1971		27th 1973		28th 1973	
	n	%	n	%	n	%	n	%
Highly pro-Palest.	(10)	34	(6)	23	(13)	52	(24)	96
Medium pro-Palest.	(2)	7	(6)	23	(2)	8	(1)	4
Intermediate	(5)	17	(8)	31	(10)	40	—	
Medium pro-Isr.	(4)	14	(4)	15	—		—	
Highly pro-Isr.	(8)	28	(2)	8	—		—	
Total*	29		26		25		25	

* Percentages and figures are based upon those countries meeting the minimum attendance levels.

These changes in African attitudes as reflected in their voting behaviour were also portrayed in the decisions of the OAU. During the emergency meeting, in November 1973, African support as expressed in OAU decisions grew stronger. This time the OAU expressed support for the Palestinian struggle for self-determination against colonialism and racial discrimination rather than the weaker reference to 'inalienable rights'. However, in general the decisions adopted by this meeting were dominated by expressions of African solidarity with the Arab states and their growing concern for Arab-African cooperation to meet the threats caused by Israel, Rhodesia, Portugal and South Africa.

It was at the OAU meeting in July 1975 in Kampala that unequivocal support for the Palestinian cause was finally expressed. At this meeting, the OAU, for the first time, adopted a separate resolution on the question of Palestine. The resolution, having reasserted recognition of the PLO as the sole and legal representatives of the Palestinian people, declared support for the Palestinian people's 'right to sovereignty over their territory' and 'their right to establish their independent authority'.[73] These decisions were in many ways adjustments to the earlier developments at the 29th Session of the General Assembly and the Non-Aligned decisions of March 1975. The OAU resolution on Palestine basically formalized the position taken by African countries in forums outside the OAU.

The Islamic countries

The Islamic countries had demonstrated strong solidarity with the Arab countries in opposing the adoption of the United Nations' partition resolution in 1947. However, this solidarity quickly eroded when, within a year of Israel's admission to the United Nations, three Islamic countries recognized Israel and two exchanged diplomatic representatives.[74] The early Islamic solidarity experienced further setbacks as all newly independent African Muslim countries, excluding the North African ones, established diplomatic relations with Israel.

This lack of unity among Islamic countries was reflected in their voting behaviour at the United Nations General Assembly. As Table 6.7 depicts most African Islamic countries remained uncommitted to thorough support for the Palestinian cause. Four of the two African countries who were supportive of the Israeli position at the 24th Session also had their embassies situated in Jerusalem rather than Tel Aviv.

Table 6.7. Distribution of Islamic support at the 24th Session by ICO and sub-group membership

	ICO	Non-Arab Africans	Non-Arab Asians
Highly pro-Palest.	10	4	6
Medium pro-Palest.	—	—	—
Intermediate	3	3	—
Medium pro-Isr.	2	2	—
Highly pro-Isr.	2	2	—
Total*	17	11	6

* Results are for those countries meeting the minimum attendance levels.

As a result of the Al-Aqsa mosque fire in Jerusalem, 25 countries met in Rabat in September 1969. The conference adopted resolutions supportive of the international status of Jerusalem and the political rights of the Palestinians[75] and as a result of Algerian and Egyptian efforts admitted the PLO as an observer. However, a Libyan proposal calling on Islamic countries to break relations with Israel was not conclusive as Iran, Turkey and African participants objected to this initiative. Hence Islamic support for the Palestinian cause stopped short of censuring Israel.

From the early 1970s the situation changed. The first Islamic summit had led to the establishment of the Islamic Conference Organization, in March 1971. This organization gave Arab governments and the PLO the opportunity to mobilize support for the Palestinian cause by raising Islamic consciousness and solidarity. Even though, in December 1970 in Karachi, the Foreign Ministers of Islamic countries had expressed support for the restoration of the legitimate rights of the Palestinians, it was not until after the October war that the majority of Islamic countries were prepared to radicalize their stand. By then, the Islamic group had reached a very high degree of cohesion in their attitudes towards the Palestinian Problem. Their voting behaviour at the 29th Session of the General Assembly suggests that all Islamic countries included in the statistical analysis fell in the highly pro-Palestinian band of support. This strong, unified pro-Palestinian stand at the United Nations was also reflected in the decisions of the 2nd Islamic Summit in February 1974, in Lahore.

At this summit members supported the right to self-determination for the Palestinian people and called for the severance of diplomatic relations with Israel, the recognition of the PLO as the sole representative of the Palestinian people and the opening of PLO offices.[76] This summit, given that the PLO participated in the following ICO meetings as a full member, also appears to have granted the PLO the status of full membership. At the following Ministerial Meeting in Jeddah in July 1975 the strength of ICO support for the Palestinian cause went as far as adopting a PLO-Syrian proposal calling members to work towards the expulsion of Israel from the United Nations. However, this decision appears not to have received the support of Iran, Turkey and some African countries.[77]

The Latin Americans

The least forthcoming Third World group in lending support to the Palestinian cause was the Latin Americans. In many ways this is not surprising. The Latin Americans had played a very crucial and decisive role in the adoption of the 'Partition Resolution' in 1947. They were also quick to follow the lead of the United States in recognizing Israel, without even waiting for her admission to the United Nations.[78] By the late 1960s, with the exception of three Caribbean states, all Latin American countries had exchanged diplomatic representatives with Israel.[79] Eleven of them actually maintained embassies in Jerusalem, making the Latin Americans supportive of Israel's claim to Jerusalem as its capital.

This very strong pro-Israeli position can also be seen in their behaviour at the United Nations General Assembly. The Latin Americans played a leading role in the politics of the Emergency Special Session of the Assembly convened after the 1967 war. They tabled a draft resolution which was perceived as strongly pro-Israeli as it did not make negotiations conditional upon complete withdrawal.[80] As Table 6.8 shows, at the 24th Session of the Assembly they were still over-whelmingly pro-Israeli with only Cuba taking a pro-Palestinian position.

This situation continued until the 28th Session when Latin American support increased in favour of the Palestinian cause. The overwhelming majority of Latin Americans who became supportive were also members of the Non-Aligned Movement, reflecting the role played by the Non-Aligned in this development.[81] The Non-Aligned Movement constituted the only regional Third World political grouping active on the Palestinian question that allowed Arab governments and the PLO access to the Latin Americans. The Group of 77 and OPEC are two other Third World political groupings that allow a similar access but these groups

Table 6.8. Distribution of Latin American support

	General Assembly Sessions					
	24th 1969		29th 1974		35th 1980	
	n	%	n	%	n	%
Highly pro-Palest.	(1)	5	(7)	43	(20)	87
Medium pro-Palest.	—		(3)	19	(1)	4
Intermediate	(5)	26	(3)	19	(2)	9
Medium pro-Isr.	(4)	22	—		—	
Highly pro-Isr.	(9)	47	(3)	19	—	
Total*	19		16		23	

* Percentages and figures are based upon those countries meeting the minimum attendance levels.

primarily operate on economic issues, and accordingly have not been included in this study.

Furthermore, the Latin Americans witnessed the process by which the Palestinian cause became absorbed by anti-colonial thinking. The cognitive linkage between the Palestinian struggle and other national liberation struggles against colonialism and racism played a crucial role in changing Latin American perceptions. The Latin Americans, particularly those associated with the Non-Aligned, in their voting at the United Nations had developed an anti-colonial tradition. This pattern progressively expanded to include all other Latin Americans. The successful integration of the Palestinian cause into anti-colonialism undoubtedly helped the process by which the Non-Aligned Latin Americans particularly came to support the Palestinian cause.

It was not until the 35th Assembly Session, in 1980, that a pro-Palestinian position among the Latin Americans emerged. It is interesting to note that some of these Latin American countries were regular observers at Non-Aligned summits. The dramatic changes in the attitudes of Bolivia, Ecuador and Uruguay may well be attributed to their steady exposure to Non-Aligned arguments on the Palestinian question. This Non-Aligned influence is, to some extent also supported by the fact that the only two Latin American countries that did not support the Palestinian cause holding instead a 'balanced' stand were the Dominican Republic and Guatemala, both of which had no relations with the Non-Aligned and continued to maintain their traditionally close relations with the United States.

It should be pointed out that, in general, this late Latin American support for the Palestinian cause never reached the levels attained by other Third World groups. Latin American support on this issue has mostly remained declaratory. Only Cuba and Guyana have followed Non-Aligned recommendations and severed relations with Israel. Similarly only 8 out of 30 Latin American countries have allowed the PLO to open offices. Jamaica a Non-Aligned country, even turned down an official request by the PLO in 1978 to open an office.[82] In general the Latin Americans have not seen their support for the Palestinian cause as incompatible with maintaining relations with Israel. But undoubtedly, the Latin

Americans constitute the group that experienced the most dramatic change in their support for the Palestinian cause.

Conclusion

In general substantial Third World support for the Palestinian cause was not mobilized in any significant way until the early 1970s. Not surprisingly the Islamic countries were the first Third World political group to commit themselves to the Palestinian cause. They were promptly followed by the Non-Aligned. The relatively easier Arab and PLO accessibility to the respective forums of these two groups enabled Arab and Palestinian delegates to pursue their diplomatic efforts. These efforts benefited from developments in the Middle East that created a conducive environment.

At the African level, member Arab governments found a much less receptive audience as the OAU, throughout the 1960s, remained reluctant to get involved in the Middle East conflict. It was only in the face of continuous Arab efforts that the Africans inched towards a more active role that culminated in the OAU mission. The failure of this mission eventually led the Africans to recognize Arab arguments. In the end for most of the African governments it was the October war itself that finally swung them firmly into the Arab fold. Once the Africans had sided with the Arabs on the Middle East conflict they also became more receptive to Palestinian demands for support. In this case the conspicuous growth in Non-Aligned support for the Palestinian cause, coupled with the steady erosion of Israel's status in the eyes of the Africans eventually ensured near unanimous support for the Palestinian cause.

The Latin Americans were the very last Third World grouping to come out in support of the Palestinian cause. The Latin Americans in general had maintained strong ties with Israel especially at the bilateral level. The Non-Aligned Movement seems to have played a central role in eroding the influence of Israel on Latin American perceptions of the Palestinian problem. This was particularly evident among those Latin Americans associated with the Non-Aligned Movement. It appears that this occured as a result of a socialization process that precipitated the need to bring Latin American perceptions of the Palestinian issue in line with the rest of the Non-Aligned. The remaining Latin Americans joined ranks with the rest gradually. Here the growth in support at the UN and the legitimization of the PLO as the representatives of the Palestinians may have played a role too.

Notes

1 Appendix II provides a complete listing of members by each grouping.
2 The construction of this index is analysed in Appendix I.
3 Willetts, P. *The Non-Aligned Movement* (Frances Pinter, London, 1978), p. 161.
4 Willetts (1978: 3); Nweke, G. *Harmonization of African Foreign Policies 1955–1975: The Political Economy of African Diplomacy* (African Studies Center, Boston University, 1980), pp. 29–30.
5 For an analysis of these meetings see Legum, C. *Pan-Africanism* (Praeger, New York, 1965), ch. III.
6 For a study of the origins of the OAU, its charter and institutional structure see Wolfers, M. *Politics in the Organization of African Unity* (Methuen, London, 1976).
7 The public perception of non-alignment in its early days appears to have stressed the concern of the Non-Aligned with the Cold War. However, Willetts (1978) challenges this

view and empirically demonstrates that anti-colonialism was a major dimension of non-alignment right from the early days.

8 According to Jansen, G. *Zionism, Israel and Asian Nationalism* (The Institute for Palestine Studies, Beirut, 1971) p. 259, it was at Bandung that new countries first heard of the Palestinian problem. This advantage is also reflected in the way in which even during a pro-Israeli period at the bilateral level, some Africans were prepared to be less supportive of Israel at multilateral gatherings, Nweke (1980: 216).

9 El-Khawas, M. 'African and The Middle Eastern Crisis', *Issue* 1975 (Spring), p. 33; Thiam, D. *The Foreign Policy of African States* (Phoenix House, London, 1965), pp. 65–6.

10 Decalo, S. 'Israeli Foreign Policy and The Third World', *Orbis* vol. II (1967), no. 3, p. 732.

11 Decraence, P. 'Is the Romance with Israel over?', *African Report* May–June 1973, p. 24.

12 For an analysis of the initiation and performance of the OAU mission to the Middle East see El-Ajouty, Y. (ed.) *The Organization of African Unity, After Ten Years* (Praeger Publications, New York, 1975) ch. 10.

13 El-Khawas (1975: 38).

14 Chibwe, E. *Arab Dollars for Africa* (Croom Helm, London, 1976), p. 26.

15 Jansen (1971: 252); Decalo (1967: 730) and Thompson, W. *Ghana's Foreign Policy, 1957–1966: Diplomacy, Ideology and the New State* (Princeton University Press, Princeton, 1969), pp. 46–7.

16 Adams, J. *The Unnatural Alliance* (Quartet Books, London, 1984), pp. 11–12.

17 Quoted in Sawant, A. 'Rivalry between Egypt and Israel in Africa South of the Sahara, 1956–1970'; *International Studies*, vol. 17 (1978), no. 2, p. 312. Also see Thompson (1969: 47) for the sympathy expressed by Ghanaian governmental circles for the Jews.

18 Sawant (1978: 312).

19 Brecher, M. *The Foreign Policy System of Israel: Setting, Images, Process* (Oxford University Press, London, 1972), p. 343.

20 See OAU Charter, Articles II (c) and (d) and III. Similarly the Bandung Conference and the First Non-Aligned Summit also set these principles as central to the development of friendly relations between countries (Jankowisch, O. and Sauvant, K. *The Third World Without Superpowers: The Collected Documents of the Non-Aligned Countries, Volumes I–IV* (Oceana Publications, Dobbs Ferry, New York, 1978), pp. LXV, LXVI and 5.

21 However, these arguments had to be put forward in a restrained manner as in the immediate aftermath of the 1967 war the majority of Africans were reluctant to discuss the Middle East conflict at the regional level. A joint Guinean/Somalian call for an emergency meeting of the OAU had been turned down as the Africans continued to believe that the Middle East problem belonged to the UN. When the OAU did meet for its 1967 summit session, the Middle East was not even on its agenda, hence the Arab arguments and efforts remained muted (Sawant, 1978: 326). Guinea was the only country to break diplomatic relations with Israel as a result of the war. She was also the only African country to take a very radical stance on the Middle East conflict during the General Assembly debates (UN Document, A/PV 1546, 3 July 1967).

22 Nweke (1980: 221).

23 Ibid.

24 See the Tanzanian delegates speech at the General Assembly (UN Document, A/PV 1530, 21 June 1967).

25 Legum, C. (ed.) *Africa Contemporary Record: Annual Survey and Documents 1972–73* (Rex Collings, London, 1973), p. C23.

26 The statistical analysis of the relationship between UN voting behaviour on the Palestinian Question and matters concerning southern Africa is examined in Kirisci, K. 'Mobilization of Support for the Palestinian Cause: A Comparative Study of Political Change at the Communal, Regional and Global Levels', unpublished doctorial thesis, The City University, London, 1986, Appendix II, pp. 396–419.

27 Although the Declaration adopted at the Bandung Conference did briefly refer to 'the rights of the Arab people of Palestine' this was done under the 'Other Problems' of the

Declaration but under the preceding section for 'Problems of Dependent Peoples' which dealt with problems of colonialism, Jankowitsch and Sauvant (1978, vol. II: LXII, LXIII).

28 El-Khawas (1975: 33).
29 See Legum (1965: 206) for the text of the resolution on Palestine. According to Legum the participants in the meeting were Ghana, Guinea, Mali, Egypt, Morocco, Libya, Ceylon and the Algerian Provisional Government.
30 El-Khawas (1975: 35–6).
31 Ibid. p. 36.
32 Akinsaya, A. 'The Afro-Arab Alliance: Dream or Reality', *African Affairs*, vol. 75 (October 1976), no. 301, p. 521.
33 Quoted in El-Khawas (1975: 39).
34 Ibid.
35 Jankowisch and Sauvant (1978, vol. I: 100).
36 Ibid., p. 109.
37 Previously, the idea of an alliance of Salisbury–Pretoria–Lisbon against the struggle for national liberation had not included Israel. (*KCA*, May 1973: 25955; Jankowisch and Sauvant, 1978, vol. I: 211).
38 Ibid., pp. 241–2.
39 Ibid., p. 243.
40 *African Contemporary Record* 1973–4, p. A9.
41 Ibid., p. A11.
42 Ibid., p. A9.
43 Ibid., p. A4.
44 Decraene (1973: 22); *The Jewish Yearbook* (1970: 161–74).
45 See Decalo, S. 'Israeli Foreign Policy and the Third World', *Orbis*, vol. II (1967), no. 3, p. 734.
46 Sawant (1978: 319, 321).
47 Schichor, Y. *The Middle East in China's Foreign Policy 1949-1977* (Cambridge University Press, Cambridge 1979), p. 52.
48 Sawant, (1978: 322).
49 However, this was achieved only after a controversial debate between Arab governments and some African countries was settled, with African liberation movements also being allowed to make speeches (Willetts, 1978: 34).
50 Jankowisch and Sauvant (1978, vol. III: 1221).
51 Schichor (1979: 117).
52 Ibid., p. 115.
53 *Arab Record and Report* (1972: 342).
54 Ibid., p. 611.
55 *ARR* (1974: 76).
56 Jankowisch and Sauvant (1978, vol. II: 437).
57 For a list of PLO offices abroad see Appendix IV.
58 *ACR* (1975–6: A87).
59 Ibid., p. C21. Even this milder version was not acceptable to some African countries. Zaïre was against the resolution while Ghana, Sierra Leone and Liberia entered reservations.
60 Jankowisch and Sauvant (1978, vol. II: 863).
61 Jankowisch and Sauvant (1978, vol. I: 5).
62 *Conference of Heads of Government of Non-Aligned Countries, Belgrade*, September 1–6, 1961 (The Publishing House, Yugoslavia, Belgrade, n.d.) pp. 45–6.
63 Ibid., p. 81.
64 Ibid., p. 124.
65 This resolution was not adopted without some opposition. A number of African countries expressed objections to it at its draft stage (Jansen, 1965: 262–3).
66 Jankowisch and Sauvant (1978, vol. I: 100).
67 Ibid., pp. 242–3.

68 Ibid., p. 209.
69 Ibid., p. 211.
70 These countries were Burma, Jamaica, Lesotho and Nepal.
71 Jankowisch and Sauvant (1978, vol. III: 1436–7).
72 Fifteen African countries supported the Latin American proposal (A/L.523 and Add.1 and 2) which did not make an immediate withdrawal a prerequiste for peace. The Non-Aligned proposal, on the other hand (A/L.522 Rev.1 and Add.1) was supported by 12 African countries and called for immediate withdrawal behind armistice lines. The Arabs held the extreme position of no recognition and no negotiations with Israel (A/PV.1526, 1529 and 1530). For a detailed and thorough analysis of the 1967 negotiations during the 1967 General Assembly Emergency Session see Lall, A. *The United Nations and the Middle East Crisis* (Colombia University Press, New York, 1968).
73 *ACR* (1975–6: C20).
74 Indonesia, Iran and Turkey recognized Israel soon after its admission to the UN. The first two exchanged diplomatic representatives with Israel. Turkey lowered its level of representation once after the Suez war and then again after Israel annexation of Jerusalem; Iran on the other hand severed its relations after the overthrow of the Shah.
75 *ARR* (1969: 398, 428).
76 *ARR* (1974: 76).
77 For Iran and Turkish objections, see 'The Campaign leading to the UN Anti-Zionism Resolution', *IJA Research Report*, no. 22 (November 1975), p. 3.
78 With the exception of Mexico which recognized Israel on April 1949, Glick, E. *Latin America and the Palestine Problem* (Theodor Herzl Foundation, New York, 1958) p. 171. For a thorough analysis of early Latin American support see Glick (1958). Similarly, Kaufman, Shapira and Barromi provide an empirically based and systematic analysis of Latin American relations up to the early 1970s. Both publications note the very strong pro-Israeli stance among Latin Americans throughout the 1950s, 1960s and early 1970s, Kaufman, E., Shapira, Y. and Barromi, J. *Israel-Latin American Relations* (Transaction Books, New Brunswick, 1979). For a more recent study covering the early 1980s see Klick, I. 'Latin America and the Palestine Question' *IJA Research Report* nos 2 and 3 (January 1986).
79 *The Europa Yearbook* (1970: 699–700).
80 UN Document A/L.523 and Add.1 and 2.
81 Kaufman, Shapira and Barromi too note the growing influence of the Non-Aligned on Latin American attitudes towards the Middle East conflict particularly from the early 1970s onwards (1979: 4, 207).
82 *ARR* (1978: 619).

7 Mobilization of Support for the Palestinian Cause among East and West European Countries

Introduction

This chapter looks at the mobilization process among those groups of countries that do not belong to the Third World. As in the previous chapter, the focus will be on the responses, emanating from the governments belonging to these two regional groupings, to the various demands put forward by Arab governments and the PLO. Unlike the previous chapter, the analysis does not rely simply on group behaviour because these two regional groupings do not have formal regional political institutions whose scope includes the Palestinian Problem and whose decisions reflect the unanimous position and attitudes of its members. The nearest thing approaching an institution with a formalized regional decision-making mechanism, which covers the Middle East too, is the European Community.

The lack of institutionalized group decisions on which to focus the analysis necessitated the study of political statements and declarations made individually by most of these governments. These statements and decisions, in particular those made during the United Nations General Assembly debates, were studied for changes in content and emphasis. This analysis was then combined with a quantitative analysis of these countries' voting behaviour in the UN General Assembly. The index of political support constructed from the voting analysis was found to be particularly useful in identifying sub-groupings.

However, this index of political support needs a word of caution. As a result of the nature of the content of the General Assembly resolutions the index is not refined enough to capture, on its own, the changing attitudes, particularly of the EC countries, in relation to the rest of the Assembly. Hence the results emerging from these countries' voting behaviour at the UN need to be carefully related to the political statements and actions made within and outside that forum.

Before proceeding to the analysis of the mobilization of support it might be useful to bear in mind a number of differences that separate these two groups from the Third World regional and political groupings in respect to the Palestinian problem.

First, some countries from both groups have had deeply entrenched historical interests in the politics and economics of the Middle East in a way no Third World country has had. This interest and involvement in the area has influenced both the emergence of the Palestinian Problem itself as well as attitudes held in these countries towards this problem. France and Britain as Mandate powers between the two World Wars and as countries with economic interests were closely involved in the politics of the region. After World War II they were, to some degree, replaced by the United States and the Soviet Union. Since the mid-1950s, factors ranging from domestic political to strategic considerations often involving matters of prestige and status have influenced the policies of these two countries towards the Palestinian Problem as well as the actual problem itself.

Second, a great number of the countries belonging to these two groups, as a result of their membership of the UN, have been exposed to the Palestinian Problem from its early days. At a time when an overwhelming majority of Asian-African countries were still colonies, these countries were participants in the General Assembly debates and roll-calls concerning the Palestinian Problem in the late 1940s and early 1950s. It was during this period that despite the Arab delegations' protests they played a central role in the process that converted the Palestinian Problem from a political one to one of resettling refugees.

Third, as a result of the Cold War the countries of the North have been split into two ideologically opposing groupings. This sustained ideological division, whose equivalent one cannot find in the Third World, has limited the emergence of the kinds of interactions between the two groups that could have benefitted the Palestinian cause. However, as the analysis below will suggest this has not necessarily led to the development of two completely separate approaches to the Palestinian Problem. Instead the attitudes of some of the countries of the Western group have overlapped with those in Eastern Europe.

In this context, the attitude of the Western group can be better characterized by a set of attitudes held by sub-groups such as the southern European countries, the Nordic countries, the EC and another group including the United States, Canada and Australia. The differences in attitudes between these Western sub-groups are reflected to some extent in their voting behaviour but more sharply in their political statements and their relations with the PLO. In contrast, the East Europeans have manifested a much more unified behaviour, particularly with regard to their voting behaviour at the UN. This strong cohesive voting behaviour, however, has not always reproduced itself in the political statements and declarations eminating from individual East European countries.

Conducive environment

Structural changes

At this level of analysis there have been few significant structural changes that have occurred with any particular consequence to the mobilization of support for the Palestinian cause. Unlike most of the Third World, after World War II, countries from the East and Western blocs developed extensive structures of communications and cooperation at both bilateral and multilateral levels. The concern and domain of these structures of communications and decision making mechanisms, particularly in the form of regional organizations, have for the most part centred around two sets of issues.

The first has covered matters relating to the maintenance of the military-political status quo between the East and Western European groups. These matters have been dealt with at the multilateral level by the respective organizations of the two military alliances. The second set of issues has encompassed matters of economic growth and economic integration. The regional organizations dealing with these issues have mostly concerned themselves with policies directed towards the promotion of greater economic growth and trade between member countries.

Other than matters of developmental aid the agendas of these multilateral forums have neither been receptive to items reflecting Third World demands for major changes in the international economic order nor to demands of political support for the resolution of a wide range of political and colonial problems of high salience to the Third World. It was only in the context of the United Nations

General Assembly and then only since the early 1960s that both the Eastern and Western Bloc countries became involved in these issues in any significant way. Until then the Western dominance of the General Assembly had prevented Third World attempts to introduce issues of concern to them to the agendas of the United Nations.

It is against this background that the emergence of the European Political Cooperation among members of the European Community and the Euro-Arab dialogue may be seen as important structural developments that brought about a conducive environment in respect to the Palestinian Problem. The EPC emerged from the adoption of the 'Luxembourg Report' in October 1970, as an inter-governmental arrangement to consult and coordinate efforts on foreign policy matters; such matters had been deliberately left outside the scope of the Rome Treaty establishing the European Community.[1]

The consequences of the EPC have been particularly stark in respect to the Palestinian Question. Countries such as France, Britain and Italy with a relatively more pro-Arab inclination since the 1967 war have left their mark by leading the formulation of a common EC stand much more sympathetic to the Palestinian cause. France has played a central role in trying to counterbalance American pressure for an Atlanticist position much less favourable to the Palestinian cause. The EPC has also exposed pro-Israeli countries such as Denmark and Holland to the Palestinian Problem.[2]

Furthermore, the particular way in which the EPC works, with its rotating chairmanship, and its demands for active involvement have forced countries, such as Ireland, with little interest in the Middle East to become involved.[3] The efficacy of this political socialization process in bringing about attitudinal changes favour-able to the Palestinian Problem can probably be best substantiated by Israel's belligerence towards the EPC.[4] The entry of Greece to the Common Market has also had its own impact on EC attitudes towards the Palestinian Problem. As an already committed ally of the Palestinian cause and with her close PLO ties, Greece injected greater urgency to the ongoing debate on the definition of the political rights of the Palestinians and the status of the PLO.

The EPC has opened the way for debates and discussions on the Palestinian Question, exposing participants to views which have come to condition their perceptions of the Palestinian problem and their attitudes towards the Palestinian cause. The EPC has also become a tangible multilateral decision-making forum to which Palestinians and Arabs have tried to gain access directly or through the Euro-Arab dialogue.

The Euro-Arab dialogue can be seen as 'a manifestation of the EPC machinery at work'that originated from the European Community Summit in Copenhagen in December 1973 attended by four Arab foreign ministers.[5] As a result of various complications encountered during the establishment of the institutions of the dialogue, it was not until June 1975 that the Euro-Arab dialogue finally got underway.

The Arabs had always wanted to involve Europe in the Middle East problem. Since the 1967 war, this view was held in the belief that once involved, Europe would develop an approach independent from the pro-Israeli position of the United States.[6] It was the 1973 war that brought about certain changes increasing the salience of the Middle East to the Europeans. The Arab oil embargo and the ensuing oil price increase quickly precipitated changes in the structures of the pre-1973 political and economic relations between Europe and the Arab world. The demonstrative effect of the ability of Arab governments to control oil supplies and the significant increase in their purchasing power forced many European governments and the EC to change their position on the Middle East in their foreign policies.

It is in this climate that the Euro-Arab dialogue was launched. Inspite of its vague terms of reference reflecting a compromise between a European desire to limit the dialogue to commercial matters and the Arab governments' insistence on a broader scope, the dialogue provided a setting within which the Europeans came to face the Palestinian Problem. This was, for example, well highlighted by the crisis that the composition of the Arab delegation precipitated. The Arab governments' insistence on including a separate PLO representation created an embarrassing problem of diplomatic recognition for the EC. The solution determined that all future meetings would be attended by a European and an Arab delegation rather than by separate, individual country delegations.

Key events

The 1967 Arab–Israeli war did not produce a direct response towards the Palestinian issue from either Eastern or Western Europe, but it did bring both sides much closer to the Arabs. The Soviet Union and the East Europeans broke relations with Israel and threw their diplomatic and political support behind the Arab side. This did not, however, immediately culminate in a climate receptive to Palestinian demands; the first signs of this did not emerge until the period immediately preceding the 1973 war.

First, the eviction of the Soviets from Egypt in July 1972 with the PLO's growing political ascendancy in the area increased the interest of the Soviet Union in the Palestinian Problem.[7] Second, a number of East European countries made themselves more accessible to the visits of PLO delegations and became supportive of the Palestinian cause. Hence, the October war came as an event that accelerated and deepened the East European move nearer to the Palestinian cause. One direct consequence of the 1973 war was to force the Soviets to take a lead in attempts to find a negotiated solution to the Palestinian Problem by putting forward the idea of a 'mini-state' at the Geneva Conference in December 1973.[8]

The 1967 war had less of an impact on Western European attitudes towards the Arab–Israeli Conflict. The only perceptible and significant change came from France. Previously a strong ally of Israel, France, under De Gaulle's leadership, moved much closer to the Arabs as the French government began to withdraw its traditional military and political support for Israel.[12] France also became one of the first leading members of the EC to advocate an approach more sympathetic to Palestinian demands.

Indirectly, the 1967 war did prepare the basis for important perceptual changes in Western Europe. First, as a result of the decisive Israeli victory in the 1967 war Israel ceased to be the 'underdog' surrounded by belligerent and numerically superior Arab countries. Second, in the face of this victory, Israel's reluctance to show magnanimity and compromise for achieving a reasonable settlement undermined European perceptions of Israel as 'one of us' ready to share the spirit of compromise that had come to characterize European politics in the post World War II era.

The impact of these two factors on West European thinking is quite evident from the importance they came to attach to Resolution 242 and to the efforts of Jarring to mediate in the Arab–Israeli Conflict. At the European Community level it was reflected in the adoption by the European ministers on May 1971 of the

Schumann Report which clearly stated the unacceptability of Israel's continued occupation of Arab territories and any changes to the status of these territories.[10] Probably the significance of the change in the cognitive environment of European decision-makers brought about by the 1967 war and the failure of the post-war diplomacy is best demonstrated by the hostility the Schumann Report received in Israel. Nevertheless, it was not until after the 1973 war that an environment more conducive to the mobilization of European support specifically for the Palestinian cause emerged. Although France, later joined by Britain, had argued the need to develop a common approach to the Middle East conflict it was the 1973 war that eventually jolted the EC into action.

Another event conducive to the mobilization of support for the PLO was the formation of the Likud government in June 1977 under the leadership of Begin. Begin's past confrontations and conflict with various European governments and his expansionist approach towards the occupied territories contributed to Europe's receptiveness to Palestinian demands and arguments.[11] This is reflected in the EC's growing readiness to respond to Palestinian demands for a 'mini-state'. With Begin in power the EC began to debate what form the expression of the political rights of the Palestinians should take. His re-election, in June 1981, and his commitment to Eretz Israel made the EC even more sceptical about Israel's goodwill. This resulted in an increase in the number of semi-official contacts between the PLO and the EC.

The signing of the Camp David agreements in March 1979 was another event that brought the EC closer to the Palestinian cause. The consensus among the members of the EC was that these agreements were a positive development albeit a partial one.[12] It was believed the agreements would not be complete until the views of the Palestinians were taken into consideration. The Autonomy plan was seen as inadequate and the extremely narrow Israeli interpretation of the meaning of autonomy was criticized. These points were reflected in the 26 March 1979 Paris Declaration which expressed the need to include Palestinian representatives in negotiations and the right of the Palestinians to a homeland.[13]

Furthermore, the aftermath of Israel's 1978 military operation in southern Lebanon and the continued policy of expanding Jewish settlements, together with a conspicuous reluctance to maintain meaningful talks, created an environment within which the urgency and relevance of Palestinian arguments and demands became very strong. It is against this background that the mobilization process culminating in the lauching of the 1980 Venice Declaration with its reference to 'the right of Palestinian people to self-determination' and to 'the need to associate the PLO with a comprehensive settlement' became possible.

By the late 1970s, as a result of these events, the EC had been led into an environment in which they had come to support the political rights of the Palestinians and the role of the PLO in a comprehensive settlement. However the definition of the political rights of the Palestinians did not go as far as a clear EC announcement in favour of the establishment of a 'state'. Similarly, the EC remained openly reluctant to recognize the PLO as the sole representative of the Palestinians. The 1980s initiated a more radical stand.

The Israeli annexation of Jerusalem, in June 1980, and the Golan Heights, in December 1981, threw serious doubts on the possibilities of achieving a comprehensive settlement based on an Israeli withdrawal from all occupied territories and the resolution of the Palestinian Problem. But probably the event that shook European governments and the public the most was the Israeli invasion of Lebanon.

The invasion, the seige of Beirut and the Sabra Chatila massacres ensured that the Palestinian Problem was kept on the formal and public agendas of European countries for many months. This urgency was reflected in the European support given to a French-Egyptian initiative at the Security Council in June 1982 and in the EC foreign ministers' declaration in September 1982.[14] The public on the other hand was engulfed with outrage and felt that, 'more urgently then ever, a homeland in Palestine is what they (Palestinians) need.'[15]

Cognitive and other linkages

It is difficult to find one or two common cognitive linkages that have influenced northern perceptions of the Palestinian issue. Instead there are a diverse set of linkages that appear to have influenced either individual governments or small groups of governments in different ways.

Anti-colonialism and anti-imperialism

Anti-colonialism and anti-imparialism have played a crucial role in mobilizing support among East European and, to a lesser extent, some West European countries. The East European countries have had a long record of involvement in the politics of decolonization, particularly at the United Nations. The nature of Marxist ideology encourages support for anti-colonial and anti-imperialist struggles; those situations that were perceived as anti-colonial and anti-imperialist struggles have usually received the political support of East European governments. In East European governmental circles the territorial gains of Israel resulting from the Arab–Israeli Conflict and American support for Israel generated sympathy for Arab allegations of the 'imperialistic and expansionist nature of Israel'.

The struggle waged by the Palestinians against Israel was seen as one against imperialism, a legitimate national liberation struggle worthy of political support. This was expressed quite clearly in a Warsaw Pact resolution of 26 November 1969 that spoke of the 'anti-imperialist national liberation struggle of the Arab people of Palestine' and a similar position received Soviet support in December 1969.[16] This position of the East Europeans is amply supported by their strong anti-colonial and pro-Palestinian voting.

For at least some East European countries it might also be possible to include the resurgence of anti-semitism as a factor in the Arab–Israeli Conflict. This is evident in the way in which the 'Arab–Israeli war of June 1967 pushed the Jewish problem into the forefront of Czechoslovak and Polish political life'.[17] The identification of Jewish communities with the Israeli victory put them into conflict with the governments of these two countries and their communist parties which had joined ranks with the Soviet Union in condemning Israel as the aggresor.

This conflict contributed to the view held by some governmental circles which attributed the political unrest of 1968 in both Poland and Czechoslovakia to an 'imperialist, revisionist and Zionist plot'.[18] This view facilitated the assessment of the situation in the Middle East in a manner favourable to the Arabs. The Arabs were seen as the victims of 'Israeli imperialism and Zionism'.

There are a number of Western countries for whom anti-colonialism also played a certain role in moulding their attitude towards the Palestinian Problem. These were some of the Scandinavian countries, Greece, Malta, Spain and Turkey. They tended to come from the fringes of European politics, in the sense they were not involved in the politics of the EC and lacked a political tradition as colonial powers. Since the early 1960s they have pursued foreign policies supportive of the rights to self-determination and of colonial peoples' struggle for independence. This is to a limited extent evident in their voting behaviour at the UN, which suggests a relatively anti-colonial position particularly in relation to the other countries in the Western European group.

Some of these countries came to perceive similarities between the Palestinian situation and struggles for independence. A growing relationship between a strong anti-colonial voting record and support for the Palestinian cause may well be indicative of this cognitive linkage. However the results of this statistical analysis must be handled with caution.[19] Unlike the Third World there is a lack of systematic evidence in the form of common declarations that unequivocally supports such a cognitive linkage.

Greece, Malta, Spain and Turkey are one such group of countries. Turkey's perception of the Palestinian struggle and its similarities to other anti-colonial struggles may well have been influenced by the debates and the decisions of the Islamic group. In a similar way Malta is a member of the Non-Aligned Movement which has endorsed and supported the Palestinian cause as an anti-colonial one. Spain has traditionally held very close and friendly ties with the Arab world. It has had a long record of policies in support of Arab and African decolonization. Hence, it has been more open to Arab and Palestinian arguments. Similarly, Greece has maintained strong ties with the Arab world: they voted against the Partition Plan in 1947 and were strongly critical of the Suez intervention. Greece's perception of the Palestinian Problem is also influenced by the similarities it draws between the occupation of Palestine and Cyprus and further strengthened by strong feelings of anti-Americanism.

To the above countries one can add Sweden, Finland and to a lesser extent Ireland. They have exhibited a voting behaviour which to some extent suggests similar levels of support for anti-colonialism and the Palestinian cause. Although all Scandinavian countries have been supportive of anti-colonialism in their voting behaviour it is only Sweden and Finland that have voted in a manner that suggests the possibility of a cognitive linkage between anti-colonialism and the legitimization of the Palestinian cause. The different behaviour of the other Scandinavian countries on the Palestinian issue may well be induced by their involvement in the politics of NATO and the EC. This may have restrained them from developing a cohesive Nordic approach towards the Palestinian issue complementing their approach to colonial matters.

Ireland's colonial background and its experience of partition has made it much more sensitive to Third World struggles for self-determination and the problems of dispossessed peoples.[20] Irish support for Egypt during the Suez crisis and for the Algerian liberation struggle can be seen as early manifestations of this anti-colonial stand favouring the Arab world.[21] Undoubtedly the same feelings may have played a role in the growth of Irish support for the Palestinian cause during the 1970s.

For the rest of the Western group, a cognitive linkage between anti-colonialism and the Palestinian cause appears to be weak because countries falling into this group have voted in four separate ways on both issues. There are those countries such as Britain, France and Austria who have tended to be relatively more supportive of the Palestinian cause than of anti-colonialism. At the opposite end of the spectrum are those Scandinavian countries that are strongly supportive of anti-colonialism but not of the Palestinian cause. The United States is the only country that has voted strongly, pro-Israeli and pro-colonial particularly since the 29th Session of the General Assembly. Finally, there are those countries, mostly EC members, that have voted neither against nor in support of either issue.

Linkages derived from legal principles

Countries belonging to the Western group have a strong tradition in international law and in the promotion of it. A number of international legal principles such as the 'inadmissability of the acquistion of territory by force', 'respect for the territorial integrity of states' and particularly those principles that make up human rights law have come to influence European perceptions of the Arab–Israeli Conflict and Israeli practices. Since the 1967 war Western attitudes influenced by these principles increasingly benefitted the Palestinian cause.

During the period prior to the 1967 war, European support for Israel, such as during the Suez war and Nasser's blockade of the straits of Tiran, had been based on arguments derived from the need to respect the existing international order governing navigation through international waterways.[22] With the 1967 war the primacy of legal principles that favoured Israel was quickly eroded. Principles such as 'respect for the territorial integrity of states' had become generally accepted in the Third World and were expressed in the decisions of the Bandung Conference, the Non-Aligned meetings and the OAU Charter. Although these principles originated from the Third World, it was partly in the context of the Arab–Israeli Conflict that they became legal norms also recognized by the Europeans. In an increasingly anti-colonial world these principles came to undermine and replace the old 'right to sovereignty by conquest'.

It is in the light of these developments that the significance of the unanimous European support for Resolution 242 should be seen. Since the adoption of this resolution the West and particularly the EC has regularly reiterated a demand for Israel's withdrawal from the occupied territories and the need for all countries in the area to respect their mutual sovereignty. The readiness of many Arab governments to accept Resolution 242 compared to Israel's reluctance weakened the earlier support that Israel had enjoyed. More importantly these measures created doubts in the minds of Europeans as to whether Israel genuinely meant to achieve lasting peace through negotiations.

The increasingly substantiated Israeli violation of human rights in the occupied territories seems to have played a role in changing European attitudes towards the Palestinian problem. Israel, in the 1950s and 1960s, had gained the admiration of large sections of the European public as well as governments. This admiration, in general, was based on the image that Israel projected of an egalitarian and socialist society. Israel was perceived as a bastion of democracy in the midst of a repressive Middle East, dominated by Nasserism and feudal monarchies, but Israeli governmental and military policies in the occupied territories gradually eroded this image. The arbitrary nature of the behaviour of Israeli authorities became increasingly difficult to accept. Groups inside Israel and in Western Europe began to express growing concern about the violation of various aspects of the Geneva Conventions and the systematic undermining of the principle of 'rule of law' so central to Western political-legal thinking. Israel's legitimacy in the occupied territories gradually eroded and enabled the West to sympathize with the plight of the Palestinians, their frustration and at times their use of violence towards the authorities.

Furthermore, similarities, however superficial, have been drawn between

Palestinian resistance to Israeli occupation and resistance to the German occupation during World War II. Particularly, in the eyes of East Europeans, the French, the Spanish and the Greeks the violence perpetrated by the Palestinians in the occupied territories came to be seen as the natural outcome of foreign occupation. The people involved in this violence were referred to as 'resistance fighters' or 'partisans' rather than terrorists.[23] This at least in the eyes of these governments signified an increase in the perceived status of Palestinian guerrilla fighters. The overall effect of this process, more importantly, was its contribution to a change in the way the Palestinian problem was seen first as a refugee problem and then as a problem of a people resisting occupation in a struggle to achieve self-determination.

Bargain linkages

The fundamental change in the European approach towards the Arab–Israeli Conflict has often been attributed to Arab oil power and to the dictations of European economic interests in the area.[24] On its face value, the announcement of the first joint EC Declaration of 6 November 1973, in the immediate aftermath of Arab oil production cuts and embargoes, may appear to lend some credence to this argument. The declaration was the first time that the EC had taken a common approach towards the Middle East and expressed the need to take an active role in search of a comprehensive settlement. It was also the first time the EC referred to the 'legitimate rights of the Palestinians'. In addition the declaration suggested the need for Israeli-Arab negotiations to take place within a UN framework, a position strongly opposed by Israel. Finally, it stressed the ties between Western Europe and the Eastern Mediterranean, and expressed interest in developing these ties, thus paving the way to the Euro-Arab dialogue.

To attribute this declaration, which received the welcome of the November 1973 Arab summit in Algiers and the very strong disapproval of Israel, to a straightforward bargain linkage between Arab governments and the EC whereby Europe was guaranteed oil and access to Arab markets in return for EC support for the Palestinian cause would be an oversimplification of a complex relationship; it would be difficult for the EC to maintain stable and healthy commercial relations with the Middle East without taking account of the political concerns of the actors in the area.

The EC, with the adoption of the Schumann Report in May 1971, had already recognized some of the concerns of the Arab countries by calling for the withdrawal of Israel from the occupied territories. Furthermore, most EC countries including traditionally pro-Israeli ones were moving towards a recognition of the political rights of the Palestinian people before the adoption of the November 1973 Brussels Declaration. The Netherlands, ironically the primary target of the oil embargo in Europe, had acknowledged the political dimension of the Palestinian problem as early as November 1970.[25] Belgium too had followed a similar pattern of behaviour and by October 1972 it expressed its concern for the future of the Palestinian people.[26] Both France and Britain, principal architects of the Brussels Declaration, had supported the 'rights and legitimate aspirations' of the Palestinians in a draft Security Council resolution in July 1973.

In this declaration the EC stopped well short of Arab and Palestinian demands. Recognition of the Palestinian dimension of the Arab–Israeli Conflict and the legitimate rights of the Palestinians did not meet Palestinian demands for a Palestinian state. It took almost a decade for most European countries to support, unambiguously, the right of Palestinian people to self-determination. And this was only as a result of a dynamic process, rather than a bargain linkage alone.

In the matter of the diplomatic recognition of the PLO, the EC remained reluctant to meet Arab demands and at no point has the EC waivered from its position of support for the Israeli state. All support that the EC has given to Palestinian political rights has always been conditional on the recognition of Israel's existence. In many ways the Europeans have skilfully exploited the significance that Arab governments and Palestinians have attached to European support in trying to moderate the PLO and some Arab governments.

Probably the most authoritative statement undermining the credibility of an argument attributing European support for the Palestinian cause purely to economic considerations came from Germany's foreign minister Genscher. In an explanation of his government's support for the principle of Palestinian self-determination he noted that a settlement of the problem was of vital concern to Europe 'even if the Arab states exported nothing but water'.[27] Economic considerations leading to bargain linkages should be seen in conjuction with other cognitive factors that have influenced European perceptions of the Palestinian problem and their attitudes towards its resolution. All in all, this bargain linkage precipitated closer dialogue between the Arabs and Europeans which, despite early reluctance, put the Palestinian Problem firmly on the agenda of the EC.

Linkages to domestic politics

Western states are not monolithic actors in world politics. Many groups contribute towards the foreign-policy-making process in these countries. In the case of foreign-policy-making on the Middle East, those representing the interest of oil companies and certain sections of the industry may be keen to promote bargain linkages in an effort to secure good relations with Arab governments. On the other hand other pressure groups such as human rights' groups, or trade unions will rely on cognitive linkages. In their attempt to persuade a government they will use arguments legitimizing the Palestinian cause by establishing linkages between the Palestinian problem and various highly prestigious principles central to political thinking in the West.

Similarly, there will be a variety of groups arguing the case of Israel, such as Jewish groups or socialist groups that identify with the dominant ideology in the Israeli political system. The aggregate impact of these pressure groups, together with governmental factors such as organizational and bureaucratic politics and environmental factors such as regional and international commitments and demands, will determine a government's foreign policy on the issue. However, there are situations when domestic political considerations feature so heavily in a governments foreign policy behaviour that it becomes possible to talk about clear linkages between the domestic and foreign policies of a country on the issue.

Linkage politics, as noted in chapter three, was a term introduced to conceptualize the relationship between the domestic political environment of a state and its international environment. Literature that was precipitated by Rosenau's work has mostly concentrated on linkages eminating from the international environment to the domestic environment or on linkages between domestic political systems.[28]

The impact that the Jewish community in the United States has on American foreign-policy-making and the international system can be seen as one such linkage. Since the early 1940s the Jewish community and the Zionist lobby in Congress has had a significant say in American policy-making towards the Middle East. The existence of the Jewish lobby has become a structural feature of the American domestic political system. It operates through a process of domestic bargain linkages which often generate inputs for the international political system. Although this linkage was to some extent weakened during and in the aftermath of the Suez war, it has gained increasing strength since the 1967 war. It has featured prominently in presidential election campaigns, in Congressional politics over various aspects of the Middle East issue and in the government's foreign policy decision making on the Palestinian problem.

However, this linkage especially since 1967 can also be likened to Roseanu's 'penetrative linkages'. Such linkages, according to Roseanu, consist in processes whereby actors from outside one state participates directly in the politics of that country.[29] Israel, it can be said, through the intermediaries of an active Jewish community and a Zionist lobby in Congress is able to bring about such linkages and influence American governmental policy. This is well demonstrated, for example, by the way in which Carter's peace plan, announced in March 1977, evoking the idea of a 'homeland' for the Palestinians had to go through a number of revisions as a result of Jewish-Israeli intervention.

Similarly, the American delegation at the UN also faced the consequences of such linkages. Andrew Young, after an unauthorized meeting in July 1979 with the PLO representative at the UN was forced to resign as a result of mounting Jewish pressure. In a later incident after the American delegation cast an affirmative vote in favour of a Security Council draft resolution strongly critical of Israeli settlement policies, President Carter 'as a result of protest from Israel and her supporters announced that the vote had been a mistake'.[30] Nevertheless, in spite of Israel's direct and indirect influence on the formation of American perceptions and attitudes towards the Palestinian Problem it would be wrong to attribute American foreign policy in the Middle East solely to this factor.

Before examining the role of strategic linkages in attitude formation toward the Middle East, the role of European socialist and labour parties in providing greater accessibility for Israeli views and a basis for favourable cognitive linkages with these views needs to be mentioned. In the 1950s and 1960s, Israel, in the eyes of the Socialist International held a special status. The moral impact of the Nazi atrocities on the European socialist movement together with the fact that 'Young Israel was seen by European socialists as a realization of the socialist dream' ensured this status.[31] This status enabled the often Labour-led Israeli government to enjoy the support and solidarity of the Socialist International on the Arab–Israeli Conflict throughout this period. However, this favourable image was gradually eroded as the membership of the Socialist International began to include groups from the Third World and anti-colonialism became absorbed in its ideology.[32]

Strategic linkages

Traditional theory in international relations makes power and power maximization central determinants of state behaviour. Accordingly American and Soviet foreign policy behaviour in the Middle East would be explained in terms of this region's place in the overall global security considerations of both countries. The United States would be expected to follow a foreign policy towards the Middle East whose primary concern would be to check Soviet expansionism, to protect vital oil fields and to maintain the strategic global status quo. Such a foreign policy would take the form of strengthening local allies of the United States and improving American capabilities to project military power to the area to meet any direct or indirect Soviet threat. The Soviet Union too would be expected to behave no differently. Its primary concern would be to try to expand its base of influence in an attempt to undermine the American position in the area. All would be done in the name of maximizing a super power's national interest, defined in terms of power.

Undoubtedly such global strategic/security considerations do enter the minds of foreign policy makers on the Middle East particularly those from the United States and the Soviet Union. Both the Global Politics approach and the Realists would break down such strategic consideration into three possible constitutent parts:

(i) prestige/status,
(ii) economic,
(iii) military/security considerations.

For the Realists prestige would be seen as a reflection of a country's 'power' usually associated with its military capabilities. For the Global Politics approach an actor's prestige can also be derived from sources other than military capabilities, as in the status given to the Pope. In this light the first consideration can be seen as an attempt on the part of the foreign policy makers to maintain a high status and prestige in the eyes of their allies in the area. This is often done by generating some degree of cognitive congruence over priority problems of the area and the means to resolve them. The United States promotes the threat of Soviet expansionism and communism as the major problem. This determines her foreign policy options. It helps the United States to justify its strong support for Israel, to mobilize support from moderate governments in the area and to promote a piecemeal approach to the solution of the Arab–Israeli Conflict. Although this is a position advocated by Israel it is not one that is shared by Arab governments. The lack of congruence over the Soviet threat to the Middle East was illustrated by Qatar's information minister when he accused the United States of 'trying to sell us the idea of danger in Afghanistan but I think Jerusalem is nearer than Kabul.'[33]

In a similar way, the Soviet Union depicts Israel and the United States as major threats to the area.[34] It has projected the struggle against the United States and Israel as an anti-imperialist and anti-Western and has sought to gain the allegiance of what it perceives to be progressive forces, which since the early 1970s have come to include the PLO.[35] The Palestinian issue has steadily gained greater centrality and has become a major problem for whose solution the Soviets have supported a comprehensive settlement. The high level of activity that has surrounded the Soviet government's desire to be involved in such a settlement can be attributed to prestige considerations.

The role of economic considerations in the Middle East is probably more central to American foreign policy than to the Soviet Union's. As important as the prestige element of checking a Soviet threat is the need to protect the economic resources of the area and ensure the accessibility of the local market to American goods and capital. At the strategic level it is believed that the loss of the area to the Soviets would endanger the continuity of the Western way of life, but foreign policy options emerging as a result of economic considerations conflict with those from earlier considerations. These options dictate the need to give greater importance to the concerns of those governments with economic leverage resulting from their control over oil supplies. The slow and painful way in which the Palestinian dimension of the Middle East problem has acquired greater attention in American foreign policy could be attributed to this conflict.

American military strategic considerations in the area are complex and at times conflicting. The credibility of the American argument of impending Soviet threat is maintained by an active American involvement in the defence of the area. This is done in two ways: first, by maintaining an American military presence, particularly a naval one in the area and second, by equiping the national defence forces of moderate friendly regimes. The latter is, however, seriously undermined by the politics surrounding American commitments to Israel. This in turn weakens American credibility and goodwill in the eyes of moderate Arab governments. Furthermore, these military considerations condition American attitudes towards the PLO. The PLO's strong ties with the Soviet Union and Syria coupled with the real and proclaimed threat the PLO constitutes towards Israel, culminates in American reluctance to recognize and maintain relations with the PLO. The close Soviet connection conditions the American stance against the idea of a Palestinian state as it 'fears that such a Palestine state would become the Cuba of the Middle East'.[36]

The Soviet Union has perceived Western and American presence in the Middle East as a threat to her security. In the late 1950s and through the 1960s ideological linkages ensured the Soviets a string of allies in the Middle East. These ideological affinities and anti-Westernism played an important role in the Soviet stance on the Arab–Israeli Conflict. It was the loss of Egypt, however, in 1972, that to some degree increased the salience of the Palestinian Problem and the PLO; the PLO became an important means of maintaining some influence in Arab politics.

Yet despite the advantages of having the PLO as an ally the Soviet Union has been surprisingly cautious in its military and political support. It was only in the 1980s that the Soviets began to talk about a Palestinian state and granted the PLO full diplomatic status. In a sense the PLO and the Palestinian issue was seen from a political rather than a military point of view. It is doubtful whether the Soviet government considered the PLO a serious military ally. This is well reflected in their reluctance to give military assistance to the PLO in an overt and consistent manner.[37]

A set of different linkages played a role in the way Northern countries approached the Palestinian problem. The cognitive linkages contributed towards the legitimization of the Palestinian cause and provided the justification for lending support for the rights of the Palestinians. For the Europeans bargain linkages increased the salience of the area and its problems that make the area unstable. In the case of the United States, domestic linkage politics and strategic considerations have conditioned its perception of the Palestinian problem. It has made the United States less accessible and less responsive to the efforts of the Arabs and Palestinians to mobilize support.

Accessiblity

This section looks at the role of accessiblity to the agendas and decision makers in Eastern and Western Europe in the mobilization process. In 1947 the ability of Zionists to reach and address themselves to Western governments in a very effective way played a crucial role in mobilizing support for the establishment of a Jewish state. In contrast this ability was conspicuously absent in Arab counter efforts.

As the matrix in Table 7.1 depicts, the Palestinian issue reached the European

Table 7.1. Access routes to European agendas

	Non-violent		Violent
Indirect	Arab governments, Euro-Arab dialogue		Resistance in the occupied territories
Direct	Formal PLO offices visits	Informal contacts	Hijackings

agendas in a number of ways. In the period between the 1967 and 1973 wars, some Arab governments tried to push the Palestinian issue on to the European agendas. Neither the East nor the West responded to it in any particularly favourable way. It was only in the aftermath of the 1973 war that the PLO began to gain access to Eastern followed by Western governments. Violence both at the local and international levels played a certain role in raising the Palestinian issue on public as well as formal agendas. Among East European and some Western countries violence at the local level came to be seen as a legitimate struggle against occupation and reprisals it precipitated led to condemnations. But it was the hijacking of aircraft belonging to Western airlines that brought the Palestinian issue on to Western public and formal agendas in a spectacular way.

Nonviolent access routes

After the October war that the Arabs gained significant access to the European political system. The Brussels Declaration of November 1973 brought the EC nearer to the Arab world and precipitated the setting up of the Euro-Arab dialogue. This dialogue increased Arab accessibility to the European scene. Once the Arab demand to include the PLO as an independent participant was resolved, the PLO was able to participate as a member of a unified Arab delegation, allowing the Palestinians access to high-ranking officials and politicians in Rome, Brussels, Bonn, Paris and other European capitals.

Following the substantial increase in the PLO status in world politics in 1973 and 1974 more direct contacts between the West and the PLO gradually developed. Most of the early contacts were of an informal kind. In late 1974 in an atmosphere generated by Arafat's appearance at the United Nations General Assembly and the adoption of resolutions supportive of the Palestinian cause, numerous Western politicians, in particular from Britain and West Germany, met with Arafat. During the same period France went further and was the first EC country to have direct official contact with the PLO. In October 1974 the French foreign minister met Arafat in Beirut and promised support for the PLO in return for moderation in the PLO's policies.[38] This encounter undoubtedly influenced France's voting behaviour at the United Nations and led Giscard D'Estaing to note that

The key to the problem is the understanding that there can be no durable peace in the Middle East if there is no just settlement of the Palestine question. Once the international community has recognized the existence of a Palestinian people, what is the natural aspiration of this people? It is to have a homeland.[39]

Unlike France, Britain, throughout the 1970s, maintained the position of not having contacts at or above the ministerial level. Contacts were limited to those taking place between the PLO and the British embassy in Beirut.[40] A slight change occurred in this policy as an EC consensus supportive of an eventual inclusion of the PLO in a negotiation process emerged. As a consequence of the Venice Declaration the EC, in an attempt to moderate the PLO and prepare the way towards a comprehensive settlement, dispatched Gaston Thorn in August 1980 and then Van der Klaauw in April 1981 to the Middle East. Both EC leaders met and had discussions with Arafat.

The minor change in Britain's policy towards contacts with the PLO came between these two visits. In early 1981 Sir J.Graham, Deputy Permanent Under Secretary, went to Beirut to meet Arafat. The purpose of the meeting was to maintain the momentum in EC efforts and also to pave the way for Lord Carrington's expected meeting with Arafat during his presidency of the EC. However, as a result of Lord Carrington's resignation over the Falklands' crisis this encounter never materialized.

His succesor Francis Pym, although expressing support for a Palestinian state as one possible way of fulfilling the Palestinians' right to self-determination,[41] did not show Lord Carrington's disposition to meet Arafat or other PLO officials.[42] In a reversal of policy in late 1982, the British government made itself even less accessible to the PLO when it refused to meet an Arab League delegation led by the PLO during their tour of permanent members of the Security Council.[43] Since then Britain has maintained its contacts with the PLO at a low level with only one meeting at ministerial level which took place in April 1983 in Tunis.[44]

The PLO gained access more readily to Europe outside the EC. Particularly, through Farouk Kaddoumi, head of the political department of the PLO, regular contacts were developed with Finland, Sweden, Austria, Portugal, Spain, Malta, Greece and Turkey. As a result of these contacts the PLO opened offices in all of these countries. With the exception of the Scandinavian countries and Portugal, the PLO was recognized as the sole representative of the Palestinians and its representatives were granted diplomatic status, giving the PLO a significant political advantage considering that some of these countries maintained no or low key relations with Israel. Furthermore, Kaddoumi's good relations with Kreisky, the Austrian chancellor, were of particular significance in gaining the support of the Socialist International. Similarly, Kreisky appears to have helped to maintain an 'indirect dialogue' between the PLO and the United States in the late 1970s.[45]

The most inaccessible government for the PLO has been the United States. This government has consistently maintained a position of not having any relations with the PLO as long as the latter refuses to recognize Israel. This was formally expressed in a gentleman's agreement reached between Kissinger and the Israeli government at the time of the signing of the Sinai disengagement agreement on 1 September 1975. Nevertheless, in spite of this uncompromising public position the United States has had some unofficial contacts with the PLO.

The first contacts between the United States and the PLO were developed by members of the Senate. Senator McGovern, chairman of the Middle East subcommittee of the senate committee on foreign affairs met Arafat in April 1975 and envisaged the possibility of an eventual independent Palestinian state. The following year Senator Stevenson held talks with Arafat and returned to the United States convinced of a moderation in Arafat's position towards the solution of the problem.[46] These visits may well have contributed to certain perceptual changes that partially precipitated a sudden upsurge of unofficial contacts between American officials and the PLO.

As early as June 1976, prior to a Security Council vote on a resolution calling for a Palestinian entity, American officials held talks with Kaddoumi.[47] Although at first denied by Kissinger, these contacts should be seen in the light of Saunders' (the assistant secretary of state for the Near East and South Asian affairs) recognition of the centrality of the Palestinian dimension of the Arab–Israeli Conflict, as well as the publication of a report prepared by the Brookings Institution which noted the need to recognize the Palestinian right to self-determination and the need for credible Palestinian representatives.[48] This report influenced the Carter administration's policy towards the Palestinian problem too. A further series of unofficial contacts took place, including a meeting between Carter and a PLO representative during a United Nations' reception in March 1977.[49] To these contacts one can also add the visits of various American senators and congressmen to Beirut.[50]

These contacts may well have been initiated by the disagreement between the United States and Israel when the former expressed readiness to accept the PLO as representing a substantial proportion of the Palestinians although not their exclusive representative.[51] Another source of disagreement was the administration's assessment that, 'without the PLO cooperation, it would be difficult perhaps impossible to solve the problems of the region'.[52] In 1978 these contacts included meetings between Arafat and various congressmen as well as Saunders' visit to the Middle East.[53] Congressman Paul Findley, on his return from direct talks with Arafat on 25 November 1978, claimed that Arafat was prepared to recognize Israel in return for a Palestinian state. Hence Findley argued in favour of putting into effect Saunders' suggestion of 28 September that the United States could establish direct contacts with the PLO if it both recognized and accepted Resolution 242.[54]

The following year these semi-official contacts received publicity when it was revealed that Andrew Young, the head of the American delegation to the United Nations, had held a private meeting with the PLO representative. The incident eventually led to his resignation in order to underline American commitment to the promise made to Israel in September 1975.[55] Although the public position of Young and the American administration was that the discussions were confined to procedural matters concerning a Security Council meeting, Young's efforts were directed more towards finding 'a common ground for an Arab-American resolution supporting both Israeli security and Palestinian rights'.[56]

In spite of this public rebuke of contacts with the PLO, the Young affair was seen by Arafat as beneficial. He alleged that the incident made the American community, particularly the blacks, more aware of the Palestinian problem.[57] Even though the PLO lacked direct and formal access to the American government the Palestinian problem found its way to the formal and public agendas of the United States. And as Campell has noted it was 'at or near the top of the Carter administration's foreign policy agenda'.[58]

The PLO gained direct access to the Soviet government at a surprisingly slow rate. The Soviets, throughout the 1960s, had treated the Palestinians as refugees and had favoured a negotiated political solution to the Arab-Israeli Conflict. This position had even led the Soviet Union to be critical of the early military activities of Palestinian groups.[59] Arafat's first contact with the Soviets came in July 1968 when he accompanied Nasser to Moscow. This visit does not appear to have inspired any particular Soviet support or change of policy in favour of Arafat and the Palestinian resistance movement. The Soviet attitude was strongly reflected in their refusal to support Palestinian guerrilla groups' demands for international legal status at the International Red Cross in Istanbul in September 1969.[60]

The second Arafat visit occurred at a period when Soviet attitudes towards the Palestinian Problem were going through a gradual change, as reflected in Kosygin's reference in December 1969 to the struggle of the Palestinians as a just national liberation and anti-imperialist struggle worthy of support.[61] As the new head of the PLO, Arafat and his delegation visited Moscow at the 'unofficial' invitation of the Soviet Committee of Solidarity with Asian and African countries.[62] A similar PLO delegation visited Moscow again in October 1971. Although both visits received wide coverage in the Arab world and were seen as a sign of growing international recognition they did not bring about any particular change in Soviet behaviour towards the Middle East other than the change reflected in Kosygin's remark and permission for 'unofficial' contacts.

A fourth visit occurred in July 1972 soon after Nasser's death and at a time when Egypt had started to weaken its ties with the Soviet Union. A change in Soviet attitude was reflected in her readiness to express support for 'the legitimate rights of the Arab people of Palestine' and military aid was promised to the PLO.[63] Even though the PLO admitted to differences on various issues with the Soviet Union[64] it was after this particular visit that the Palestinian issue began to take concrete form on Soviet public and formal agendas. Arafat went to the Soviet Union in late November 1973 where he was, for the last time, received on an 'unofficial' basis. During this meeting, the Soviets appear to have tried to put pressure on Arafat to participate in the Geneva Conference and accept the idea of a 'mini state'. At the same time it promised its support for the Palestinians and described the PLO as 'the only legitimate representative of the Palestinian people'.[65] This position did not, however, culminate in official Soviet recognition of the PLO.

The move towards the establishment of official ties came in March 1974 when Gromyko 'extended to Arafat the latter's first official invitation to the Soviet Union from the Soviet government.'[66] Arafat's visit was preceded by wide media coverage. At the end of the visit the Soviets acknowledged the worldwide recognition that the PLO was receiving as 'the sole legitimate representative of the Arab people of Palestine' and agreed to allow the PLO to open an office in Moscow.[67]

Although Arafat, on his way back from attending the General Assembly in 1974, met with Gromyko and the Soviet premier Kosygin, implying a further increase in the status of the contacts, formal Soviet recognition of the PLO did not come until November 1978.[68] Until then the Soviet Union's behaviour and policy suggested a *de facto* recognition of the PLO particularly strengthened by Brezhnev's reference to the PLO as the 'head' of the Palestinian people's struggle during his meeting with Arafat in March 1978.[69] From the PLO's point of view it was in October 1981 that the major breakthrough came: the PLO was granted full diplomatic status at the end of Arafat's state visit to the Soviet Union.

The East Europeans, with the exception of Romania, broke diplomatic relations with Israel after the war of 1967 as an expression of solidarity with the Arab countries. This did not, however, immediately change the East European treatment of the Palestinian Question as a refugee problem. To alter this, the PLO, from the early 1970s, tried to gain access to East Europe. The responses of the East Europeans were varied.

The first contacts were of an 'unofficial' nature mostly between East European trade unions and various groups from the Palestine resistance movement.

Bulgarians and especially East Germans appear to have played a leading role in expanding these contacts with Palestinian representatives during 1972.[70] By early 1973, these 'unofficial contacts' were becoming visits. One such visit occurred in February 1973 when a PLO delegation visited both Bulgaria and East Germany.[71] In Bulgaria the visit received some official character when Arafat was met by the secretary general of the Bulgarian communist party.[72]

The first official Arafat visit to East Germany came in July 1973. The way was prepared for this visit by an East German delegation that came to have talks with Arafat.[73] The consequence of this first visit to East Germany is significant in a number of ways. The visit and the Palestinian Problem received wide media coverage putting the Palestinian cause on the public agenda. Second, Arafat was received by Honecker with whom he signed an agreement which allowed the PLO to open its first office in East Europe.[74] This recognition granted to the PLO is particularly significant considering that at that time the PLO had not been recognized by the Arab League as the 'sole representative of the Palestinian people'.

In marked contrast to its accessibility to Bulgaria and East Germany the PLO could not develop any meaningful contacts with the other East Europeans until after the 1973 war. The first breakthrough for the PLO came with Romania, when the latter consented to the opening of a PLO office.[75] This development had particular significance as less than two years before Romania had received Golda Meir and there had been no reference to the rights of the Palestinians.[76] The importance of this development was further highlighted when the Romanian Foreign Minister's visit to Israel prior to Arafat's visit to the UN, was concluded without the announcement of a joint communiqué as a result of deep differences between the two countries over the Palestinian problem.[77]

In the case of other East Europeans the first official contacts occurred in June 1974 when all East European ambassadors in Damascus held talks with Arafat.[78] These talks may have provided the basis for the preliminary arrangements that culminated in a major PLO tour of Eastern Europe in August–September 1974, as a part of a worldwide campaign to mobilize support for the Palestinian position at the coming 29th General Assembly Session.[79] The East Europeans lent their full support for all the resolutions supporting the Palestinian cause including their right to national independence and sovereignty, but how far one can attribute this to the PLO's campaign is much more difficult to establish. Nevertheless, these developments did pave the way to the eventual establishment of official relations with the PLO. The PLO was allowed to open an office in Hungary in September 1974 followed by the ones in Czechoslovakia and Poland in May 1975 and March 1976, respectively.

The increase in status and frequency of PLO contacts with Eastern Europe strongly coincides with a growth in East European support for the Palestinian cause. However, how much of this can be directly attributed to the PLO's accessibility to the East Europeans governments is very difficult to say. The early unofficial contacts between Palestinian representatives and Bulgarian/East German trade unions must have played a certain role in the formation of public opinion about the Palestinian Problem. To these informal Palestinian contacts one must also add the role of Arab governments with strong ties, such as Syria and Iraq, in raising the problem with East European countries. It may not be a coincidence that early breakthroughs in East European governmental support for the Palestinian cause tended to be announced during official talks between these countries.[80]

Probably the most difficult factor to assess is the role of the Soviet Union in this process. The peculiar relationship between the Soviet Union and Eastern Europe, has led to assertions that East European attitudes towards the Palestinian Question are more or less a result of Soviet directives.[81] It is not within the scope of this book to test the validity of such assertions. Suffice it to say that the Soviet Union, just as the United States, has a capacity to mobilize greater resources in aggregating support for its positions. This factor may have played a certain role in determining East European attitudes and decisions on these issues. However, it would be wrong to assume that this influence is a strictly one-way flow and that the Soviet decision-making process is a closed system completely insensitive to inputs from its environment. It is also difficult to substantiate such an assumption considering that most East European governments have been systematically ahead of the Soviet Union in their recognition of the PLO as 'the sole representative of the Palestinian people'.

Violence as an access route

Both local and international violence played a role in bringing the Palestinian problem to the attention of Europeans. From the late 1960s onwards the Soviet Union joined ranks with some East Europeans in lending public support for the resistance activities of Palestinian guerrillas. As Golan notes,

A decided stamp of approval was given when the Soviets began to use the word 'partisans' in connection with these operations, explaining that the Palestinian actions were legitimate acts of self-defence similar to the resistance movements in Nazi-occupied territories during World War Two.[82]

In the case of Western countries, in particular the EC bloc and the United States, it was the hijacking of international airliners in the late 1960s and early 1970s that brought the Palestinian Problem to the attention of the public and governments. The nature of the events that involved Western airliners ensured wide media coverage. Although these acts met generally with public condemnation they also served to bring the motives behind these actions to public notice. The fact that the hijackings involved airplanes and passengers from the West created an atmosphere of crisis for the governments involved. The grievances expressed by the hijackers became items at the very top of the formal agendas, at least for the duration of the crisis. As Mortimer notes,

Just as de Gaulle with his infuriating and absurd obstinacy managed to keep France on the political map of the world during the Nazi occupation, so the PLO resistance groups with all their terrorism and posturing have kept Palestine on the map—indeed have put it back there after a period when its existence even as a geographical expression had virtually lapsed outside the Arab world.[83]

Local violence did not affect Western Europe in a major way until the 1978 and 1982 Israeli invasions of Lebanon. Both invasions were seen as unjustifiable and disproportionate retaliations to isolated acts of terrorism leading to unnecessary and unacceptable levels of human sufferings. In Western Europe the invasion of 1982 was taken up formally by governments as well as the EC.[84] The impact of the invasion was reflected in the EC's support for a Franco-Egyptian draft resolution in the Security Council on 28 July 1982 which expanded on Resolution 242 and called for 'mutual and simultaneous recognition of the parties concerned' and accepted the existence of the PLO without granting it official status.[85]

The invasion also led the American government to acknowledge the centrality of the Palestinian Problem and its linkage to a secure Israel. Reagan noted this when he accepted that

The war in Lebanon has demonstrated another reality in this region. The departure of the Palestinians from Beirut makes even more dramatic than ever the lack of a homeland for the Palestinian people. The Palestinians are convinced that their problem is more than a refugee problem.[86]

In this concluding part of the chapter the change in attitudes towards the Palestinian Problem and the growth in support among East and Western European countries will be examined. This change should be seen as the outcome of a dynamic mobilization process whose constitutent parts were introduced in the preceding sections. A method similar to that used to look at the mobilization process among Third World groupings has been employed to substantiate the change in European perceptions of the Palestinian problem. First, the content of political statements made by major governments and the EC has been examined to establish whether a change in attitudes and declared support has occurred. Second, an index of political support constructed from these countries' voting behaviour at the United Nations has been used to supplement the above analysis.

Growth of support

Eastern Europe and the Soviet Union

In the immediate aftermath of the 1967 Arab–Israeli war the East Europeans, except Romania, broke their diplomatic relations with Israel in an expression of political solidarity with the Arab world. However, a survey of East European and Soviet commentaries on the war indicates no reference to the rights of the Palestinians.[87]

For almost twenty-five years, East European countries made no use of the terms 'Palestine' or 'Palestinian'. Whenever the subject of the Middle East conflict was treated, it was invariably 'refugees' and not 'Palestinians' for whom concern or pity were expressed.[88]

The Soviets, too, did not refer to the rights of the Palestinians other than to their rights as refugees. This was quite evident in a Soviet sponsored peace proposal in early 1969 which referred to the right of the Arab refugees to return to their homes.[89] Towards the end of the same year the situation began to change. In November 1969, in a Warsaw Pact Declaration the East Europeans recognized the political nature of the Palestinian Problem and declared it a national liberation struggle.[90]

This breakthrough in East European perceptions should be seen in the light of two developments. First, at the local level, Palestinian guerrilla groups had intensified their use of violence and become more assertive. Second, the Palestinian resistance movement appeared to be gaining support among the Palestinians particularly after the Karameh battle in March 1968. The linkage between this violence and the change in Soviet perception was noted by Kosygin in December 1969: 'The Soviet people considers the struggle of the Palestinian organizations . . . as a just national liberation and anti-imperialist struggle and supports it.'[91]

Furthermore, at the international level the political rights of the Palestinians were included in the debates and decisions of the United Nations General Assembly. East European delegations participated in the relevant debates and lent their full support to the resolutions ensuring their adoption albeit with narrow margins. From 1969 onwards, although the East European voting behaviour was highly cohesive and they remained the only group in full agreement with the Arabs, their behaviour outside the United Nations suggested a different picture.

An analysis of East European statements, made in relation to the political rights of the Palestinians, particularly their right to establish a state and their behaviour towards the PLO, suggests that East European attitudes developed along two separate lines until they converged into a unified position by the mid- to late 1970s. The first approach emerged among East Germany and Bulgaria, and later joined by Romania and Czechoslovakia. Bulgaria and East Germany became the first countries to refer to the Palestinians as a 'people' and develop contacts with the Palestinians and the PLO.[92] This happened early in 1972; at the same time the other East European countries continued to ignore the Palestinian dimension of the Arab–Israeli Conflict[93]; the Soviet Union limited itself to expressing support for the restoration of 'the legitimate rights of the Palestinians'.[94] Bulgarian and East German contacts with the Palestinians quickly intensified.

As promised during Arafat's visit to lobby the East Europeans, Romania, Czechoslovakia and Bulgaria in their speeches at the 29th Session of the General Assembly unambiguously referred to the Palestinians' right to an independent state.[95] The position of East Germany was rather confusing. In spite of the alleged support expressed for a Palestinian state the East Germans were more restrained at the United Nations. There they referred to 'the lawful right of the Palestinian Arabs to their own statehood'.[96] This wording was rather similar to that of the Soviets[97] which fell short of unambiguous support for a state. The situation changed two days after the adoption of Resolution 3236 (XIX) when the East German leader, Honecker, spoke of 'the right of the Arab people of Palestine to found an independent state'.[98]

The situation with the remaining East European countries—Poland and Hungary—was somewhat different. Even though these countries had voted in favour of Resolution 3236 (XIX) they remained reluctant to express public support for a 'Palestinian state' and recognize the PLO as 'the sole representative of the Palestinians'. Poland during the debates only referred to 'the legitimate rights of the Arab people of Palestine to self-determination and existence as a nation'.[99] Hungary expressed support for the 'creation of an independent Palestinian national power'.[100] During the visit of Arafat to Hungary in October 1974 the Hungarians were reluctant to go any further than speak of 'the creation of an independent Palestinian national rule', and not surprisingly did not put into effect their alleged promise to allow the PLO to establish a mission in Budapest until October 1975.[101] Poland too followed a similar pattern, only allowing the PLO to open an office as late as March 1976 and so becoming the last East European country to do so.[102]

The Soviet Union, in spite of its strong support for the Palestinian cause at the United Nations, has hesitantly recognized the right of the Palestinians to establish a state and the PLO as their sole representative.[103] The Soviets, in 1971, responded sceptically to the idea of a separate Palestinian state, particularly if it were created at the expense of Israel.[104] The Soviet Union's position towards Israel's right to exist has been one of the most consistent features of its policies towards the Palestinian Problem and has conditioned its attitudes towards the Palestinians' right to self-determination. Soviet support for Palestinian self-determination began to emerge along with Soviet efforts to influence the PLO to accept the idea of a mini-state, in the immediate aftermath of the 1973 Arab–Israeli war. It is not surprising that the first public references to a Palestinian state by high Soviet officials occurred after the 12th Palestinian National Council's decision to endorse the idea of a mini-state.[105]

To the PNC decision one must also add the role of Arafat's visit to Moscow in July–August 1974 and his discussions with politburo member Ponomarev in mobilizing Soviet support.[106] It was in this climate that on 8 September 1974 the Soviet president Podgorny referred to the need to take into account the right of the Palestinians 'to establish their own statehood in one form or another' in the context of finding a solution to the Arab–Israeli Conflict.[107] Only after the Arab League decisions at Rabat and the adoption of Resolution 3236 (XIX) was the ambiguity in Podgorny's reference to 'a statehood in one form or another' removed by Brezhnev; on 26 November Brezhnev unambiguously referred to the rights of the Palestinians to a state.[108]

Even though they did refer to the right of the Palestinians to their own state the Soviets appeared to have consciously refrained from actually calling for its establishment. Eventual Soviet support for a Palestinian state came only at the end of a series of visits by Arafat to Moscow between April 1977 and November 1979 and in a conducive environment brought about by the announcement of the Camp David Agreements in March 1979.[109] The communiqué concluding Arafat's visit on November 1979 resolved both the issue of support for a Palestinian state and the related matter of the recognition of the PLO as the 'sole representative of the Palestinians'.[110] Soviet support became even clearer when Gromyko at the end of the America–Soviet summit in Vienna, 15–18 June 1979, called for a Palestinian state.[111]

Western Europe

During the period under study the size of the EC increased from six to nine then to ten. It would be difficult to take the evolution of each country's attitude towards the question of Palestine separately. Instead the EC countries will be examined as a group using their declarations as the basis for determining their position on the issue. Where there have been major departures from the common EC position these will be mentioned.

In the aftermath of the 1967 war, the members of the EC like other West and East European countries saw the Palestinian problem exclusively as a humanitarian problem concerning 'Arab refugees'. This was strongly reflected in the Schumann report of 13 May 1971 which defined EC policy towards the Middle East Conflict, referring to the 'Arab refugees' and their right either to return to their home or to be indemnified.[112] The report did not suggest a perceptible change in the common position of the EC. By the time of the next EC declaration the situation had changed substantively. This was precipitated by developments in the Middle East such as the October 1973 war, the growth of Palestinian nationalism, the oil embargo as well as greater Arab accessibility and the enlargement of the community which brought in two relatively pro-Arab countries—Britain and Ireland. The EC in November 1973 adopted a French-British sponsored text that recognized 'the legitimate rights of the Palestinians' by expressing the need to take these rights into consideration in a global settlement.[113] Change is also reflected in the voting behaviour of the EC members. They moved from a position of support for Israel at the 24th General Assembly Session to a balanced position at the 28th Session.

The period between November 1973 and the next EC Declaration in December 1977 was one of substantive change, particularly with regard to the form the 'legitimate rights of the Palestinians' was to take. The French, who in their voting during the 29th Session had taken a relatively pro-Palestinian position, defined these rights in a way that led it to take into account 'the legitimacy of a Palestinian homeland', while Britain limited itself to stressing the need 'for any settlement to provide for a personality for the Palestinian people'.[114] Italy and The Netherlands for their part noted the need for the Palestinian people to express their 'national identity' and Genscher, the West German foreign minister, spoke of 'the right of self-determination of the Palestinian people including the right to establish a State authority . . .'[115]

The vagueness inherent in these references to a 'homeland', 'national identity' and 'a state authority' was to a certain degree resolved when the London Declaration of the EC, in December 1977, stated that the 'legitimate rights of the Palestinians should take the form of a homeland for the Palestinian people'. The reference to a homeland, at least for some Jewish circles, was synonymous with 'state'. This is not surprising considering that the history of the establishment of Israel was marked by the Zionist movement's struggle to mobilize support for a 'Jewish homeland' that eventually came to mean a state. However, at the time of the London Declaration the linkage did not necessarily exist for the EC members. This is reflected in the observation of Dr Owen, the British foreign secretary that 'The statment was not referring to a Palestinian state. It was referring to the need for a Palestinian homeland.'[116]

After the London Declaration the EC countries edged their way closer to the Palestinian cause and the PLO. The PLO gained increasing access through the Euro-Arab dialogue as well as directly to European countries. Although no EC country went as far as recognizing the PLO, there was a growing realization of the need to include the PLO in efforts to find a comprehensive settlement for the Middle East conflict especially in the immediate aftermath of the announcement of the Camp David Agreements. The Europeans found these agreements positive, but inadequate: the Palestinians had been excluded.

The speech of O'Kennedy, the Irish foreign minister and spokesman for the EC, at the 34th Session of the United Nations General Assembly came as a turning point.[117] In this speech the EC, for the first time, officially referred to the role that the PLO could play in attempts to achieve peace in the Middle East. The need to include representatives of the Palestinian people in negotiations had been mentioned before in the London Declaration as well as in the declaration put out by the EC on 26 March 1979. However, this was the first time that the name of the PLO had been introduced.

The pressures arising for a more active EC role in the Middle East, the weaknesses of the Camp David Agreements and the growing realization of the need to involve the PLO in future negotiations culminated in the Venice Declaration of 13 June 1980. The declaration noted a readiness to work in a more concrete way toward peace and the need to associate the PLO with negotiations. Furthermore it stressed that:

A just solution must finally be found to the Palestinian Problem, which is not simply one of refugees. The Palestinian people, which is conscious of existing as such, must be placed in a position, by an appropriate process defined within the framework of the comprehensive peace settlement, to exercise fully its right to self-determination.[118]

In less than a decade the EC changed its group perception of Palestinians as 'Arab refugees' to people entitled to self-determination. The Venice Declaration remained ambiguous about whether self-determination meant the establishment of a state even though Greece, France and Ireland had wanted to see a clear reference to 'a state formula of their own choice'.[119] French foreign minister Cheysson after his meeting with Arafat reiterated France's support for Palestinian self-determination and alluded to the establishment of an eventual Palestinian state.[120] On 14 December 1981 his position became clearer when he declared that a main principle of his government's approach to the Middle East was based on the Palestinians' right to a state.[121]

Even though the EC has not supported a Palestinian state in an unambiguous manner, the extent of the change in its perception of the Palestinian Problem and its support for the political rights of the Palestinian people is often underestimated. Two significant changes have been blurred by European demands. First, the EC has supported the political rights of the Palestinians without prejudice to Israel's existence in its pre-1967 borders, a position not very unlike that of the East Europeans. It is in this respect that the index of support for the Palestinian cause does not do justice to the EC support. The relatively low reading for the EC on the index is because the wording of the resolutions on which the roll-calls are based has seldom included a clear and explicit reference to Israel's right to existence. Second, the EC countries have consistently demanded from the PLO that it should recognize Israel, express support for a political solution and denounce violence. It has tried to use the issue of recognition as a separate leverage on the PLO again giving a superficial impression that the EC is unsupportive of the rights of the Palestinian people.

In this research West European countries outside the EC are ranged in two groups. The Mediterranean countries together with Austria form a reasonably cohesive group characterized by a conspicuous support for the Palestinian cause and the PLO. The Scandinavian countries can be sub-divided into two. The first sub-group has Sweden and Finland who follow a policy closer to the southern European countries, particularly at the United Nations; Norway and Iceland are somewhere between the EC stance and the American position.

Table 7.2 depicts the way in which the Mediterranean countries have gradually coalesced around a position highly supportive of the Palestinian cause which, after the 29th Session of the General Assembly, included the right of the Palestinians to self-determination. Spain, Greece and Turkey have followed the development of the Palestinian issue at the UN from a highly supportive stance.[122] Portugal, after the 1974 change in regime, joined their ranks at the 29th Session.

Recognition of the PLO as the sole representative of the Palestinian people is another common denominator for the south European countries. These countries together with Finland voted in favour of resolutions inviting Arafat to the United Nations and granting the PLO observer status. They did not develop official relations with the PLO until the late 1970s. The Spanish government was the first European country to receive Arafat officially shortly followed by Turkey.[123] In Greece, Papandreau in his first day in office invited Arafat to an official visit in October 1981. The PLO maintains diplomatic missions, of varying and at times unclear status, in all these countries except Portugal.[124]

The Scandinavian countries in their voting behaviour on the Palestinian question at the 24th Session of the General Assembly were generally supportive of the Israeli position. During the period preceding the 29th Session Scandinavian attitudes began to change. As Table 7.2 suggests Finland and Sweden at the 29th Session supported the Palestinian cause while Norway and Iceland continued to maintain their earlier positions. Sweden's behaviour at the United Nations Security Council is particularly remarkable too. In December 1975, during the

Table 7.2. Distribution of support across sessions for West European countries outside the EC

	24th Session 1969	29th Session 1974	35th Session 1980
Highly pro-Palest.	Spain, Greece, Turkey	Spain, Portugal, Finland, Turkey	Spain, Malta, Portugal Greece, Turkey
Medium pro-Palest.	—	Austria Greece, Sweden, New Zealand	Austria, Sweden, Finland
Intermediate	—	Australia	Canada, Norway, New Zealand, Iceland
Medium pro-Israel	Austria, Norway, Finland, Sweden, Iceland, Portugal Australia, New Zealand	Norway, Iceland, Canada	Australia
Highly pro-Israel	USA, Canada	USA	USA
Low attenders	Malta	Malta	

vote on whether to allow the PLO to participate in the work of the Security Council Sweden cast the only Western vote that settled the matter in favour of the PLO.[125] Sweden and Finland unlike the other Scandinavians have not hesitated to project their anti-colonial values to the Palestinian Problem. In the case of Norway and Iceland military alliance commitments may well have restricted their foreign policy options on the Middle East.[126]

The Nordic Council statement of 27–8 March 1980 on the Middle East has a strong resemblance to the Venice Declaration. The content of this statement suggests the possibility of a compromise brokered by Denmark to bridge the gap between Sweden and Finland on the one hand and Norway and Iceland on the other.[127] Denmark appears to be holding the middle ground between the two groups, particularly since it declared that the Venice Declaration did not imply a recognition of a Palestinian state.[128] Such a position is roughly midway between Norway's 'American'-like position expressing support for the 'legitimate interests and rights of the Palestinians'[129] and Sweden and Finland who in their 1980 voting demonstrated a position more supportive of the Palestinian cause, not unlike that of France.

The remaining countries within the Western group are Australia, New Zealand, Canada and most importantly the United States. Unlike the other three the United States has been involved in the Palestinian Problem from its early days. During World War II the United States became a committed supporter of the Zionist cause. Once established the United States developed close ties with Israel. Although the United States had strongly lobbied in favour of the partition of Palestine into two separate states, in the aftermath of the establishment of Israel the Arabs of Palestine were perceived as refugees. The United States maintained this image of the Palestinians as refugees well into the 1970s becoming the last and most reluctant Western country to recognize the minimum political rights of the Palestinians.

The first suggestion that the Americans might regard the Palestinian Problem as something more than one of refugees came on 24 June 1973. The communiqué issued at the end of Brezhnev's visit to the United States noted that a Middle East settlement 'should take into due account the legitimate interests of the Palestinian people'.[130] Even though the reference was to the milder 'interests' rather than 'rights', the problem had nevertheless been put on the agenda and the referents were 'the Palestinian people' rather than 'Arab refugees'. However, the United States did not hesitate to veto a Security Council draft resolution noting the need to take the legitimate aspirations/rights of the Palestinians into account in the resolution of the Middle East conflict. The United States after the 1973 war continued to remain unimpressed by the growing recognition of the political rights of the Palestinian people and the PLO. The American position as elaborated by Kissinger was that the problem was one to be settled between Israel and Jordan, and that recent developments favouring the Palestinians were impediments to the achievement of peace between the Arab states and Israel.

A major breakthrough in American perceptions came on 12 November 1975, when Saunders, assistant secretary of state for Near East and South Asian Affairs, noted 'the legitimate interest of the Palestinian Arabs must be taken into account in the negotiations of an Arab–Israeli peace. In many ways, the Palestinian dimension of the Arab–Israeli conflict is the heart of that conflict.'[131]

The Carter administration began at a time when the Palestinian dimension of the Arab–Israeli Conflict had also been recognized by a report prepared by the Brookings Institute in December 1975.[132] The report stressed the importance of taking into account the Palestinian right to self-determination in a viable peace settlement in the Middle East. The report had two possible scenarios. The first one suggested a Palestinian state and the second a Palestinian entity associated with Jordan. It was the second which appeared to win the interest of the Carter administration.

This was reflected in what has become known as the Carter plan. Rouleau summarized thus:

A homeland would have to be set apart for the Palestinian people. It would be either an independent entity (a solution Carter is said to have misgivings about, because of the opening it would provide for Soviet infiltration) or an integral part of Jordan, or again a component state of a federation along with Jordan and Syria.[133]

In the face of mounting Jewish pressure Carter had to make it quite clear that his reference to a Palestinian entity or homeland did not add up to an acceptance of the Palestinian right to self-determination.[134] In an interview given on the eve of Israel's 30th anniversary he plainly said, 'my belief is that a permanent settlement will not include an independent nation on the West Bank' and declared 'I have never favoured an independent Palestinian state'.[135] This retraction by the Carter administration did not come as a surprise to Kaddoumi. In an interview he maintained that the 'Carter Plan' in his view had already reflected a certain degree of retraction from the Saunders' position.[136]

During the Camp David peace process repeated references to the 'concerns of the Palestinians' did not go as far as recognizing their political rights in an unambiguous manner. In September 1978 there was a framework agreement between Carter, Sadat and Begin to recognize the legitimate rights of the Palestinian people and their just requirements and the determination to achieve full autonomy for the inhabitants. The negotiations as prescribed by the framework did not get anywhere as the parties remained deeply divided on what 'full autonomy' entailed and on who was to represent the Palestinians.[137]

In spite of a growing realization, particularly among state department officials and some politicians, of the need to include the PLO in efforts to achieve a settlement in the Middle East, domestic political considerations have prevented the United States from introducing major changes to its foreign policy on the Palestinian Problem. The constraining role of this domestic linkage on American options is well demonstrated by Carter's unrestrained reference, on his return from Sadat's funeral, to the need to include the PLO in efforts to resolve the Palestinian Problem.[138] This was in marked contrast to the requirments of an election campaign that had led Carter, only a few months earlier, to stress his opposition to an independent Palestinian state and the recognition of the PLO.[139]

The late 1970s was nevertheless a period when the Palestinian Problem was high on the American foreign policy agenda. It was a period which saw a marked increase in 'unofficial' contacts with the PLO in an attempt to persuade the latter to accept Resolution 242 to enable it to play its role in setting the Palestinian Problem. Furthermore this was also a period when

Disagreements between the US and Israel now appeared on a wide range of issues. The US, criticising Israeli raids on Palestinian bases in Southern Lebanon, said that Israel 'may have' broken the US law by using American supplied weapons for other than defensive puposes. Dissatisfaction was expressed about Israeli settlements in the West Bank and the slow progress of autonomy talks.[140]

This was probably the period when the PLO achieved its highest standing in the United States, evident in the administration's desire to see the PLO involved in a negotiation process and in the implementation of the 'autonomy plan' that would emerge from it. In the end, however, the United States fell back to its traditionally pro-Israeli stance.[141]

The Reagan plan, as it was called, recognized the need of a homeland for the Palestinian people and hence the need to attain autonomy for the Palestinians in association with Jordan. He made it quite clear that this did not entail a state but he announced simultaneously the categorical rejection of annexation: 'In comparison with the traditional position of the US, Reagan's speech constituted a turning point in the American Palestinian Problem.'[142] In spite of this development the United States, during the period under study, has remained strongly pro-Israeli and has consistently stopped short of recognizing 'the Palestinian people's right to self-determination'.

Of the remaining three countries in this group, Australia and Canada have held attitudes towards the Palestinian Problem not unlike the United States, while New Zealand has gone in a very different direction. Although Canada, in its voting behaviour between 1969 and 1980 moved from a strongly pro-Israeli position to an intermediate one, this transformation did not reach the point of a clear and unambiguous recognition of the Palestinians' right to self-determination. Instead the Canadian speech at the Seventh Emergency Special Session of the Assembly did not go any further than expressing the view that any settlement of the

Palestinian Problem would have to take 'into account the existence of a Palestinian national consciousness, and unless there is a recognition of the legitimate rights of the Palestinian people, peace will not prevail'.[143] Furthermore, this speech did not seem to envisage any role for the Palestinians in a negotiation process to reach such a settlement.

The Australians appear to have taken a similar position. Except during the 29th Session of the Assembly when the Australian delegate referred to his government's support for the applicability of 'the principle of the right of peoples to self-determination and independence' to the Palestinian Arab people they have in their voting behaviour maintained a pro-Israeli position.[144] This is particularly evident in the way in which the Australian delegation to the 30th Session of the General Assembly retracted from its position in 1974 and was not prepared to endorse anything stronger than 'the need to recognise and respect the legitimate rights of the Palestinians' in achieving an eventual settlement.

New Zealand experienced a significant change in its attitude towards the Palestinian Problem. While together with the United States, Canada and Australia it had voted strongly pro-Israeli at the 24th Session of the General Assembly in 1969, by the 29th Session their stance had changed quite dramatically. This was reflected in a readiness to support the resolutions inviting Arafat to address the Assembly and granting the PLO permanent observership. This change in attitude had consolidated itself to such an extent that by 1980 the New Zealand delegation was prepared to argue that:

Palestine is not simply a refugee problem. It is also a political problem for which a solution must be found. The search for a solution must involve the participation of the Palestinian people, including the PLO, along with the other parties directly concerned. The rights of the Palestinian people include the right of self-determination. That is not something as limited as local autonomy. It means that the Palestinians must have the right to set up an independent Arab State of Palestine, as was envisaged in the 1947 partition resolution, if that is their wish.[145]

Conclusion

As it has been suggested in the preceding sections both the Western and East Europeans governments continued to perceive the Palestinian Problem as a refugee problem subsumed within the Arab–Israeli Conflict well into the late 1960s. Furthermore, the perceptual changes towards the Palestinian Problem that followed did not develop in a uniform manner in both regions.

In Eastern Europe, the Bulgarians and East Germans were the first to respond to Arab and Palestinian efforts to mobilize support. In spite of their cohesive and pro-Palestinian voting at the United Nations, it was not until the mid-1970s that a general East European consensus, supportive of a 'Palestinian state' and of the PLO as the 'sole representative of the Palestinian people' emerged. For the East Europeans cognitive linkages based on anti-colonial and anti-imperialist thinking played an important role in the process that altered their perceptions of the Palestinians from refugees to people fighting a national liberation struggle. Palestinian violence at the local level played a role in bringing about this breakthrough.

The countries within the Western group also saw the Palestinians as refugees in the aftermath of the 1967 War and the changes in attitudes within that group were even more diverse and also in some cases slower and more limited than in the East

Europeans. First, within this group there were southern European countries—to some extent joined by countries such as Finland, Sweden and Austria—that lent full support to the Palestinian cause, and countries such as the United States, Canada and Australia which remained very reluctant to recognize anything stronger than 'the legitimate rights and interest of the Palestinians'. In the case of the first group, cognitive linkages based on anti-colonialism and geographical proximity contributed to their readiness to go as far as supporting a 'Palestinian state' and recognizing the PLO. While in the case of the United States, domestic political considerations coupled with strategic ones made any change in governmental attitudes much more limited.

The position of the EC, which included some traditionally pro-Israeli countries, experienced a very slow change in opinion. This change is reflected in the difference in the contents of the Schumann Report of May 1971 which did not recognize the Palestinian dimension of the Arab–Israeli Conflict and the June 1980 Venice Declaration recognizing the Palestinian right to self-determination and the need to include the PLO in any settlement effort. This change was also marked by a relative increase in the cohesion of the group. The group, which once included pro-Israeli and relatively pro-Arab countries together with uncommitted members, as a result of the EPC and the Euro-Arab dialogue developed a more unified position increasingly favourable to the Palestinian cause. This relatively more cohesive and pro-Palestinian position did not, however, reflect itself in the EC countries' voting behaviour at the UN. Some members would not support resolutions recognizing the political rights of the Palestinians without a clear reference to Israel's right to existence within recognized borders, while others were content, just like the East Europeans, with an implicit recognition of Israel's rights.

Notes

1 For a study of the origins and development of the EPC see Wallace, W. and Allen, D. 'Political Cooperation: procedure as a substitute for policy', in Wallace, H. and Webbs, C. (eds) *Policy Making in the European Communities* (Wiley, London, 1977); Allen, D. Rummel, R. and Wessels, W. (eds) *European Political Cooperation* (Butterworth, London, 1982).

2 Haagerup, N. and Thune, C. 'Denmark: the European pragmatist', in Hill, C. (ed.) *National Foreign Policies and European Political Cooperation* (George Allen and Unwin, London, 1983) p. 110; Edwards, G. 'Britain' in Allen, D. and Pijpers, A. *European Foreign Policy-Making and The Arab–Israeli Conflict* (Martinus Nijhoff, The Hague, 1984) p. 40.

3 For EPC influence on Ireland see Keatinge, P. 'Ireland', in Allen and Pijpers (eds) (1984: 19).

4 Ibid., p. 165.

5 Allen, D. 'The Euro-Arab Dialogue', *Journal of Common Market Studies*, vol. XVI (1978), no. 4, pp. 323 and 325. For a discussion of the institutions and meetings of the Euro-Arab dialogue see Taylor, A. 'The Euro-Arab Dialogue: Quest for Interregional Partnership', *The Middle Eastern Journal*, Autumn 1978, pp. 429-43.

6 Frangi, A. *The PLO and Palestine* (Zed Books, London, 1983), p. 159.

7 Golan, G. *The Soviet Union and The Palestine Liberation Organization: An Uneasy Alliance* (Praeger, New York, 1980), pp. 46–7.

8 Ibid., p. 87.

9 For the sudden switch in French policy towards the Middle East see Feuer, G. 'La politique de la France', *Revue Française de Sciences Politique*, vol. 19 (1969), no. 2, and Auri, N. and Hevener, N. 'France and the Middle East 1967–1968', *The Middle East Journal*, vol. 23 (Autumn 1969), no. 4.

10 For a text of the Schumann Report see *Le Monde*, 15 May 1971.
11 Greilsammer, I. and Weiler, J. 'European Political Cooperation and the Palestinian-Israeli Conflict: an Israeli perspective' in Allen and Pjipers (eds) (1984: 184).
12 Artner, S. 'The Middle East: A Chance for Europe?' *International Affairs*, Summer 1980, p. 435.
13 *Le Monde*, 28 March 1979.
14 *United Nations Security Council Official Records*, 37th year, S/15317. For the EC foreign ministers' declaration see *The Times*, 22 September 1982.
15 *The Times*, 20 September 1982.
16 Golan (1980: 10–11) and for a study of change in Soviet perceptions of Palestinian guerrilla warfare see Freedman, R. 'Soviet policy towards International Terrorism' in Alexander, Y. (ed.) *International Terrorism* (Praeger, New York, 1976).
17 Fejto, F. *A History of the People's Democracies* (Pelican Books, Harmondsworth, 1974), p. 297.
18 Ibid., p. 298–9.
19 For the details of the statistical analysis of the relationship between voting on the Palestinian Question and on colonial matters at the UN see Kirisci, K. 'Mobilisation of Support for the Palestinian Cause' (Ph.D. thesis, The City University, London, 1986), Appendix II.
20 Keatinge, P. 'Ireland: neutrality inside EPC', in Hill (ed.) (1983: 143–4); Keatinge in Allen and Pijpers (eds) (1984: 19).
21 Ibid. A relatively anti-colonial Irish behaviour among the West European group at the United Nations in the mid-1950s is also supported by Reiselbach, R. 'Quantitative Techniques for Studying Voting Behaviour in the UN General Assembly', *International Organization*, vol. 14 (1960), p. 300–1.
22 Soetendrop, B. 'The Netherlands', and Raeymaeker, O. 'Denmark', in Allen and Pijpers (eds) (1984: 39, 64).
23 For details of speeches at the Security Council by these countries see chapter eight, note 52; also see O'Neill, B. *Armed Struggle in Palestine: A Political-Military Analysis* (Westview, Boulder, 1978) p. 195 for a similar observation.
24 In her visit to European leaders in the aftermath of the 1973 war Golda Meir accused them of deserting Israel and claimed that no one had responded to her because 'Their throats are choked with oil', Meir, G. *My Life* (Weidenfeld and Nicolson, London, 1975), p. 376. Similarly, 'Israel's UN representative Blum, Y. complained about the growing number of "sorry parades of nations supplicating the Arab oil gods". In some cases that may be true. Yet Blum's comment reflects a dangerous misapprehension on the part of the Begin government—namely, that support for Palestinian rights is based solely on a fearful lust of Middle East oil supplies' (*Economist*, 14 April 1980, p. 10).
25 Soetendrop in Allen and Pijpers (eds) (1984: 40).
26 Raeymaeker in ibid., p. 66.
27 Quoted in Artner (1980: 439).
28 Rosenau, J. (ed.) *Linkage Politics: Essays on the Convergence of National and International Systems* (Free Press, New York, 1969); *The Scientific Study of Foreign Policy* (Frances Pinter, London, 1980), chapter 15.
29 For Rosenau's definition of penetrative linkages see Rosenau, J. 'Toward the Study of National-International Linkages' in Rosenau (ed.) (1969: 46).
30 Yodfat, A. and Arnon-Ohanna, Y. *PLO Strategy and Tactics* (Croom Helm, London, 1981) p. 129; also see Nicol, D. 'Andrew Young at the United Nations: A Major Role for the UN in US Foreign Policy' in Nicol, D. (ed.) *Paths to Peace: The UN Security Council and Its Presidency* (Pergamon Press, New York, 1981) p. 324.
31 Peri, Y. 'The Fall From Favour: Israel and the Socialist International' *IJA Research Report*, nos 21 and 22 (December 1980), p. 2.
32 For an analysis of this change and the impact it had on attitudes held by the Socialist International towards the Palestinian Problem see ibid.
33 *Middle East Magazine*, October 1982.
34 Golan (1980: 52).

35 Ibid., p. 45.
36 *The Guardian*, 14 October 1982.
37 For Soviet attitudes on military aid to the Palestinians see Golan (1980: 214–27).
38 *Arab Report Record* (1974: 468).
39 The French delegation not only supported the invitation to the PLO but in their speech directly referred to Giscard's speech (UN Document (Provisional) A/PV 2292, p. 46, 20 November 1974).
40 Blumenkrantz, A. 'Britain and Israel: the Carrington era and after', *IJA Research Report* (September 1982), no. 9.
41 *The Guardian*, 12 October 1982.
42 Carrington had expressed interest in meeting Arafat in the belief that it would serve the cause of peace. Allen, D. and Smith, M. 'Europe, the United States and the Arab–Israeli conflict', in Allen and Pijpers (eds) (1984: 217).
43 In July 1982, when such a visit was first raised, London had expressed no objections (*The Guardian*, 24 November 1982) and PLO representatives within the Arab League delegation had met Douglas Hurd, Minister of State at the Foreign and Commonwealth Office in the summer of 1982 (Edwards in Allen and Pijpers (eds) 1984: 54).
44 Edwards, in Allen and Pijpers (eds) (1984: 54).
45 Yodfat and Arnon-Ohanna (1981: 115). The Palestinians also developed close contacts through various non-governmental organizations in Europe. For some of these contacts see Cobban, H. *The Palestinian Liberation Organization: People, Power and Politics* (Cambridge University Press, Cambridge, 1984) pp. 232–4.
46 *Facts on File*, 28 February 1976, p. 161; see also 'Arab Reports and Analysis: "Changing American Attitudes to the Palestinians"', *Journal of Palestine Studies*, vol. IV (Summer 1975), pp. 155–6.
47 *ARR* (1976: 400, 470).
48 Yodfat *et al.* (1981: 109).
49 *ARR* (1977: 184).
50 *ARR* (1977: 620).
51 *ARR* (1977: 809, 757).
52 Yodfat *et al.* (1981: 111).
53 *ARR* (1978: 31, 794).
54 'Views from Abroad: "An opening of US-PLO talks"', *Journal of Palestine Studies*, vol. VIII (Winter 1979), no. 2, pp. 173–5.
55 Finger, M. *Your Man at the United Nations: People, Politics and Bureaucracy in the Making of Foreign Policy* (New York University Press, New York, 1980) p. 284–5.
56 Artner (1980: 429).
57 'Interview with Arafat' in *Journal of Palestine Studies*, vol. IX (Winter 1980), no. 2.
58 Campbell, J. 'The Middle East: A House of Containment Built On Shifting Sands', *Foreign Affairs*, 1981, p. 612.
59 Golan (1980: 7–8).
60 Schiff, Z. and Rothstein, R. *Fedayeen; The Story of the Palestinian Guerrilla* (Valentine-Mitchell, London, 1972) p. 215.
61 Golan (1980: 11).
62 Yodfat *et al.* (1981: 87).
63 *ARR* (1972: 365).
64 *ARR* (1972: 443).
65 Yodfat *et al.* (1981: 90).
66 Golan (1980: 231).
67 *ARR* (1974: 311, 337) However, the office was not opened until June 1976 (*ARR*, 1976: 400).
68 Golan, G. 'The Soviet Union and the Palestine Liberation Organization' in Kaupi, M. and Nation, C. (eds), *The Soviet Union and the Middle East in the 1980s* (Lexington Books, Lexington, Mass., 1983) p. 190.
69 Golan (1980: 234–43).
70 Hazan, B. 'Involvement by Proxy—Eastern Europe and the PLO 1971–1975' in Ben-

Gor, G. (ed.) *The Palestinians and the Conflict* (Turtle Dove Press, Ramat Gan, 1979) p. 324.
71 *ARR* (1973: 71).
72 Hazan in Ben-Gor (ed.) (1979: 326).
73 *ARR* (1973: 310).
74 *ARR* (1973: 287).
75 *ARR* (1974: 161).
76 *ARR* (1972: 243).
77 *ARR* (1974: 388).
78 *ARR* (1974: 266).
79 *ARR* (1974: 363).
80 Hazan in Ben-Gor (ed.) (1979: 333).
81 Golan (1980: 59 and 235–6) also see Hazan in Ben-Gor (ed.) (1979: 322, 328).
82 Golan (1980: 8).
83 *The Times*, 29 January 1974.
84 Documents and source material: 'Statement on the Mideast issued by leaders of the Common Market, 29 June 1982', *Journal of Palestine Studies*, vols XI–XII (Summer/ Fall 1982), p. 343.
85 UN Doc., S/15317 and Keatinge in Allen and Pijpers (eds) (1984: 30, note 24).
86 Documents and source material:'Middle East Peace Proposal of President Reagan, September 1, 1982', *Journal for Palestine Studies*, vols XI–XII (Summer/Fall 1982), pp. 340–3.
87 'Eastern Europe and the Middle East Crisis–II' *IJA Background Papers*, no. 6 (August 1967).
88 Hazan in Ben-Dor (ed.) (1979: 320).
89 *ARR* (1969: 23).
90 Golan (1980: 11).
91 Quoted in Golan (1980: 11).
92 Hazan in Ben-Gor (ed.) (1979: 323–5).
93 Ibid., p. 323.
94 *ARR* (1972: 292).
95 For Romania see UN Document (Provisional) A/PV 2289 November 1974, pp. 7, 18; for Czechoslovakia see UN Document (Provisional) A/PV 2292 November 1974, pp. 27, 20; and for Bulgaria see UN Document (Provisional) A/PV 2295, 21 November, pp. 36, 45
96 UN Document (Provisional) A/PV 2286, 15 November 1974, p. 80.
97 UN Document (Provisional) A/PV 2287, 15 November 1974, p. 102.
98 Cited in Hazan in Ben-Gor (ed.) (1979: 333).
99 UN Document (Provisional) A/PV 2291, 19 November 1974, p. 12.
100 UN Document (Provisional) A/PV 2287, 15 November 1974, p. 61.
101 Hazan in Ben-Gor (ed.) (1979: 334–5).
102 *ARR* (1976: 169).
103 See Golan (1980: 56–7; and ch. 2) for an analysis of Soviet attitudes towards Palestinian statehood.
104 'The Soviet Attitude to the Palestinian Problem; from the records of the Syrian Communist Party, 1971–1972', *Journal of Palestine Studies* vol. II (Autumn 1972), pp. 187–212.
105 Soviets openly praised those involved in the decision. (Golan 1980: 87–8).
106 During this visit Arafat was allegedly promised support for an independent state (Golan, 1980: 55, footnote 15). However, the communiqué released after the Arafat–Ponomarev meeting referred only to 'the attainment of the legal national rights of the Palestinian Arab people'; 'Joint Palestinian–Soviet Communiqué August 4, 1974', *Journal of Palestine Studies*, vol. IV (Autumn 1974), no. 1 , pp. 202–3. Previously, the Soviets referred to 'the legitimate rights of the Palestinian people'; 'Text of the Joint Soviet–Palestinian Communiqué, Moscow, July 28, 1972', *Journal of Palestine Studies*, vol. II (Autumn 1972), no. 1, pp. 183–4.

107 Yodfat *et al.* (1981: 91).
108 'Joint Palestinian– Soviet Statement', *Journal of Palestine Studies*, vol. V (Spring/ Summer 1976) nos 3–4, pp. 255–6.
109 'Joint Soviet–Palestinian Communiqué, April 8, 1977' *Journal of Palestine Studies*, vol. VI (Summer 1977), no. 4, pp. 178–9.
110 Yodfat *et al.* (1980: 101).
111 Yodfat *et al.* (1981: 102).
112 *Le Monde*, 15 May 1971. Although the report was far from recognizing the political rights of the Palestinians, Israel nevertheless lobbied very hard against its adoption in the belief that the gradual reconciliation of the divergent views of the EC countries would culminate in a position closer to France's. *Le Monde*, 14 May 1971.
113 *Le Monde*, 7 November 1973.
114 UN Document (Provisional) A/PV 2292, 20 November 1974, pp. 47, 28.
115 UN Documents (Provisional) A/PV 2423, 2 December 1975, p. 42; A/31/PV.7, 28 September 1976, pp. 77, 81. In 1974 West Germany was the first EC country to refer to the right of self-determination of the Palestinian people and to 'recognise the right of the Palestinian people to decide itself whether to establish an independent authority'. UN Document (Provisional) A/PV 2291, 19 November 1974, p. 6.
116 Quoted in 'European Stance on the Palestinian Issue: EEC Statement Analysed', *IJA Research Report*, no. 3 (August 1977), p. 4.
117 UN Document A/34/PV.8, 25 September 1979.
118 *The Times*, 14 June 1980.
119 Franck, C. 'Belgium: committed multilateralism' in Hill (ed.) (1983: 99).
120 *Le Monde*, 1 September 1981.
121 Moisi, D. 'La France de Mitterand et le conflict du Proche-Orient comment concilier emotion et politique', *Politique Etrangere*, vol. 47 (1982), no. 2, p. 396.
122 Malta, which has been excluded from the statistical analysis because of low attendance, can also be included in this group.
123 Greilsammer, I. 'The impact of Enlargment: Spain, Portugal and the Arab–Israeli Conflict', in Allen and Pijpers (eds) (1984: 228).
124 Ibid., p. 234.
125 Furthermore at the General Assembly Sweden spoke of the PLO as 'the most authoritative spokesman for the Palestinian Arabs'. UN Document (Provisional) A/PV 2295, 21 November 1974, p. 88).
126 The influence of such consideration on Norwegian and Icelandic policies towards political problems in the Third World is also noted by Rudebeck: 'Norway is a member of the Atlantic pact (NATO), whereas Sweden is neutral. This made it possible for Sweden, for instance, to come out earlier and more strongly than Norway in support of national liberation movements in Indochina and in Portugal's former African colonies ... Iceland is also a strategic link in the NATO system which puts some implicit restrictions on its freedom of action in international politics' (Rudebeck, L. 'Nordic Policies Towards the Third World', in Sundelieus, B. (ed.) *Foreign Policies of Northern Europe* (Westview, Boulder, 1982), pp. 167, 171.)
127 Haagerup and Thune in Hill (ed.) also note Denmark's influence in getting the Nordic Council to a position closer to the EC's (Hill (ed), 1983: 112).
128 Thune, C. 'Denmark', in Allen and Pijpers (eds) (1984: 84).
129 UN Document (Provisional) A/PV 2296, 22 November 1974, pp. 18–20.
130 Stebbins, R. and Adam, E. (eds) *American Foreign Relations 1973; A Documentary Record* (New York University Press, New York, 1976), p. 279.
131 For a thorough analysis of the origins and the making of the Saunders' statement see Buheiry, M. 'The Saunders Document', *Journal of Palestine Studies* vol. VIII (Autumn 1978), no. 1, pp. 28–40.
132 A copy of the report can be found in 'The Brookings Report on the Middle East', *Journal of Palestine Studies*, vol. VI (Winter 1977), no. 2, pp. 195–205.
133 E. Rouleau in a series of articles in the July editions of the *Guardian Weekly* as reported

in 'Views From Abroad': 'US–Israel relations', *Journal of Palestine Studies*, vol. VI (Summer 1977), no. 4, pp. 170–1.

134 Ibid., p. 174.

135 The interview was conducted by T. Feldman in *The New York Post*, 1 May 1978. The article is cited in 'Views From Abroad'; *Journal of Palestine Studies*, vol. VII (Summer 1978), no. 4, p. 168.

136 'Interview with Farouq Al-Qaddumi' in 'Shu'un Filastiniya', Beirut, June 1977 reproduced in *Journal of Palestine Studies*, vol. VI (Summer 1977), no. 4, pp. 181–90.

137 According to Hurewitz, 'Egyptians expected the autonomy to unfold by stages into full self-government for the Palestinians. For the Israelis the evolution into a state of the projected Palestinian "self-governing authority (administrative council) was wholly excluded." Furthermore Begin advocated autonomy for the population but not the territories, a thinly disguised intent of maintaining sovereignty over the West Bank and the Gaza Strip.' Hurewitz, J. 'The Middle East: A Year of Turmoil', *Foreign Affairs*, vol. 59 (1980), no. 3.

138 Campbell (1978: 616).

139 Yodfat *et al.* (1980: 129).

140 Ibid., p. 116.

141 Ibid., p. 116–17.

142 'Middle East Peace Proposal of President Reagan, September 1, 1982', *Journal of Palestine Studies*, vols XI–XII (Summer/Fall 1982), no. 4, pp. 340–3.

143 UN Document A/ES-7/PV.11, 30 July 1980.

144 UN Document (Provisional) A/PV/2294, 21 November 1974.

145 UN Document A/ES-7/PV.4, 24 July 1980.

8 Mobilization of Support at the UN Level

So far we have examined the mobilization process across local and regional levels of analysis. Now the analysis will be extended to the global level. This level is best represented by the United Nations with its near universal membership. Particular attention will be paid to the General Assembly and the Security Council and to the politics that surround the changes in the contents of their agendas and the outputs that emerge from them.

The introductory chapter looked briefly at the Palestinian question in its early days at the United Nations. An attempt was made to point to some of the processes that gradually led the United Nations at that time to define the Palestinian Problem as one of refugees. The occasional challenges made by Arab countries, attempting to undermine this definition, were unsuccessful; the refugee image remained firm in the minds of many until the late 1960s. The first challenges made by non-Arab delegations began to surface during the debates on the June 1967 war in the Middle East. The analysis of the mobilization process that eventually changed the definition of the Palestinian Problem from one of refugees to one of self-determination will begin from 1967 and cover the period up to 1980.

The year 1980 was chosen for substantive as well as practical reasons. By then an overwhelming majority of the members had come to favour the Palestinian right to self-determination and a general consensus had developed on the inadequacy of the provisions of the Camp David Agreements relating to the rights of the Palestinians. This was also the year when the last major regional grouping, the European Community, formally joined ranks in recognizing the right of the Palestinian people to self-determination. Similarly, it was in 1980 that the Latin Americans reached a high degree of cohesion in their support for the Palestinian cause. The practical reasons emanate from the fact that post-1980 voting data in a machine readable form were not available when the research for the book began. Since then voting patterns on the Palestinian Question appear to have remained stable.

Conducive environment

The first task will be to identify a series of developments during the 1960s that brought about changes in the structure of the United Nations' political system making it more conducive to the mobilization of support for the Palestinian cause. Four such developments can be identified.

Growth in Third World membership

When the United Nations came into being it was an organization dominated by what was known as the Western bloc. The bloc, which included the Latin Americans, commanded a majority of the membership well into the late 1950s, a factor which influenced both the nature of issues that were taken up as well as the resulting decisions. During the first decade, the agendas were dominated by items that reflected the high centrality of the Cold War to the majority of the membership. In a similar way, decisions on this issue tended to be determined by the almost automatic majority that the Western bloc could master.

As Table 8.1 depicts, the composition of the United Nations began to change from 1955 onwards as Afro-Asian countries joined in increasing numbers. A particularly dramatic increase occurred in 1960 when 17 newly independent countries became members. It is not surprising that this was also the year that saw the adoption of the 'Declaration On The Granting Of Independence To Colonial Countries And Peoples', an indication that decolonization was becoming an issue of great importance to a growing number of members and hence a dominant item on the United Nations' agenda.

Table 8.1. Change in distribution of United Nations' membership by region between 1945 and 1980

Year	Latin America		Western Europe		Eastern Europe		Asia (Arabs)		Africa (Arabs)		Total
	%		%		%		%		%		
1945	20	39	14	27	6	11	8(4)	16	3(1)	6	51
1950	20	33	17	28	6	10	14(5)	23	3(1)	5	60
1955	20	26	23	30	10	13	19(6)	25	4(2)	5	76
1960	20	20	23	23	10	10	21(5)	21	25(5)	25	99
1965	22	19	24	20	10	9	25(7)	21	36(6)	31	117
1970	24	19	24	19	10	8	28(8)	22	41(6)	32	127
1975	27	19	25	17	11	7	35(12)	24	46(8)	32	144
1980	29	19	25	16	11	7	38(12)	25	50(9)	33	153

One of the consequences of this salience given to decolonization was that issues that could be treated as problems of decolonization stood a better chance of receiving attention and benefiting from the prestige that anti-colonialism offered. It is mostly in this context that the growth of Third World membership provided a more favourable basis for the mobilization of support for the Palestinian cause.

Changes in the distribution of elected posts

The Assembly elects the countries to fill the seats of the elected bodies of the UN as well as the president and vice-presidents of the Assembly and the chairmen of the main committees. One major consequence of the growth of Third World membership has been an increase in the demands for better Third World representation to these elected posts. Previously, the distribution of the elected posts of the General Assembly and non-permanent seats on the Security Council tended to favour Western and Latin American countries. However, Resolution 1990 (XVIII), in December 1963 and Resolution 33/138 in 1978 increased the number of vice-presidents and reorganized their distribution across geographical regions in a way that allowed greater Third World representation. These resolutions also rearranged the distribution of main committee officers. These changes are depicted in Tables 8.2 and 8.3.

Table 8.2. Geographical distribution of vice-presidents before and after resolutions 1990 (XVIII) and 33/138

	Before 1963	After 1963	After 1978
Africa and Asia	4	7	11 (5)
Latin America	2	3	3
East Europe	1	1	1
Western and others	2	2	2
Permanent members	5	5	5
Total	13	17	21

Note: The number in brackets indicates Asian states.

Table 8.3. Distribution of main committee chairmanships before and after resolutions 1990 (XVIII) and 33/138

	Before 1963	After 1963	After 1978
Africa and Asia	2	3	3 (1)
Latin America	2	1	1
East Europe	1	1	1
Western and others	2	1	1
Total	7	6*	6*

* The seventh chairmanship rotates every alternate year between representatives of States belonging to second and third groups. The numbers in brackets indicate Asian states.

These changes appear to have had two consequences for the politics of the General Assembly. First, the composition of the General Committee changed from a Western dominated body to one with enlarged representation for the Third World. It is particularly with regard to the politics surrounding the inclusion and exclusion of certain items and the allocation of the agenda items to various parts of the Assembly that the composition of the General Committee can play a significant role. A General Committee with a larger Third World representation will naturally act more favourably towards matters of greater concern to the Third World. The General Committee's decisions on the agenda, conditional upon Assembly approval, will determine 'whether a particular item will go through the remaining ... phases of "parliamentary diplomacy" and be considered by the Assembly'.[2]

Second, although the influence that presiding officers have on the course of debates and decision making is difficult to ascertain, these officers, particularly the chairmen of the main committees, can exercise a certain degree of influence in steering a debate.[3] Similarly, the president of the Assembly can at times take the initiative. One example of this was during the 29th Assembly Session when the Algerian president did not hesitate to ensure that the chairman of the PLO, Arafat, was escorted from the rostrum by the chief of protocol, an honour usually reserved only for heads of states.[4]

Another structural change was precipitated by Resolution 1991 (XIII) which endorsed Third World demands for more equitable representation on the Security Council. The resolution not only increased the number of non-permanent seats from six to ten but also introduced, for the first time, a formalized geographical distribution of elected seats. Previously the seats were distributed according to a 'gentleman's agreement' reached during the first session of the Assembly.[5] From its early days, this formula had been a problem as the West, in the context of the Cold War, employed the agreement 'to have the Security Council so constituted that there are always seven members which can be relied upon to stand together in the case of threats to the peace.'[6]

It was not the Soviet bloc's challenges to the way this 'gentleman's agreement' was interpreted that undermined the arrangement. Instead, it was the inability of the original pattern of geographical distribution of seats to accommodate a growing number of Third World countries that led to the adoption of Resolution 1991 (XIII).[7] This resolution rearranged and formalized the geographical regions into Western Europe and others, Eastern Europe, Latin America and Africa-Asia, allotting five seats to the last group. This change in the arithmetic of seat distributions appears to have influenced Security Council decision making in a number of ways.

First, seven seats gives the Third World the opportunity to block majority decisions. Conversely and more importantly, the Third World with the support of only two other members can achieve a majority. This has made Third World views highly influential in relation to procedural decisions which require only simple majorities without the veto being used. This advantage, in the context of the Palestinian Problem, was well demonstrated when the Security Council, in December 1975, invited the PLO to participate in its work.[8]

The emergence of political groupings

Another important aspect of the growth of Third World membership was the strengthening of existing political groupings and the emergence of new groupings with Third World membership. These groups perform a wide range of functions including the exchange of information on all or part of the agenda, developing common general positions on important agenda items and undertaking joint action for or against a proposal.[9]

These functions enable group members to pool resources for an effective voice in General Assembly decision making; the existence of political groupings provides members with the opportunity to raise issues of high salience to them and seek the cooperation of the group. The group hence plays an important role as an access route to the larger assembly.

The opportunity of lobbying other groups is facilitated by political groupings with overlapping membership. For example, the Latin American group is not directly accessible to the Arab countries. However, growing Latin American membership in the Non-Aligned movement has paved the way for the Arabs to gain access to the larger Latin American audience. Similarly, the Afro-Asian and Islamic groups constitute a channel through which Arab representatives can influence the position of the Turkish delegation who in turn may have an impact on the West European group in which it also participates. The same things can be said for the overlapping memberships of the Afro-Asian/Non-Aligned groups with the Commonwealth group.

Another important aspect of overlapping membership is that it can facilitate the development and recognition of common political values. These values then play a crucial role in guiding group perceptions and attitudes toward issues. As it unfolds this process culminates in cross-cutting loyalties and hence forms a crucial basis for the mobilization of support.

National liberation movements and the United Nations

A final factor that contributed towards a conducive environment for the mobilization of support for the Palestinian cause was a growing acceptance that non-governmental actors, in particular national liberation movements, had a legitimate role to play in UN politics. The basis for direct national liberation movements' participation can be traced to the adoption of Resolution 1514 and the reluctance of Portugal and South African governments to accept eventual independence for African territories under their control.

The Fourth Committee of the General Assembly in the wider context of decolonization had already developed a practice of granting hearings to petitioners.[10] However, it was not until the late 1960s that direct contacts between the United Nations and the national liberation movements began to develop. The basis of these developments lay in the contacts between the special committee on decolonization and national liberation movements during its visits to Africa and particularly in a Bulgarian initiative calling for a more active United Nations' involvement in the process of decolonization.[11] The Bulgarian initiative culminated in the adoption of Resolution 2311 (XXII) which opened the way to contacts between the specialized agencies and the national liberation movements.

The special committee for its part adopted, after contacts with African liberation movement leaders in September 1970, a programme for the 10th anniversary of the adoption of Resolution 1514 in 1960.[12] This programme, *inter alia*, called for the participation of liberation movements in United Nations' proceedings related to their countries. The endorsement of these points by the General Assembly laid the ground for further developments in the following two sessions.[13] First, the specialized agencies were called on to examine procedures for national liberation movement participation and second, Resolution 2874 (XXVI) prepared the way for these movements to obtain observer status at the General Assembly.[14] It was the special committee that first invited the liberation movements to participate in its deliberations and then its chairman suggested that the movements be allowed to participate in the work of the fourth committee as observers.[15] These developments were subsequently endorsed by the Assembly in 1974 when an invitation—to all liberation movements recognized by the OAU—to participate in the work of its main committees and subsidary bodies was adopted.[16]

The impact of the structural changes

All these developments are important for the mobilization process in a number of ways. First, the growth in Third World membership and the changes in certain aspects of the structure of the General Assembly and the Security Council were significant because they broadened the basis of potential allies for Arabs and also enabled both Arabs and Third World delegations to have a greater say in the politics of the UN. Second, the emergence of political groupings opened the possibility for the Arabs and later on the Palestinians to gain access to growing numbers of delegations. It enabled them to caucus the non-Arab membership of these groupings. It also enabled the Arabs and Palestinians to contribute to the development of ideological guidelines for the inclusion and processing of various issues on the United Nations' agendas. Third, the gradual incorporation of national liberation movements set a precedent for the PLO's eventual participation, allowing it to gain access to various parts of the organization and hence have a direct impact on the politics of the Palestinian Problem.

These developments, although they brought about a conducive environment, did not necessarily generate instant support. Take for example the sudden increase in Third World membership in 1960 and the adoption of Resolution 1514 which did not generate immediate support for demands made by the Arabs. At the 16th Session of the Assembly, this was reflected quite starkly in the reluctance of some African and most Latin American countries to support the Arab position on Algeria.[17]

Hence, the conducive environment as described above should not be equated to support *per se*. Instead it should be seen as a series of structural changes that increased the chances to generate support for the Palestinian cause by allowing Arab/Palestinian access to a potentially favourable audience and for them to argue in favour of cognitive linkages between the Palestinian issue and other issues already enjoying the UN's support. In the following two sections those aspects of the mobilization process at the United Nations will be examined.

Accessibility

Indirect access

When the Palestinian Problem first came to the United Nations the Palestinian Arabs had enjoyed indirect access to that forum through Arab countries that tended to support their cause. Once the Palestinian Question at the United Nations lost, in the early 1950s, its political dimension it became very difficult for the Arab delegations to maintain debates on the political rights of the Palestinian Arabs let alone ensure recognition of them.

This situation remained unchanged until the late 1960s when some African and other non-Arab Islamic countries began to make references in their speeches to the rights of the Palestinian Arabs. For example Mali was the only delegation during the Security Council debates on the Middle East war of 1967 to refer to the Palestinian dimension of the Arab–Israeli Conflict.[18] It was not until the 24th Session of the Assembly that this growing recognition gathered adequate strength to translate itself into a recognition of 'the inalienable rights of the Palestinians'.

During this initial period in addition to the delegations' role, members of the Secretariat enabled the Palestinian Arabs to gain indirect access to the Assembly. A remarkable development came in 1968 when the Secretary General, in his address to the special political committee, deplored the inability of the General Assembly to take any significant steps towards a solution of the problem of Palestine refugees who still, he noted, 'had no homeland, no future and no hope'.[19]

The special committee to investigate Israeli practices affecting the human rights of the population of the occupied territories, set up in December 1969, was another body that allowed the Palestinians indirect access to the United Nations.[20] During its visits to the Middle East it interviewed and consulted many Palestinian Arabs and its first report reflected the frustration felt by the Palestinian Arabs of living under occupation without enjoying the right to self-determination.[21]

The impact of the reports prepared by UNRWA and the special committee should not be underestimated. These reports injected new and particularly detailed information on aspects of Palestinian life in the refugee camps and the occupied territories into the general debate on the Palestinian Problem. By exposing delegations to new aspects of the Palestinian Problem and forcing them to develop and express opinions, the information presented took the content of the Assembly debates well beyond the usual deliberations on the narrow humanitarian and technical aspects of the refugee problem that had characterized most of the earlier debates.

Direct access

The Palestinian Arabs also experienced direct access soon after the Palestinian Question was brought to the attention of the United Nations. The Arab Higher Committee together with the Jewish Agency had been invited to participate in the work of the Assembly concerning the question of Palestine. However, this situation did not last very long. Once Resolution 181 (II) was adopted, Palestinian Arabs speaking on behalf of their own political organizations did not reappear until 1965. The special political committee of the Assembly, which traditionally has debated issues pertaining to the refugees in the Near East, began, after a long procedural debate, to invite the PLO and another group of Palestinians calling themselves the Palestine Arab Delegation to address the committee. The invitations to the PLO and the Palestine Arab Delegation were extended on the clear understanding that they did not imply recognition of the organizations, and they were limited to addressing the special political committee of the Assembly.[22] It nevertheless did give representatives of these organizations the chance to express the views of the Palestinian Arabs and participate in the more informal aspects of the politics surrounding the debate.

The direct participation of the representatives from these two organizations affected politics at the General Assembly in two ways. First, both delegations injected the political dimension of the problem into the debates and contributed towards a radicalization of opinions and views on the Palestinian question. This to a certain extent was reflected in the increasing number of Arab, followed by Islamic and African, countries' systematic references to the colonial nature of the problem and the Palestinian Arabs rights to self-determination. Second, as Table 8.4 depicts the number of delegations sponsoring the renewed requests to invite the PLO steadily increased. This growing support for the PLO prepared the way for its eventual observer status.

Table 8.4. Number of countries sponsoring PLO's participation in the work of the SPC

	1965	1970	1971	1972	1973	1974
Arabs	13	14	17	18	18	19
Asians	—	3	8	10	9	9
Africans	—	6	5	7	27	29
L. Americans	—	1	1	2	6	4
East Europe	—	2	10	10	11	10
West Europe	—	—	—	—	—	1
Total	13	26	41	47	71	72

It has already been noted that the General Assembly had begun to look favourably at the participation of African national liberation movement in the work of the United Nations. The major breakthrough for the PLO came about as a result of the adoption of Resolutions 3210 (XIX) on 14 October 1974 and 3237 (XIX) on 22 November 1974. These resolutions amounted to the granting of a status of observership that went beyond the privileges enjoyed by other national liberation movements.[23]

Unlike the other national liberation movements, this status gave the PLO the opportunity to participate in all sessions and debates of the Assembly. In practice, this came to include the right to make speeches, to circulate and receive documents, and to table draft resolutions with the cooperation of 'friendly' delegations. Although this status did not include the right to vote, it nevertheless opened the way to participation in and influencing all stages of decision making at the Assembly. Furthermore, this status also allowed the PLO to bring up the issue of Palestinian rights in relation to other items on the agenda, such as matters concerning Southern Africa, and in the context of forums of specialized agencies.

The Security Council is the other major main organ to which the PLO gained access. The PLO's participation in the work of the Security Council was first endorsed in the November 1975 majority statement delivered by the president of the Council which noted that the PLO would be invited to the next meeting of the Council.[24] The nature of the PLO's participation, which was not clarified, became a highly contested issue when the Council next met in December 1975.[25] After a long procedural debate and by a vote of nine to three, with three abstentions, it was agreed that the PLO would be invited to the debates with 'the same rights of participation as are conferred when a Member State is invited to participate under rule 37'.[26] This practice, which was repeated on numerous occasions, enabled the PLO to participate in the Security Council debates concerning the Middle East and the rights of the Palestinians. Although none of these meetings adopted resolutions recognizing the political rights of the Palestinians, they nevertheless enabled the PLO to interact directly with other representatives present at the Security Council debates.

Local and international violence

From 1965 local violence by the Palestinian resistance movement directed towards Israel from neighbouring countries and international violence in the late 1960s and early 1970s led to the frequent calling of Security Council meetings. During these meetings the Arab delegates were able to raise and argue the point that the political dimension of the Palestinian Problem was the cause of this violence. The membership of the Council became receptive to these arguments particularly after the 1967 Middle East war. Until then, most of the members of the Council had concurred with the Israeli view that armed operations into Israel were breaches of armistice agreements between her and neighbouring Arab countries. In the aftermath of the 1967 war a different climate emerged which made Arab arguments that portrayed these operations as reactions to alien domination more acceptable.

Armed Palestinian operations at the local and international levels were also mentioned during discussions on the 'Implementation of the Declaration on the Granting of Independence to Colonial Countries and Peoples'. One tangible consequence of these discussions was reflected in the adoption by the Assembly of Resolution 2649 (XXV), which recognized the legitimacy of the struggles of peoples under colonial and alien domination and condemned 'those Governments that denied the right to self-determination of peoples recognized as being entitled to it, especially the peoples of South Africa and Palestine'.[27] The phrase 'alien domination' which had not been included in the previous session's resolution on the same issue, is generally agreed to have been introduced to cover the Palestinian case.[28]

Furthermore, the use of international violence by the Palestinian resistance movement was a major factor in airing the Palestinian Problem at the Assembly's Legal Committee and Plenary debates on terrorism in 1972.[29] Some delegations referred to aspects of the Palestinian Problem that related it to recognized national liberation struggles elsewhere.

These three different sets of access routes enabled the Palestinian Problem to appear on the United Nations' agendas. They played an important role in increasing delegates' awareness of the issue and also provided an opportunity of working towards cognitive linkages with other legitimized issues. This in itself contributed to influencing the perceptions of growing numbers of delegations in such a way that it led them to apply their criteria of legitimacy during the mobilization of support for the Palestinian cause.

Cognitive linkages

This section, to avoid any duplication with previous chapters, will primarily examine the decision-making process that extended the coverage of the decolonization struggle to include the Palestinian cause. Therefore, the emphasis will be on the inputs, in the form of significant speeches and draft resolutions, into the decision-making process and emerging outputs in the form of adopted resolutions, rather than an analysis of each delegation's voting behaviour.

The 15th Session of the General Assembly was a crucial year in the struggle against decolonization and in the development of anti-colonial thinking because it saw 17 newly independent countries join the UN as well as the adoption of Resolution 1514 (XV), the Declaration on the Granting of Independence to Colonial Countries. This resolution noted that 'All peoples have the right to self-determination' and proclaimed, 'the necessity of bringing to a speedy and unconditional end to colonialism in all its forms and manifestations'.[30] The adoption of this resolution, without any opposition, is generally regarded as an indication of the change in attitudes towards the right to self-determination and also a landmark in the recognition of the growing legitimacy of the struggle for decolonization.[31]

At the time this Declaration was particularly concerned with the situation arising from the policies of the Portuguese, South African and Rhodesian governments. The Palestinian struggle was excluded until 1970. This is not surprising considering that as late as in 1967 the Assembly still considered the Palestinians as refugees and victims of the conflict between Israel and the Arab states; this refugee status was reinforced by the adoption of Security Council Resolution 242.

Although the 24th Session saw an intensification of the arguments stressing the anti-colonial nature of the Palestinians' struggle for self-determination, it was not until the 25th Session that this became recognized by the Assembly. During the deliberation on the agenda item entitled 'Implementation of Recommendations of the International Conference on Human Rights' the third committee recommended to the Assembly an Afro-Asian resolution which, *inter alia*, condemned governments which deny the right to self-determination to peoples 'recognized as being entitled to it, especially the peoples of Southern Africa and Palestine.'[32] The inclusion of the word 'Palestine' had been challenged by Israel but at a subsequent vote requested by Costa Rica the whole phrase 'especially by the peoples of South Africa and Palestine' was then retained by a vote of 49 to 22, with 35 abstentions.[33]

Some further weight to the linkage between colonial struggles and the Palestinian one was added when the Assembly, at the recommendation of the fourth committee, adopted Resolution 2708 (XX), on 14 December 1970, which reaffirmed the Assembly's 'recognition of the legitimacy of the struggle of the colonial peoples and peoples under alien domination to exercise their right to self-determination'. The phrase 'alien domination' was inserted at the request of the Afghan delegation and was generally meant to cover the Palestinian people.[34] During the following session the Assembly endorsed 'the legality and the legitimacy of the struggle of the Palestinian people for self-determination' in an explicit manner when it adopted Resolution 2787 (XXVI) on 6 December 1971.[35]

By the 26th Session, non-Arab delegations, too, began to note in their speeches similarities between the regimes of South Africa and Israel. The Belorussian representative drew parallels between what they described as 'the policies of racial and national superiority' pursued by South Africa and by Israel. He noted that Israel was pursuing a policy similar to the policy of Bantustans in South Africa.[36] The most dramatic development in respect to the assertion of similarities between South Africa and Israel came in 1973.

First, Resolution 3175 (XXVIII) of 17 December 1973 that had been sponsored by Non-Aligned countries was very critical of Israel's policies in the occupied territories and in its last paragraph declared that the principles mentioned in the resolution were applicable to 'all states, territories and peoples under foreign occupation, colonial rule and apartheid'. Second, the political implications of the last paragraph were further strengthened when the representatives of Upper Volta asked for a separate vote and declared the purpose of the vote to be a means for identifying the unshakable supporters of Portugal and South Africa.[37] Ninety-four countries supported the motion while Israel, Nicaragua, Portugal and the United States opposed it. In the light of this it is not surprising that a large number of African and Asian countries supported the inclusion, in Resolution 3151 G (XXVIII), of an amendment condemning the 'unholy alliance between Portugese colonialism, South African racism, Zionism and Israeli imperialism'.[38]

The establishment of cognitive linkages between the problems of South Africa and Palestine was a major factor that contributed to the growth of support for the Palestinians. For the Third World, East Europeans and some West Europeans anti-colonialism as a belief system had become a primary source of reference in defining their attitudes towards a variety of problems. Once similarities between the situation in the occupied territories and particularly South Africa were accepted a growing number of delegations began to apply their anti-colonial criteria to their perceptions and decisions concerning the nature of the Palestinian Problem. In this context the Palestinian Problem ceased to be a refugee problem. Instead, it became a problem of a people struggling to achieve self-determination not unlike the national liberation struggles of various peoples in southern Africa.

Furthermore, the policies of Israel particularly in the West Bank and the Gaza Strip were increasingly seen as policies designed to deny the Palestinians their right to self-determination. This contributed towards a change in Third World perceptions of Israel. Furthermore, links between Israel and South Africa became increasingly singled out for criticism as signs of an alliance to perpetuate repression in these two parts of the world. These points were expressed in a stark manner in Resolution 3324 E (XXIX) which condemned relations between the two countries and received the overwhelming support of the Third World with the exception of a few Latin Americans.[39] As Israel was likened more and more to South Africa, its favourable image was eroded at the cost of increased support for the Palestinian cause. The process gained so much strength that to continue to support Israel while condemning South Africa was anomaly in itself, a position incompatible with anti-colonial thinking and behaviour.[40]

Growth of support

The period from 1947 to 1967

The political rights of the Palestinian Arabs had been recognized by Resolution 181 (II); very quickly, however, these rights drifted into obscurity. By the 3rd Session of the Assembly, the Palestinian Question was tranformed from one that sought a 'future government of Palestine' to one that sought a solution to the refugee problem as defined in Resolution 194 (III). The Assembly did not stop there; during the 5th Session it adopted Resolution 394 (V) that recommended a solution to the 'refugee problem' not through repatriation but by resettling substantial numbers of Palestinian Arab refugees. This new position was much closer to the Israeli view that claimed the Palestinians had the whole Arab World to settle in. By the 7th Session the process of redefining the issue reached a climax when 'the Question of Palestine', an agenda item that had originally symbolized the search to satisfy the political aspirations of both the Palestinian Arabs and Jewish people, was dropped.[41] The Western European and Latin American members even attempted to invalidate the applicability of previous resolutions particularly Resolutions 181 (II) and 194 (III).[42] Although this attempt failed, in practical terms the Western countries had set the parameters defining the problem.

In the mid-1960s there had been some signs of the beginnings of a change in attitudes towards the acceptance of the definition of the Palestinian Problem in its prevailing form. The Palestinian Arabs had begun to appear before the special political committee and argued strongly in favour of the political nature of the refugee problem. By the 20th Session their arguments had gained some ground as Afghanistan and Malaysia sponsored a draft resolution favourable to the Palestinian Arabs.[43] However, in general the Assembly, including many Africans, remained reluctant to recognize the Palestinian Problem as anything other than an off-shoot of the Arab–Israeli Conflict. This is strongly reflected in the way in which some Africans did not hesitate to join West European countries in supporting the idea of direct Arab–Israeli negotiations, during the 18th Session.[44]

Furthermore, the 1967 war reinforced in the eyes of the majority of the Assembly the centrality of the Arab–Israeli Conflict. Lall, in his study of the speeches of the delegates during the Fifth Emergency Special Session in 1967 identified seven different approches towards the possible solution of the crisis.[45] These were mostly related to positions taken on matters concerning the withdrawal of Israel from occupied territories, the means of achieving a just and durable peace and the issue of freedom of navigation through the straits of Aqaba. None of the approaches, however, tackled the Palestinian question in a form other than the expression, particularly on the part of West European and Latin American delegations, of humanitarian concern for the refugees.[46]

The Arabs, during the deliberations of the Emergency Special Session, did not separately articulate the political rights of the Palestinian Arabs.[47] Although in the past there had been some references on the part of Arab representatives to the right of self-determination of the Palestinian Arabs it seemed these rights were not taken up separately.[48] Instead, they were subsumed within the uncompromising challenge offered to the very existence of Israel whose presence in their midst was described as an aggression in itself.[49] During the Security Council deliberations in November 1967 this situation began to change as the political rights of the Palestinians received greater attention from Arab delegations.

In this, the role of the Arab Summit at Khartoum in August 1967 needs to be noted. After an eventful debate centred around the Palestinian Problem, a resolution was adopted that determined the guidelines for future policies towards Israel which among other points included 'an insistence on the rights of the Palestinian people in their own country'.[50] It was against this background that Egypt argued that the central issue in the Middle Eastern conflict was the expulsion of the people of Palestine and the need to ensure 'the Palestinian Arabs' right to self-determination'.[51] This line of argument only received support from the Mali representative who called for the need to restore the inalienable rights of the people of Palestine. Thus, there was inadequate support to influence the content and eventual adoption of Resolution 242, which continued to treat the Palestinian Problem as a by product of the Arab–Israeli Conflict.

The period between the wars of 1967 and 1973

The period between the two Middle Eastern wars was marked by a rapid change in attitudes towards the nature of the Palestinian Problem, which, from as early as 1968, began to occupy the attention of various parts of the United Nations. The increased resistance operations of the Palestinian guerrilla groups and Israeli reprisals led to numerous Security Council meetings between 1966 and 1973, precipitating debates on the causes of violence in the area. Growing numbers of non-Arab delegations participating in the debates argued that the acts of violence were a natural reaction to occupation.[52] Some African delegations joined the Arabs in arguing that resistance operations represented the Palestinians' struggle to achieve their right to self-determination while Israeli reprisals reflected the colonial nature of its regime.[53] By 1973 there was general agreement even among some permanent members of the Security Council that the Palestinian Problem was political in its essence and that Resolution 242 needed to be modified.[54]

These developments took a concrete form during a Security Council debate in June 1973. At this meeting a Non-Aligned-sponsored draft resolution was tabled.[55] The resolution, *inter alia*, expressed its conviction that a just and peaceful solution to the problem of the Middle East could be achieved only on the basis of 'respect for national sovereignity, territorial integrity, the rights of all states in the area and for the rights and legitimate aspirations of the Palestinians'. The draft resolution, which reflected a compromise between the position of radical Arab countries such as Algeria and Syria and the content of Resolution 242, failed when the United States cast the only opposing vote.

The General Assembly became the forum within which various aspects of the Palestinian Problem were debated, views expressed and opinions formulated and which culminated in the growth of support for the Palestinian cause. The deliberations surrounding particularly the agenda item entitled 'Assistance to refugees in the Near East' transformed the special political committee into a major forum for the discussion of the political aspects of the Palestinian Problem. This became quite evident during the 24th Session of the Assembly. Until then the resolutions recommended by the special political committee had not gone beyond the expression of support for the refugees' right to return to their homes.

It was at this session that the arguments put forward by the Palestinian Arabs and Arab delegations stressing the political nature of the Palestinian Problem began to bear fruit. First, a number of non-Arab delegations made speeches indicating a change in attitudes towards the Palestinian Problem, probably best reflected in the position taken by France and the Soviet Union. Both delegations, while continuing to express support for Resolution 242, also acknowledged the essentially political nature of the Palestinian Problem.[56] The Soviet Union went even further and, for the first time, noted that the Palestinian Arabs had the right to exercise self-determination as much as Israel had the right to exist.[57] Second, the Assembly saw the adoption of Resolution 2535 B (XXIV) on 10 December 1969. Even though this resolution was adopted with a very small majority, it nevertheless was the first to refer explicitly to 'the inalienable rights of the Palestinians'.

At the 25th Session the Assembly, in Resolution 2672 C (XXV) of 8 December 1970, expanded the 'inalienable rights' of the Palestinian people to include the right to self-determination and in Resolution 2628 (XXV) of 4 November 1970 declared the need to respect the rights of the Palestinian people in establishing a just and lasting peace in the Middle East. This session also saw the Palestinian Problem taken up by the third committee during its deliberation of the agenda item concerning the implementation of the recommendations of the International Conference on Human Rights. On the recommendation of the third committee the Assembly adopted Resolution 2649 (XXV) of 30 November 1970 which extended the application of the Declaration on Decolonization to the Palestinian Problem by recognizing the Palestinians as a people entitled to self-determination.

Between the 24th and 28th Sessions of the Assembly the content of resolutions supportive of the political rights of the Palestinians became more and more comprehensive as well as receiving growing support. The growing support of the Assembly is depicted in Tables 8.5 to 8.7. Both the Africans and Asians increasingly lent their support to the Palestinian cause. Among the Third World countries it was the Latin Americans who remained reluctant to extend full support to the Palestinians as a group. They were generally divided with substantial sections either supporting or maintaining an intermediate position. This is not surprising considering that as late as the 26th Session the Latin Americans were prepared to

Table 8.5. Distribution of support by regional groupings at the 24th Session*

	West European	Latin American	Africa	Asia	East Europe
	%	%	%	%	%
Highly Pro-Palest.	14	5	34	71	100
Medium Pro-Palest.	—	7	—	—	—
Intermediate	10	26	17	21	—
Medium Pro-Isr.	67	21	14	7	—
Highly Pro-Isr.	10	47	28	—	—
No. of countries	21	19	29	14	10

* Percentages are based upon countries meeting the minimum attendance levels.

Table 8.6. Distribution of support by regional groupings at the 26th Session*

	West European	Latin American	Africa	Asia	East Europe
	%	%	%	%	%
Highly Pro-Palest.	14	10	23	58	100
Medium Pro-Palest.	33	5	23	24	—
Intermediate	14	35	31	18	—
Medium Pro-Isr.	29	15	15	—	—
Highly Pro-Isr.	10	35	8	—	—
No. of countries	21	20	26	17	9

Table 8.7. Distribution of support by regional groupings at the 28th Session*

	West European	Latin American	Africa	Asia	East Europe
	%	%	%	%	%
Highly Pro-Palest.	14	39	96	81	100
Medium Pro-Palest.	14	11	4	19	—
Intermediate	68	22	—	—	—
Medium Pro-Isr.	—	11	—	—	—
Highly Pro-Isr.	4	17	—	—	—
No. of countries	21	18	25	16	10

* Percentages are based upon countries meeting the minimum attendance levels.

table a resolution supported by Israel. This draft resolution, if adopted, would have called for direct negotiations between the Arab governments and Israel.[58]

The Western Europeans, on the other hand, moved away from a position whereby a substantial proportion remained supportive of the Israelis to one that was slightly favourable to the Palestinians. The East Europeans constituted the only non-Arab group that throughout the period maintained a pro-Palestinian position.

Post-1973

If the previous period was characterized by a rapid change in attitudes towards the nature of the Palestinian Problem and growth of support for the Palestinian right to self-determination, the post 1973 period was one during which the recognition of the political rights of the Palestinians not only became consolidated but was also clearly elaborated to include the right to establish a state. The 'Palestinian Question' as an independent item was reintroduced to the plenary level of the Assembly and the problem was also taken up by the Security Council, ECOSOC and the specialized agencies. Furthermore, this was the period when the PLO became recognized as 'the legitimate representative of the Palestinian people' and was granted the right to participate in the work of practically all the bodies making up the United Nations' system.

The Security Council deliberations following the October War had attracted some speeches supporting the need to take into consideration the rights of the Palestinians, but the eventual Security Council decision that emerged did not mention the political rights of the Palestinians in any way. Instead Resolution 338 (1973) on 22 October 1973 called for a cease-fire and the implementation of Resolution 242, setting the limits for future Security Council decisions. Although numerous broadly supported attempts to expand Resolution 242 to include the political rights of the Palestinians were made between 1973 and 1980, American vetoes ensured that such proposals did not get adopted.[59]

It would be misleading to suggest that the Palestinian Problem did not receive any recognition at all just because the United States prevented the adoption of formal decisions recognizing the political rights of the Palestinians. Although the political and legal weight of a Council resolution can not be denied, the position of the remaining members of the Council did play a certain role in relation to attitude formation and the mobilization process.

The post-1973 period became the one during which the Palestinian question entered the agenda of the Security Council and most members acknowledged the right of the Palestinians to self-determination in one form or another. The Security Council debate in January 1976 is a good case in point. On this occasion a variety of formulations on the question of self-determination emerged. France held the view that the Palestinian people's right to 'an independent homeland' had to be recognized. The Soviet Union took a stronger view and noted that it was 'a legitimate national right of the Palestinians to create their own state', while the United Kingdom limited itself to the necessity of recognizing 'the right of the Palestinian people to express their national identity' without indicating what form this expression was to take. The East Europeans and Non-Aligned countries who participated in the debate mostly supported the idea of an independent Palestinian State. This became especially evident when Romania and Non-Aligned countries tabled a draft resolution which called for, among other things, respect for the Palestinian people's 'right to establish a State in Palestine'. Nine countries including France supported the draft resolution while the United States voted against with the other West Europeans abstaining.[60]

The obstacle caused by the American vetoes throughout the second half of the 1970s finally precipitated the calling of an Emergency Special Session of the General Assembly in July 1980. The Security Council had met in March and April during which a large number of delegations had made repeated calls for a resolution going beyond the provisions of Resolution 242.[61] However, a Tunisian draft resolution reflecting these positions was vetoed by the United States.[62] Subsequently, Senegal called for the convening of an Emergency Special Session invoking the 'Uniting for Peace' Resolution. The session met in July and adopted Resolution ES 7/2 by a vote of 112 to 7 against, with 24 abstentions which recognized the right of the Palestinian people 'to exercise their right to self-determination including the right to an independent state.'[63]

In addition to the Security Council becoming a forum where the Palestinian Problem was discussed one other development occurred with important implications for the mobilization process. The procedural decisions on the participation in the Council of states, bodies and persons from outside the Council call only for nine votes and are not subject to a veto. This enabled the Council to allow the PLO to participate in its deliberations. In itself this can be regarded as a significant development in respect to the Palestinian Problem. First, the invitation accorded to the PLO can be seen as a recognition of the PLO's centrality to the question.

Second, it gave the PLO the opportunity to raise the rights of the Palestinians directly in the most prestigious organ of the United Nations. Hence it gained effective status for lobbying and mobilizing support for the cause it represents. Third, to invite a non-state entity to participate in the work of the Council as if it were a state can be regarded as according a significant degree of prestige to the PLO.

It was the General Assembly which became the major focus of attention. The 29th Session began with two significant developments that set a pattern for the post 1973 period. First, the Assembly, at the request of 56 countries, asked the secretary general to include an item entitled 'Question of Palestine' on the agenda.[64] Second, the Assembly was also asked to consider a proposal put forward by 72 delegations inviting the PLO as the representative of the Palestinian people to participate in the Assembly's deliberations concerning the item.[65] The proposal was adopted by 105 votes to 4, with 20 abstentions as Resolution 3210 (XXIX) on 14 October 1974.

These developments were significant for three reasons. First, the 'Question of Palestine', after having been excluded from the formal agenda of the General Assembly since the 7th Session, was reintroduced. Second, the high salience of the issue to a large majority in the Assembly was evident in the allocation of the item to the plenary and in the active participation of a great number of delegations in the debate. Third, it culminated in the adoption of resolutions recognizing the right of the Palestinian people to national independence and granting the PLO observer status with the Assembly.

Resolution 3236 (XXIX) of 22 November 1974 affirmed 'the inalienable rights of the Palestinian people' including their 'right to national independence'. This resolution adopted by a vote of 89 to 8 with 37 abstentions took the political rights of the Palestinians one significant step further. Although in the previous session Resolution 3089 D (XVIII) referring to the political rights of the Palestinians had received approximately the same level of support in a vote of 87 to 6, with 33 abstentions, the new one was different.

It recognized: (i) the right to national independence and sovereignty rather than the more general reference to 'the right to self-determination'; (ii) the inalienable rights of the Palestinian people are indispensable for the solution of the Question of Palestine and that the Palestinian people are a principal party in the establishment of a just and lasting peace previously the 'Palestinian people' were not referred to as 'the principal body'; (iii) the right of the Palestinian people to regain its rights by all means in accordance with the purposes and principles of the Charter of the United Nations; and (iv) it appealed to all states and international organizations to extend their support to the Palestinian people in its struggle to restore their rights in accordance with the Charter.

The first two points expanded and redefined the political rights of the Palestinians while the last two were completely new elements. Resolutions on the 'Importance of the Universal Realization of the Right to Self-Determination' and 'the Implementation of the Declaration on the Granting of Independence to Colonial Countries and Peoples' had regularly raised these last two points in respect to people under colonial and alien domination. However, it was the first time that these points had been raised directly within the context of the 'Question of Palestine'.

In the second new development, in 1974, the Assembly adopted, by a vote of 95 to 17, with 19 abstentions, a resolution which accorded the PLO the status of a permanent observer. The PLO, as it was noted earlier on, had already been invited to attend a number of UN Conferences and had also been participating in the work of a number of Third World regional organizations. In the context of the United Nations, this resolution enabled the PLO to participate 'in the sessions and the work of the General Assembly, ... of all international conferences convened under the auspices of the Assembly and of other organs' in the capacity of a permanent observer.[66]

This development had two consequences. First, it meant that the PLO gained access to practically all sections of the United Nations, enabling it to raise various aspects of the Palestinian Problem in a variety of forums.[67] Second, it has also meant that the PLO has had to develop and articulate policy on many issues. The first factor ensured that the Palestinian issue reached numerous United Nations' agendas and opened up possibilities for the PLO delegations to develop networks of communications and engage in a wide range of lobbying. The second consequence meant that the PLO, through their delegations at the United Nations, became absorbed in a socialization process that favoured the achievement of a solution to the Palestinian Problem by diplomatic rather than violent means.[68]

Two further developments occurred during the remaining parts of the period under study. First, by Resolution 3375 (XXX) of 10 November 1975, the PLO was invited to participate in all UN efforts to solve the Middle East problem, on an equal footing with other parties. The Palestinian Problem was no longer a by-product of Arab-Israeli wars but the main and central element in the conflict. Second, the Assembly in Resolution 3376 (XXX) of 10 November 1975, having declared the Palestinian Problem a threat to international peace, decided to establish the Committee on the Exercise of the Inalienable Rights of the Palestinian People. The committee which was composed of 22 members, subsequently enlarged to 24, was given the duty of considering and recommending to the General Assembly a programme for the implementation of the rights of the Palestinian people.

The committee, which was composed mostly of Non-Aligned countries, played a crucial role in the further expansion of the political rights of the Palestinian people from 'the right to national independence' to the clearer and firmer expression of 'the right to establish a State'. Over the years during the discussions of the reports prepared by the committee, an increasing number of delegations began to refer to an 'independent Palestinian State'. These points were eventually taken up by the 7th Emergency Special Session resolution in July 1980. Although, this resolution was far from receiving unanimous support it nevertheless recognized and defined the basis of a future Palestinian state that would be established in parts of Palestine occupied by Israel in June 1967.

A further development was the spread of the Palestinian Problem to other parts of the United Nations. It did not remain an issue limited to the General Assembly in plenary and to the Security Council. As Sharif notes, the Palestinian issue came 'to permeate all major United Nations General Assembly Committees, subsidiary committees and commissions as well as agencies'.[69] Figure 8.1 shows the areas which have dealt with the Palestinian issue. Sharif's version of the diagram excludes certain parts of the United Nations that ought to be included to produce a more complete picture of the relationship between various United Nations' bodies and the Palestinian Problem.

First, Sharif appears to exclude the Sixth Committee of the General Assembly, the Legal Committee, from his diagram. However, considering that this committee took up the problem of terrorism which led certain delegations to bring up the Palestinian Problem it seems that the figure ought to be enlarged to include the Legal Committee as well. Second, as a result of the implementations of

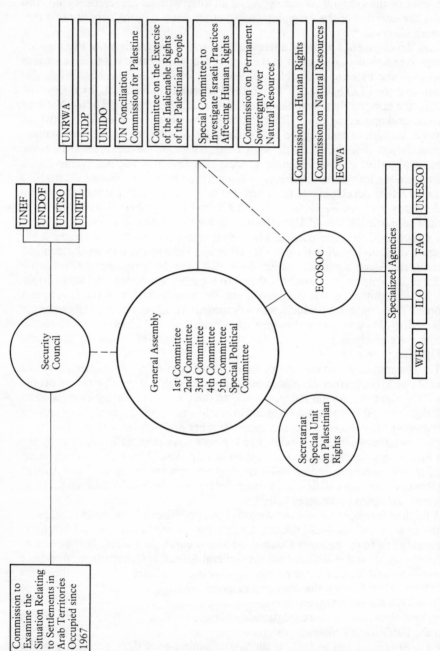

Figure 8.1. The United Nations system as it relates to the Palestinian Problem [70]

Resolutions 3237 (XXIX) and 3247 (XXIX) the PLO gained access to practically all specialised agencies with the exception of GATT, the IMF and the World Bank. The fact that the nature of this access gave the PLO the chance to raise their problem formally as well as informally warrants the inclusion of the other agencies, which have been omitted. Finally, Resolution 3237 (XIX) also entitled the PLO to participate in the work of United Nations conferences called under the auspices of the General Assembly. The above additions should be made to complete the picture that shows the extent to which the Palestinian issue has penetrated the United Nations' system.

As Table 8.8 shows, in addition to the Palestinian Problem becoming a major issue on the United Nations agenda and the content of Assembly resolutions growing in strength throughout the 1970s, the political support expressed in votes for the Palestinian cause increased too. The major changes occurred among the divided 'West Europeans and others Group' and the Latin Americans. In the case of the Western group, substantive numbers of relatively pro-Israeli countries

Table 8.8. Distribution of support across two sessions*

	West Europe		Latin America		Africa		Asia	
	1974	1980	1974	1980	1974	1980	1974	1980
	%	%	%	%	%	%	%	%
Highly Pro-Palest.	19	22	43	87	96	98	88	91
Medium Pro-Palest.	24	17	19	4	—	2	12	9
Intermediate	24	52	19	9	4	—	—	—
Medium Pro-Isr.	29	4	—	—	—	—	—	—
Highly Pro-Isr.	4	4	19	—	—	—	—	—
No. of countries	21	23	16	23	23	36	17	23

* Percentages are based upon countries meeting the minimum attendance levels.

moved to a 'intermediate' position while a group of mostly south Europeans continued to maintain their pro-Palestinian position. It should be noted that the group of countries with a intermediate position were mostly European Community countries. In their Venice Declaration of June 1980 they had formally recognized 'the right of the Palestinians to self-determination' but then abstained on most General Assembly resolutions because they believed these resolutions did not adequately state the right of Israel to exist.

The change in Latin American views was of a particularly dramatic nature as 87 per cent of Latin American countries had become pro-Palestinian by 1980 compared to 43 per cent in 1974. Furthermore, many Latin American countries which had been pro-Israeli in the previous period and had maintained strong diplomatic ties with Israel moved to a intermediate position.[71] No doubt the influence of the Non-Aligned Movement, particularly in getting some Latin American members of the Movement to recognize the cognitive linkage between colonial struggles and the Palestinian struggle was central to this. One also needs to add the pressure generated by high support for the Palestinian cause among the rest of the Third

World. This has resulted, on the part of some Latin Americans, in a concern about being associated with positions regarded as untenable within the anti-colonial stance of the Non-aligned Movement.

Conclusion

From the very early days of the United Nations the Palestinians enjoyed either direct or indirect access to the General Assembly. However, in a Western and Latin American dominated forum this accessibility was not enough to prevent the Palestinian Problem from losing its political nature. Third World membership of the United Nations began to increase at a time when the Palestinian Problem was firmly entrenched as a by-product of the Arab–Israeli Conflict that required a technical-humanitarian solution. The increase in Third World membership did not therefore immediately change the attitudes held. Instead it precipitated a process that began to change the structure as well as the concerns of the United Nations.

Most issues of concern to the North, such as Cold War questions, were overtaken by matters concerning decolonization and economic development. The change in the membership precipitated structural changes that led the Third World to have a greater say in decision making as well as in attitude formation. This brought about a conducive environment for a mobilization process to alter the image held of the Palestinian Problem.

It was also during the 1960s that a new Palestinian national movement began to emerge. The Palestinian delegations from this movement coupled with radical Arab delegations began to project a different image of the Palestinian Problem. They began to stress the political nature of the problem and in the context of the growing resistance movement in Palestine described the problem as one of national liberation against occupation and a struggle for self-determination. As these delegations voiced the similarities between the situation in Palestine and in other places experiencing colonial domination their arguments gradually found a receptive audience prepared to use their anti-colonial values in judging the nature of the Palestinian Problem.

The establishment of a cognitive linkage between the Palestinian Problem and other colonial problems became a source of support for the Palestinian cause. Naturally, this did not happen overnight. The first signs in the form of Assembly decisions appeared in the late 1960s when with small majorities the Palestinian Arabs were recognized as a people entitled to self-determination as guaranteed by the Decolonization Declaration. To begin with it was mostly countries closely associated with the Arabs and in the forefront of the anti-colonial struggle that lent their support. From this basis of the Palestinians gained access to a larger audience. Their efforts were directed towards achieving some degree of cognitive congruence between perceptions of southern Africa and Palestine.

In this chapter the mobilization process that changed the image of the Palestinian Problem held by the Assembly has been examined with very little attention given to the possible impact of interactions between mobilization at different levels. In the final chapter this interaction will be examined to see whether the mobilization process was of a linear nature or whether all levels interacted and fed upon each other.

Notes

1 For a distribution of presidents and Security Council seats up to 1959–1960 see respectively: Bailey, B. *The General Assembly of the United Nations; A study of Procedure and Practice* (Stevens and Sons Limited, London, 1960) Table IX on p. 54 and Hovet, T. *Bloc Politics in the United Nations* (Harvard University Press, Cambridge, 1960) p. 6.

2 Xydis, S. 'The General Assembly' in Barros, J. (ed.) *The United Nations: Past, Present and Future* (The Free Press, New York, 1972) p. 81.

3 For a discussion of the function and role of elected officers of the Assembly see Werners, S. *The Presiding Officers in the United Nations* (F. Bohn, Haarlem, 1967).

4 *Arab Report and Record* (1974: 499).

5 For a discussion of the origins and the politics flowing from the 'gentleman's agreement' see Goodwin, G. *Britain and the United Nations* (Oxford University Press, London, 1957) pp. 240–1 and Bailey (1960: 164–5).

6 Bailey (1960: 167).

7 The general pattern that emerged from the first election of non-permanent members to the Security Council was:

Latin America	2
Middle East	1
East Europe	1
West Europe	1
Commonwealth	1

Goodwin (1957: 40); Hovet (1960: 5). The inadequacy of these criteria in meeting Third Third World demands for better representation becomes quite evident from the fact that by 1965 it excluded 36 of the 117 United Nations' members from being eligible for elections. There were 11 Asian, 4 North African, 18 Francophone African and 3 other Africa countries which did not fit into any of the above geographical groupings.

8 UN Doc. S/PV 1859, 4 December 1975, p. 3. On the issue of PLO participation in the Security Council debates it is interesting to note the role of the president (who was the representative of the Soviet Union), in the adoption of a majority statement. He said it 'is the understanding of the majority of the Security Council that when it reconvenes on 12 January 1976 in accordance with paragraph (a) of resolution 381 (1975) the representatives of the Palestine Liberation Organization will be invited to participate in the debate' (UN Doc. S/PV 1856, 30 November 1975, p. 16). The significance of this statement in terms of prejudging a future meeting in a way favourable to the Third World position is made quite evident by West European representatives' statements critical of the decision. The UK representative's remark summarizes the Western European position that 'in accordance with the established procedures and rules of the Council the question of participation in any meetings of the Council is a matter which has to be decided at the time of those meetings themselves' (UN Doc. S/PV 1856, 30 November 1975, p. 41). For a report on the politics around this statement see 'Mandate of Golan Heights Force Renewed; PLO invitation to Mid-East Favored' *UN Monthly Chronicle*, no. 11 (December 1975).

9 Kaufmann, J. *United Nations Decision Making* (Sijthoff & Noordhoof, Alphen van der Rijn, 1980) pp. 90–2.

10 For a discussion of the participation of petitioners in the work of the General Assembly on decolonisation see, Zuijdwijk, T. *Petitioning the United Nations* (St. Martin's Press, New York, 1982) Chapter V.

11 UN Doc. A/6835, 20 September 1967.

12 UN. Doc. A/8086 and Add. 1, 2 October 1970.

13 Resolution 2621 (XXV), 12 October 1970.

14 Resolution 2874, 20 December 1971.

15 Zuijdwijk (1982: 213); UN Doc. A/C.4/744, 22 September 1972.

16 Resolution 3280 (XIX), 10 December 1974.

17 Twelve Latin Americans and 6 Africans joined the West Europeans in abstaining from

this crucial resolution which had received 61 votes in favour to 34 against, with France not participating (*General Assembly Official Records*, Annexes, 16th Session, vol. 3, pp. 3–4). For a discussion of the Algerian problem at the United Nations particularly in relation to African countries see Nweke, G. A. *Harmonization of African Foreign Policies, 1955–1975* (African Studies Center, Boston University, Boston, 1980) pp. 39–44.

18 Security Council Official Records, 22nd year, meeting 1382, 22 November 1967.

19 General Assembly Official Records, 23rd session, Special Political Committee, meeting 612, 11 November 1968.

20 'The Special Committee to Investigate Israeli Practices Affecting the Human Rights of the Population of the Occupied Territories' was established pursuant to Resolution 2443 (XIII) of 19 December 1968.

21 UN Doc., A/8089 October 1970. See *GAOR*, 25th Session, SPC meetings 727, pp. 744–51, December 1970 for a summary of the first report and the debate surrounding it.

22 The full debate and the decision can be found GAOR Twelfth Session, SPC 434th to 437th meetings, November 1965. Prior to November 1965 various Palestinian individuals had been invited to address the SPC. For an account of these invitations see Kirisci, K. 'Mobilization of Support for the Palestinian Cause', Ph.D. thesis, The City University, p. 335–6, note 36.

23 Travers, P. 'The Legal Effect of United Nations Action In Support of the Palestine Liberation Organization and the National Liberation Movements of Africa', *Harvard International Law Journal*, vol. 17 (Summer 1976), no. 3 p. 570.

24 UN Doc. S/PV 1856, 30 November 1975.

25 UN Doc. S/11893, December 1975. For a detailed study of the Security Council's decision see, Gross, L. 'Voting in the Security Council and the PLO" *American Journal of International Law*, vol. 70 (1976), no. 3.

26 UN Doc. S/PV 1859, 4 December 1975. Rule 37 of the Rules of Procedure of the Security Council states that: 'Any Member of the United Nations which is not a member of the Security Council may be invited, as a result of the decision of the Security Council, to participate, without vote, in the discussion of any question brought before the Security Council, when the Security Council considers that the interests of that Member are specially affected, or when a Member brings a matter to the attention of the Security Council in accordance with Article 35(1) of the Charter'.

27 UN Doc. A/8163, November 1970.

28 In the context of a discussion of the politics surrounding the participation of national liberation movements in the 1974 Diplomatic Conference on Humanitarian Law Baxter notes that 'peoples fighting against ... alien occupation' were Palestinians. Baxter, R. 'Humanitarian Law or Humanitarian Politics: The 1974 Diplomatic Conference on Humanitarian Law', *Harvard International Law Journal*, vol. 16 (1975), p. 12.

29 The Sixth Committee during the 27th Session was allocated an additional item concerning the prevention of international terrorism. However, a Saudi amendment to its title ensured an examination of the 'underlying causes' of terrorism (A/L.673, September 1972). This opened the way for various Arab and non-Arab delegations to link aspects of international terrorism to the situation prevailing in Palestine. For speeches including such points, see GAOR, 27th Session, Sixth Committee meetings 1311–1314, September 1972 and meetings 1355–1370, 1372 November 1972 and 1386–1390 in December 1972. Also speeches critical of attempts to describe the struggle of Palestinian and African peoples to achieve independence as terrorism were delivered. See for example the speeches of Oman, Zambia and Mauritania during the 1370th meeting of the Sixth Committee, November 1972 and the Chinese speech during the 1368th meeting.

30 Resolution 1514(XV), 14 December 1969.

31 For a short discussion of differing views on the legal status of Resolution 1514 see Bos, M. 'The Recognized Manifestations of International Law; A New Theory of "Sources"', *German Yearbook on International Law*, vol. 20, pp. 66–7.

32 Resolution 2649 (XXV), 30 November 1970.

33 *The Yearbook of the United Nations* 1970 p. 532. The vote was taken in response to an Israeli amendment to delete the word 'Palestine'. (A/C.3/L.1804, 4 November 1968).

34 The Afghani amendment to insert 'and the peoples under alien domination' was adopted by a vote of 65 in favour to 2 against, with 39 abstentions (A/L.622, 14 December 1970).
35 Resolution 2787 (XXVI) 6 December 1971 was adopted by a vote of 76 in favour to 10 against, with 33 abstentions. A series of amendments to ECOSOC Resolution 1592(L) inserted the Palestinian issue. However, this did not pass unchallenged. Barbados and Uganda tried to remove direct references to Palestine (A/C.3/L.1888, A/C.3/1889). However, these attempts were defeated by 47 in favour to 26 against, with 41 abstentions when the Committee voted on a Moroccan oral amendment reintroducing the references to Palestine (GAOR, 26th Session, Annexes, agenda item 55, pp. 3–5).
36 GAOR, 26th Session, SPC 801st meeting, 15 December 1971.
37 Ibid., and GAOR, 28th Session, Second Committee, 1580th meeting, 7 December 1973.
38 Resolution 3151 G, Burundi amendment A/9232/Add.1, paragraph 28 adopted by 63 in favour to 31 against with 27 abstentions (GAOR, 28th Session, annexes, agenda item 42, p. 10).
39 See *The Yearbook of the United Nations*, 1974 p. 133 and GAOR, 29th Session, Plenary 2320th meeting, 16 December 1974.
40 It should be noted that, during the 30th Session, an attempt to get Zionism declared as 'a form of racism and racial discrimination' did not go unchallenged. Firstly, Sierra Leone and Zambia proposed to defer the consideration of the matter to the next session. This is a practice usually employed with potentially embarrassing and contentious issues. Secondly, Ivory Coast and Liberia voted against the resolution with twelve African delegations abstaining. Although Resolution 3379 (XXX) of 10 November 1975 was adopted, the controversial nature of its content was evident in the distribution of votes: 72 in favour to 35 against with 32 abstentions (GAOR, 30th Session, Third Committee 2132–2134th meetings and Plenary 2400th meeting).
41 See pp. 6–7 and Tomeh, G. 'When the UN Dropped the Palestinian Question', *Journal of Palestine Studies*, vol. IV (1974 Autumn), no. 1.
42 A/AC.61/L.23/Rev.3, 8 December 1952. GAOR, 7th Session, SPC, 36th meeting.
43 A/SPC/L.116, 17 November 1965 failed by a vote of 34 in favour to 38 against, with 23 abstentions (GAOR, 20th Session, SPC, 459th meeting).
44 A/SPC/L.100 and Add.1, 21 November 1963. This draft resolution supported by 15 Third World countries was later withdrawn.
45 Lall, A. *The United Nations and the Middle East Crisis, 1967* (Columbia University Press, New York, 1968) pp. 128–68.
46 Ibid., p. 156.
47 Ibid., pp. 134–5.
48 For references to the Palestinian Arabs' right to self-determination (see GAOR, 18th Session, SPC, 398–416th meetings). Most Arab countries referred to the 'right of the Palestinians' without specifying the right to 'self-determination'. The refugees' right to return was frequently mentioned. Iraq was one of the few Arab countries to refer to the Palestinians' right to 'self-determination and national independence' (meetings 403 of 11 November and 405 of 12 November).
49 This was best captured by the foreign minister of Tunisia: 'Today, in spite of affirmations of support and sympathy, the horizon is clouded by the majority of nations represented here particularly by the four great Powers, none of which has ever called into question the actual existence of Israel as a State, whereas in our eyes it is the very existence of Israel which constitutes permanent aggression' (Lall, 1980: 181).
50 For the divisions among Arabs and the reluctance of the summit to accept PLO proposals put forward by Shukairy calling for 'a refusal to negotiate even indirectly with Israel, recognize even the pre-June 5 status-quo, or reach any settlement that may affect the Palestinian cause', see Quandt, W., Jabber, F. and Lesch, A. *The Politics of Palestinian Nationalism* (University of California Press, Berkeley, 1973) p. 185.
51 SCOR, 22nd year, 1373th meeting, 9 November 1967.
52 Speeches arguing that resistance was a natural reaction to occupation were made by the representatives of the Soviet Union and Hungary in August 1968 (SCOR, 23rd Year, 1434–1440th meetings, August 1968) again by the Soviet Union and Spain in March

1969 (SCOR, 24th Year, 1482–1485th meetings, March 1969); by France, Yugoslavia and the Soviet Union in February 1972 (SCOR, 27 Year, 1643–1644th, 1648–1650th meetings).

53 Examples of such arguments can be seen in the speeches of Guinea (SCOR, 27th Year, 1644th meeting, February 1972), India (SCOR, 28th Year, 1718th meeting, June 1973).

54 See speeches of France and the Soviet Union on the need to expand Resolution 242 (SCOR, 28th Year, 1723th–1724th meetings, June 1973 and 1735th meeting July 1973).

55 Draft Resolution S/10974, 26 July 1973.

56 *The Yearbook of the United Nations*, 1969, p. 235–7.

57 Ibid., p. 237.

58 UN Doc. A/L.652 and Add.1, 10 December 1971, A/L.652/Rev.1, 13 December 1971.

59 Below is a list of failed attempts at the Security Council to adopt resolutions recognizing the political rights of the Palestinians.

(1) S/10974, 26 July 1973, sponsored by Non-Aligned countries, referred to the 'rights and legitimate aspirations of the Palestinians', vetoed by the United States.

(2) S/11898, 8 December 1975, sponsored by Non-Aligned countries, referred to the Palestinians 'right to national independence and sovereignity in Palestine', vetoed by the United States with Costa Rica abstaining.

(3) S/11940, 26 January 1976, sponsored by Non-Aligned countries and Romania, referred to the Palestinians' 'right to establish a State in Palestine', vetoed by the United States, with Italy, Sweden and the United Kingdom abstaining.

(4) S/12119, 29 June 1976, sponsored by Non-Aligned countries, referred to the Palestinians 'right to national independence and sovereignity in Palestine', vetoed by the United States, with France, Italy, Sweden and the United Kingdom abstaining.

(5) S/13514, 24 August 1979, sponsored by Senegal, content same as above; not submitted to a vote.

(6) S/13911, 28 April 1980, sponsored by Tunisia, referred to the Palestinians' 'right to establish an independent State', vetoed by the United States, with France, Norway, Portugal and the United Kingdom abstaining.

60 SCOR, 30th year, 11–26 January, meetings 1870–1879. A United Kingdom amendment to draft resolution S/11940 drawing attention to Resolution 242 and 338 was rejected by a vote of 4 in favour to 2 against with 9 abstentions.

61 SCOR, 30th year, 31 March–9 April, 29 and 30 April, meetings 2204–2208, 2219, 2220.

62 Tunisian draft resolution S/13911, 28 April 1980.

63 UN Doc. A/ES-7/L.1/Rev.1, 29 July 1980.

64 The initiative for the inclusion of the 'Question of Palestine' had come from Arafat during the Arab summit in October 1974 when the Arab Ministers had agreed to take up the issue of placing the item on the Assembly's agenda (see Silverburg, R. 'The Palestine Liberation Organisation in the United Nations: Implications for International Law and Relations', *Israeli Law Review* vol. 12 (1977), no. 3, p. 372). Also see 'Report on Rabat Arab Summit Secret Sessions' in Yodfat, A. and Ornan-Ohanna, Y. *PLO Strategy and Tactics* (Croom Helm, London, 1981) pp. 176–9.

65 The initiative in this case had also come from Arafat and had the initial objection of Egypt 'on two accounts; first, the lack of precedent on this matter; second, it (would) get the Arab delegations into a procedural wrangle with those opposed to it from Western and some Latin American countries'. (Correspondence with a Palestinian representative of a Gulf state United Nations' delegation.)

66 Resolution 3237 (XXIX), 22 November 1974.

67 See Appendix V for a list of specialised agencies which have maintained contacts with the PLO and have allowed the PLO to participate in their work as an observer. The exceptions were the International Monetary Fund, the World Bank and the GATT.

68 Similar points are also made by Freudenschuss, H. 'Legal and Political Aspects of the Recognition of National Liberation Movements' *Millenium: Journal of International Studies*, vol. 11, no. 2 and Fisher, R. 'Following in Another's Footsteps: The Acquisition of International Legal Standing by the Palestine Liberation Organization', *Syracuse Journal of International Law Commerce*, vol. 3 (Spring 1975), p. 238.

69 Sharif, R. 'The United Nations and Palestinian Rights, 1974–1979', *Journal of Palestine Studies*, vol. 9 (Autumn 1979), no. 1, p. 23.
70 Sharif (1979: 39).
71 The strong ties of Latin Americans were evidenced in their tendency to maintain their embassies in Jerusalem. Bolivia, Chile, Colombia, Costa Rica, the Dominican Republic, Ecuador, El Salvador, Haiti, Guatemala, Panama, Uruguay, Venezuela kept their embassies in Jerusalem until the Security Council adopted Resolution 476, 20 August 1980, asking members to move their embassies from Jerusalem. All the above together with only the Netherlands, complied with this decision (S/14248, 11 November 1980).

9 Conclusion

Introduction

So far, in the second part of this book the mobilization process aimed at changing governmental attitudes towards the Palestinian Problem and the aggregation of support associated with this process has been examined. This was done by applying the mobilization process model, developed in chapter three, to the Palestinian, the regional and the United Nations' levels of analysis. During this analysis neither the interaction between individual levels of mobilization nor the feedback processes within each level were studied in detail. It is the main purpose of this concluding chapter to examine these two aspects of the mobilization process. Furthermore, the chapter will also reconsider certain parts of the mobilization model in the light of insights obtained from its application to the Palestinian case. This will be done in an effort to achieve a better conceptualization of how issues are raised on the political agenda. Finally, to complete the general picture of how an item reaches the global political agenda the need to expand the analysis beyond governmental actors will be noted.

Interactive nature of the growth of support

One striking conclusion that emerges from the application of the mobilization process model to the Palestinian case is that the aggregation of support across the different levels of analysis was far from uniform and hierarchical. During the earlier stages of this research, it was expected that the mobilization of support for the Palestinian cause would grow in a multi step manner, i.e. from one level of analysis to another. As depicted in Figure 9.1 it was assumed that the Palestinian community would be the first group to become mobilized, followed by the Arabs

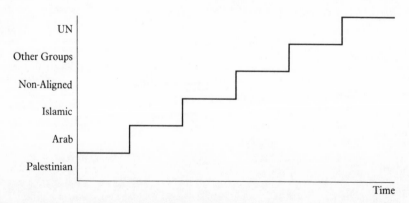

Figure 9.1. Growth of support across different levels represented as multi step-function

then those groups such as the Islamic world, the Non-Aligned and the Third World at large. This, it was thought, would continue until adequate global support was mobilized to reflect itself at the United Nations' level.

The analysis emerging from the preceding chapters has, however, to a large extent undermined this line of thought. Instead, a more complex and fluid picture of the mobilization process has emerged, one that is rather difficult to represent by a multi step-function aggregation of support and one where the different levels appear to interact with each other in a dynamic manner. That is, expressions of support at both a lower level as well as at a higher level appear to influence each other. It is possible to group these interactions into three. Those that occur:

(i) from a lower level to a higher one,
(ii) between regional levels,
(iii) from a higher level to a lower one.

From a lower level to a higher one

The best example of a flow of support from a lower level to a higher one is represented by the aggregation of votes to change policy in an international organization. This process is quite evident in the workings of the General Assembly. In organizations where no votes are taken this process usually takes the form of consensus building in favour of a change in attitudes as reflected in the decision-making processes of the OAU and the Non-Aligned Movement.

The second type of interaction occurs when an actor belonging to a lower level of analysis, such as the PLO, is capable of demonstrating to an actor belonging to higher level of analysis, such as an Arab government or a regional political grouping, that it is the recipient of a high level of Palestinian support, leading to this actor expressing support in favour of the PLO and/or the Palestinian cause. An example of such a process is the recognition of the PLO by the Non-Aligned as 'the sole representative of the Palestinian people' at their Algiers summit in September 1973. This expression of support for the PLO accompanied by the granting of observer status seems to have been significantly influenced by the growing strength of the PLO among the Palestinians which was conspicuously expressed during demonstrations precipitated by the deaths of three prominent PLO officials in April 1973, in Beirut. A more vivid example of this type of interaction was the Egyptian call, in May 1976, to grant the PLO full membership of the Arab League in the wake of the West Bank mayoral elections in April of that year whose results had been generally interpreted as an expression of support for the PLO.[1]

Interaction between regional levels

It is interesting to note that this Arab League meeting appears, at the same time, to have been influenced by an earlier expression of support coming from another regional group. The influence that the promotion of the PLO, to the status of a full participant at the Non-Aligned foreign ministers' meeting in Lima in August 1975, had on this Arab League decision constitutes an example of the second type of interaction that occurs between two groupings at the regional level.

It is possible to prepare a long list of examples to illustrate such a process. Here we shall limit ourself to a few significant and more apparent ones. In chapter six, it was mentioned that the Non-Aligned Movement played an important role in encouraging wide Latin American support for the Palestinian cause and the PLO. This type of interaction is also evident between Northern regional groupings and countries. For example, it seems Soviet support and commitment to the Palestinian cause played a central role in influencing the American administration to recognize, in June 1973, that a settlement in the Middle East 'should take into due account the legitimate interests of the Palestinian people'.[2] Similarly, according to Golan, the Soviet Union actually appears to have claimed credit in 1977 for a further favourable shift in the position of the United States towards the Palestinians.[3]

The EC's readiness, as expressed in the Venice Declaration of June 1980, to see the PLO associated with any negotiations towards the solution of the Palestinian Problem appears to have been influenced by the decisions of the Arab League. This shift in the EC's position was also affected by the growing prestige of the PLO as well as by pro-Palestinian developments at the United Nations. This last type of interaction between expressions of support at the United Nations and the mobilization of West European support brings us to the final type of interaction.

From a higher to a lower level

The recognition and support that the PLO and the Palestinian cause has received at the United Nations has influenced mobilization processes at lower levels. Primarily, it increased the standing of the PLO among the Palestinian community. Frangi notes that 'Yasser Arafat's speech to the United Nations ... led to a series of sympathy demonstrations for the PLO and protests against Israeli occupation' and that growing international recognition accorded to the PLO had a direct impact on the results of the 1976 mayoral elections in the West Bank.[4]

Probably the most significant aspect of the role of the United Nations in the mobilization of support is that in the long run it legitimizes certain issue-positions at the expense of others. Jeane Kirkpatrick, president Reagan's ex-envoy to the United Nations, also makes this point. 'The cumulative impact of decisions of the U.N. bodies influence opinions all over the world about what is legitimate, what is acceptable.'[5]

Fisher applies this argument to the role that international recognition of the national liberation movements has had when he notes that such recognition,

allows a people officially to become part of the international decision-making process and gives a sense of illegitimacy to agreements reached without them. It enhances the prestige of their representative entity ... Finally, recognition puts pressure upon states which previously had withheld from dealing with that entity, to reconsider their positions.'[6]

To support his argument Fisher offers the case of the Indian government which, in January 1975, less than two months after the adoption of Resolutions 3236 (XIX) and 3237 (XIX) responded to a PLO request, reportedly made 'some time back', and recognized the PLO.[7] It is also interesting to note that the adoption of Resolution 3210 (XIX), on 14 October 1974, inviting Arafat to address the Assembly, preceded the Arab summit decision to recognize the PLO as 'the sole and legitimate representative of the Palestinian people' by less than two weeks.

Another less spectacular but nevertheless important example of the influence that developments at the United Nations can have on the aggregation of support concerns the United States. American perceptions of the nature of the Palestinian Problem and its salience to the settlement of the Middle East conflict may well have been influenced by the United Nations. Both senator Percy, once a member of the American delegation in 1974 and the American envoy to the UN, Yost, in 1975 recognized the need to take into account 'the legitimate concerns and aspirations of the Palestinians.' This change of attitude away from one that was uncritically supportive of Israel is attributed by Lilienthal, to the impact that the United Nations has had on their thinking.[8] Similarly, to a large extent it was again the necessity of fulfilling the expected role of the president of the Security Council that induced Young, another American representative to the UN, to have talks with the PLO observer there.[9]

But probably the most important impact the United Nations had on the United States in general, was the way in which the invitation to Arafat to address the General Assembly attracted high media attention. This opened up a debate on the Palestinian question and put the problem squarely on the public agenda in a way that otherwise might have not happened. It is perhaps not surprising that it was in the aftermath of this period that the first major American study of the Palestinian Problem, which came to play an important role in the formation of American governmental attitudes, was prepared by a prestigious institute with close ties to successive administrations.[10]

This type of interaction is not limited to the ones between the United Nations and lower levels. It can also occur between regional and governmental levels. An example is the way in which the Arab League influenced the position of Jordan on the question of the PLO's status in relation to the Palestinians residing in the West Bank. It is possible to point to a similar process between the EC and some EC members such as Denmark, the Netherlands and Belgium. These countries that had traditionally held pro-Israeli positions changed their perceptions of the Palestinian Question as a result of EC influence. The same process is evident in the relationship between the OAU and some conservative African governments such as Gabon, Ivory Coast and Liberia.

So far, we have tried to demonstrate how support for the Palestinian cause and the PLO at one particular level has had an impact on the mobilization process at another level. Although the examples above are not exhaustive they should be enough to demonstrate the interactive nature of the mobilization of support for the Palestinian cause. Before we proceed to look at the dynamic nature of the mobilization arising from 'positive feedback' processes at each level, there remains one other aspect of the interactive process that needs to be examined.

Convergence of issue-positions

Another weakness in depicting the aggregation of support as a multi step-function is that it naturally fails to account for the moderating effect that the above inter-active process has on the demands put forward by the initiators. To assume that support is simply either lent or withheld from initiators' demands that remain unchanged throughout the mobilization process is too simplistic. In chapter three, it was mentioned that those groups trying either to put a new item on a political agenda or modify the definition of an existing item will frequently find themselves moderating their demands in an attempt to broaden their basis of support. This process is quite evident in the case of the Palestinian Problem at all levels of analysis.

That is, the PLO as the main initiator has had to modify its stance on a number of crucial issues. Two such issues have arisen from the territorial aspects of an eventual settlement of the Palestinian Problem and the methods to be followed in order to achieve this settlement. The position held by the PLO in the 1960s had been one that stressed the unity of Palestine and the primacy of armed struggle to achieve it. This position began to change in the early 1970s as the PLO interacted with actors from all the three levels in its efforts to gain support. These were mostly actors that favoured a solution to the Palestinian Problem that did not jeopardise the existence of Israel within some recognized boundaries.

It is important to point out that most of these actors in the 1960s had once seen the Palestinian question as a by-product of the Arab–Israeli Conflict and treated it as a refugee problem that basically needed humanitarian and technical solutions. Yet by the 1970s many of these actors had reconsidered their perceptions of the Palestinian Problem and had demonstrated a tendency to support the political rights of the Palestinian people. This seems to point towards a situation whereby as a result of the mobilization process the PLO and the prospective supporters of the Palestinian cause have converged towards a relatively common new issue position. Below we shall offer examples from each level to illustrate this particular dimension of the interactive aspect of the mobilization process.

Convergence on issue-positions

Convergence at the communal level

The initial advocacy and use of armed struggle by various Palestinian guerrilla groups had played an important role in putting the Palestinian Problem on the political agenda and in awakening a Palestinian national consciousness. However, it appears that the gradual acceptance by the PLO of the idea of a Palestinian state alongside Israel played a crucial role in expanding its basis of support within the Palestinian community. The acceptance of this idea by the PLO constitutes an interesting example of the interaction between the PLO and other actors from the Palestinian community supportive of that idea. The process appears to have led to a compromise on the part of the PLO in return for broader Palestinian support.

It is rather difficult to determine where the idea of an 'independent national authority' or a 'mini-state' first originated. But, by the early 1970s, the debate concerning the possibility of replacing the idea of a 'secular democratic state' through armed struggle with the idea of a 'mini-state' as the eventual goal of the PLO had already gathered some momentum. It seems that at the Palestinian community level the idea first began to gain some ground in the West Bank. This, for example, is evident in the support lent to the idea of a 'mini-state' by the mayor of Hebron in July 1973 followed by an official endoresment of it by the Palestinian National Front soon after the October 1973 Arab–Israeli war.[11]

The earlier categorical rejections of this idea in PLO circles began to change in the face of these developments. In December 1973[12] the PDFLP became the first guerrilla group within the PLO to adopt the idea, followed by Al-Fatah and Saiqa[13] and eventually by the Palestinian National Council in June 1974. As Coban notes, there was no doubt that the PNF 'had made some contribution to the Twelfth PNC's decision, in June/July 1974, to pursue a political option based on the call for establishing a 'Palestinian national authority' on any parts of Palestine evacuated by Israel.'[14]

It was not just inputs eminating from the West Bank that brought about a moderation in the policies of the PLO. Similar clear demands were being made from both Arab countries and the Soviet Union. It is possible to argue that the PLO was able to receive greater support from the Arab League and the Soviets as a result of the compromise arising from its readiness to recognize the possibility of achieving the establishment of a 'mini-state' through diplomatic means. Again the mobilization process brought the participants closer to each other than they had been previously.

Convergence at the regional levels

In the aftermath of the June 1967 Arab–Israeli war, Arab governments agreed in September 1967 to a policy of 'no negotiation and no recognition' of Israel. Nevertheless, they were reluctant to include Shukairy's more dramatic demands that would have amounted to a commitment to liquidate Israel.[15] This reluctance and hence the gap between the PLO and some Arab governments had become more evident when Egypt and Jordan accepted Resolution 242 in November 1967 joined by Syria in March 1972. The preparedness of Arab governments to enter peace negotiations became real in July 1970 when first Egypt then Jordan accepted the Rogers Plan announced in June 1970 and also later cooperated with Jarring's and the OAU mediation missions to the Middle East. Throughout this period fundamental differences remained between the PLO and these Arab governments.

This situation began to change after the October 1973 war. Resolution 338, of 22 October 1973, had been accepted by Egypt and Israel and preparations towards the convening of a peace conference in Geneva had also gained the support of the Arab summit in Algiers in November 1973. From then on, the PLO came under increasing pressure to participate in peace negotiations as well as to accept the idea of a 'mini-state'. The Egyptians had already circulated these ideas in June 1973 but had then met the opposition of the PLO.[16] Although the PLO continued to reject similar efforts well into 1974 the combined pressure eminating from the West Bank and the major Arab governments coupled with the effect of growing international recognition of the PLO as the 'sole representative of the Palestinians' began to make inroads into PLO thinking on these matters. A number of scholars have attributed the growing Arab governmental support for the PLO and the eventual withdrawal of Jordanian objections to the status of the PLO, as expressed in the decisions of the Arab summit in Rabat in October 1974, to the readiness of the PLO to moderate its policies.[17]

The Soviet Union also appears to have put effective demands on the PLO for moderation and then extended greater support as a consequence of the change in the PLO's overall approach. Soviet pressure on the PLO to show a willingness to participate in peace talks and to aim for a 'mini-state' alongside Israel took a conspicuous form during a visit of a PLO delegation to Moscow in November 1973.[18] According to Golan, the Soviet Union seems to have used its recognition of the PLO and the opening of a PLO office in Moscow as a lever.[19] This is supported to some extent by the fact that there was a marked increase in Soviet support for the PLO when Arafat was received in Moscow by governmental officials immediately after the Twelfth PNC. Previously, PLO delegations had been invited to Moscow in an 'unofficial capacity' by the Soviet Afro-Asian Committee.[20] It was also during this vist that the Soviets announced an agreement for the opening of a PLO office in Moscow.[21]

It is possible to offer a much longer list of examples that point towards a growing convergence between positions held by the PLO and actors from various regions culminating in a growth of support for the Palestinian cause. In this respect, 1977 was a particularly interesting year. It was marked by the 13th PNC decision to redefine the rather ambiguous term of 'independent national authority' to an 'independent state'.[22] The Soviet Union seems to have played a role in this by its repeated efforts to bring the PLO to make this change.[23] This change was formalized in March 1977 during the 13th PNC session when the idea of the establishment of an independent Palestinian state by means of a political settlement was endorsed.[24] One concrete expression of Soviet support resulting from this development was an invitation to Arafat to visit Moscow in April when he also got to meet Brezhnev for the first time.[25]

Many West European governments were also influenced by the PLO's growing readiness to compromise and moderate its policies and demands. They moved closer to the PLO and lent greater support to the Palestinian cause during this period. Prior to the Twelfth PNC meeting the French foreign minister actually held talks with PNC leaders and promised support for a homeland in return for a PLO commitment to a political solution.[26] After the PNC meeting and Kaddoumi's declaration expressing a readiness to participate in the Geneva peace talks, increasing contacts between the PLO and Western European governments took place. These contacts increased the prestige of the PLO but also encouraged it to adopt conciliatory measures.

For example, in May 1977, Arafat met the Austrian chancellor Kreisky while Kaddoumi met the French foreign minister, expressing the possibility of accepting Resolution 242 if some amendments were introduced.[27] This moderation also made it possible for the PLO to participate in the Euro-Arab dialogue as a part of the Arab delegation. Even the American position appears to have been influenced by these developments. Various congressmen and senators visited Arafat in the Middle East while Carter, throughout 1977, made statements relatively favourable to the Palestinian cause compared to earlier ones. Finally, in October 1977, in a American-Soviet statement, the American government was prepared to take another step and recognize the legitimate 'rights' rather than the 'aspirations' of the Palestinians and the need to include representatives of the Palestinian people in a renewed Geneva conference.

Convergence at the United Nations level

Similar forces were also evident at the United Nations level. It would be difficult to imagine that Arafat could have addressed the General Assembly if the PLO had continued to maintain its earlier goal of liquidating Israel through armed struggle. Furthermore, the PLO's participation in the work of the United Nations appears to have had a quite an impact on its policies. This participation has meant that Palestinian representatives have become exposed to an institution and a socialization process that are inherently biased in favour of negotiation and conciliation.

The consequence of this is evident in the way in which the PLO at the Security Council has found itself participating in efforts for the adoption of draft resolutions recognizing the Palestinian people's right to self-determination together with the provisions of Resolution 242. The General Assembly too has had its own impact on the PLO. It has extended growing support for the Palestinian cause but at the same time it has obliged the PLO to articulate its objectives and the means to achieve than in a way compatible with the Assembly's values. This became particularly evident after the establishment of the Committee on the Exercise of the Inalienable Rights of the Palestinian People in 1975.

The committee, which was charged with the duty to consider and recommend to the General Assembly a programme for the implementation of the rights of the Palestinian people, played a crucial role in getting the PLO to agree and contribute towards the drawing up and the eventual adoption of a precisely formulated plan. This plan provided for the evacuation of the Israeli occupied areas followed by United Nations supervision until the establishment of a Palestinian government. Hence as O.Carre notes, 'the more the Palestinian cause is accepted in the United Nations, the more precise, and consequently moderate, does the Palestinian' demands become'.[28]

Figure 9.2 is an attempt to illustrate this convergence in issue positions held by the PLO and selected regional groupings. The figure represents a field of changing issue positions projected from two axes. The vertical axis (AB) represents different definitions of the Palestinian Problem accompanied by associated solutions. At one end of the axis (A) the problem is defined as a refugee problem, a by-product of the Arab–Israeli war, and humanitarian solutions are advocated within an overall solution of the Arab-Israeli Conflict. The other end of the axis (B) defines the problem as political and sees its solution in the creation of a 'secular-democtratic' Palestinian state. The horizontal axis, on the other hand, represents the types of methods advocated to achieve the envisaged solutions. It represents a continuum ranging from the advocation of diplomatic means (C) to armed struggle (D).

Various intermediary positions on both axes can be plotted. For example, the idea of a 'mini-state' could be placed towards the centre on the AB axis. Similarly, the advocation of multi-lateral diplomacy rather than direct negotiations could be placed in a similar position on the CD axis. The position of each actor on the field can then be plotted by projecting its place on each axis to a point on the field where they meet. The exercise can be repeated at specific intervals to see changes that are actually occurring. Figure 9.2 depicts the change that has occurred in the position

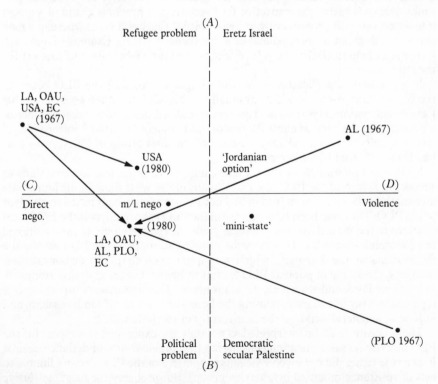

Figure 9.2. Convergence of issue positions on the Palestinian Question

of selected actors in respect to positions represented on both axes. Visually it displays the convergence that has taken place from positions all over the field towards positions in the middle of the bottom left quadrant.

So far, we have seen how the PLO, in its efforts to mobilize support for its demands, has had to respond to pressures from all levels to adopt more realistic goals and policies. One major consequence has been that the Palestinian cause, once defined by the PLO as the armed struggle to achieve a 'secular democratic state' in the whole of Palestine, has been redefined as the establishment of a 'mini-Palestinian state' in parts of Palestine evacuated by Israel. It is to this Palestinian cause that the overwhelming majority of world governments have lent their support.

Dynamic nature of the growth of support; the role of feedback processes

The interactive aspect of the mobilization process, which we examined earlier on, demonstrated the way different levels influenced each other. Consideration of the dynamic aspect of the mobilization process is intended to capture the feedback through which an already existing level of support facilitates further support at the same level. This growth can be in the form of an expansion of the domain of the support and/or an intensification of the commitment to that support. Here the assumption is that an actor trying to expand its basis of support at a particular level will benefit from support that has already been mobilized. Naturally, the greater the level of existing support the greater the urgency for others to join ranks. Hence it seems the impact of feedback from a previous round of support into a new one will progressively increase until it reaches a point where one may begin to talk about a 'snowballing' or a 'bandwagon effect'. Examples from each level might help to clarify the role of feedback in the mobilization of support for the Palestinian cause.

It was among the Palestinians in the refugee camps that the PLO began to receive its first support, which gradually expanded to other sections of the Palestinian community at large. This was evidenced in the increasing number of enrolments in the various guerrilla groups, particularly Al-Fatah. Violence played a central role in raising the consciousness of this first group of Palestinians that had been displaced by earlier wars.

While the Palestinians of the refugee camps were beginning to show signs of support in favour of the PLO, the Palestinians of the West Bank in the immediate aftermath of the civil war in Jordan had not yet completely committed themselves to the PLO. They had been reluctant to follow PLO calls to boycott the 1972 local elections in the West Bank which basically saw the reinstatement of the traditional pro-Jordanian leadership. However, the growing strength of the PLO among the Palestinians in the Lebanon, which was quite evident in the demonstrations following the killing of popular PLO leaders in Beirut, triggered similar responses in the West Bank and elsewhere. As Amos notes: 'This nationalist outpouring was repeated in May in a march opposing the Israeli military parade in Jerusalem, and in June in a general strike on the anniversary of the June war.'[29]

These events could be interpreted as not only the expression of support for the PLO but also its intensification considering that previous acts of defiance against Israeli rule either did not involve slogans supportive of the PLO or were limited to acts of resistance mounted by guerrilla groups. But probably the most conclusive example of an intensified support for the PLO, at least partially attributable to a feedback from earlier levels of Palestinian support, was provided by the results of the 1976 West Bank local elections. It was on this occassion that the West Bank chose to elect mayors closely associated with the PLO and endorsed the desire to see the PLO, even though indirectly, involved in the administrative aspects of their day-to-day lives.

The last group of Palestinians to be mobilized were those who live within Israel. It is with regard to these Palestinians that growing support for the PLO elsewhere in the Palestinian community appears to have been an essential prerequisite for their mobilization. The Palestinians in Israel remained under the influence of a traditional leadership until the early 1970s. From 1973 onwards they became increasingly pro-PLO. This is evident in their growing tendency during Israeli elections to vote in favour of political parties that either recognized the PLO or were supportive of the Palestinian cause. It is in this context that one can argue that growing support from previous rounds has fed back into a following round helping to expand its domain and range.

At the Arab regional level, consideration of the effect of positive feedback from Arab governmental support for the PLO at the Arab summit in Algiers in 1973 to the one at Rabat in 1974 provides a more complete picture of the change in the nature and quality of this support from one summit to the other. The impact of feedback on this change is particularly evident in the case of the change in Jordan's position towards the PLO. The role of the already existing support for the PLO among the Arab governments in influencing Jordan's position on the PLO's status is to some extent implicitly acknowledged in a statement made by King Hussein that:

we shall also respect the collective Arab will if it is the wish of the Arab countries and their leaders to create a new situation in which the Palestine Liberation Organization is made fully responsible for discussing, striving and working for the recovery of the occupied Arab territories, including the West Bank and Jerusalem, and the recovery of Palestinian rights . . . We shall . . . regard it [such a decision] as absolving us of our reponsibilities.[30]

Subsequently at Rabat, Jordan withdrew its objection to the PLO being the 'sole representative of the Palestinian people'.

It is interesting to note that at the Rabat summit support for the PLO not only expanded with the inclusion of Jordan but also grew in intensity. During the previous Arab summit the decision to recognize the PLO as 'the sole representative of the Palestinian people' had been a secret one. At Rabat this recognition was included in a public declaration and was also strengthened by the addition of the word 'legitimate' to the provisions determining the status of the PLO.

It is probably only at the UN level that one can begin to ponder some possibilities for developing a formal model, composed of a set of equations representing each session, that could capture the feedback from one session to another. However, in this case, too, it would be very difficult to separate the effect that support from other levels may have on the UN (which sometimes becomes as evident as the actual citing of decisions of other regional organizations). Nevertheless, at this level it is easier to find a wide range of examples illustrating the dynamic nature of the mobilization of support from one round to another, influencing both the range and the intensity of fresh support. Some of the evidence for this is actually evident in the wording of resolutions as well as in the speeches of delegations.

For example, when it granted the PLO the status of permanent observer Resolution 3237 (XIX) cited the previous UN decisions inviting the PLO to participate in the work of certain conferences held earlier in that year. Similarly, the procedural decision of the Security Council in November 1975 to invite the PLO to participate in its work, with privileges similar to ones accorded to member states being invited under rule 37 of the Rules of Procedure of the Council, was influenced by the support expressed for the PLO in the previous decisions of the General Assembly. This was quite evident in some of the speeches made during the procedural debate.

The evidence for the impact of a feedback process becomes more noticeable when a delegation actually acknowledges, in a speech, the role of the position of other delegations. For example, the United Kingdom delegation had voted against allowing the PLO to participate in the work of the Security Council in December 1975. However they abstained when the matter next came up at the Security Council meeting in January 1976. On this occasion their representative noted that their earlier position was not shared by the majority hence 'they did not think it right to press . . . objections to the point of voting against the proposal.'[31]

Furthermore, it seems it would not be too unrealistic to suggest that the PLO and its allies will, in their attempts to persuade potential supporters, point out the already existing level of support during the lobbying that precedes most debates and votes at the UN. Unfortunately, UN documentation does not provide any information about this process. But according to a Palestinian diplomat it appears that those Non-Aligned countries that had been reluctant to support Resolution 3237 on legal grounds found themselves revising their position in the face of the sponsors' arguments pointing out the already existing support for it.[32]

Even more interesting is the General Assembly where there has been a steady growth in the number of countries voting in favour of resolutions supportive of Palestinian political rights. This growth in support together with the usage of stronger language in the wording of resolutions seems to be indicative of a positive feedback mechanism that lends greater legitimacy to the Palestinian cause and to the PLO's representative status over the years.

The interactive and dynamic aspects of the aggregation of support between various levels were introduced to enhance the analysis emerging from the application of the mobilization process model to each level offered in the previous chapters. The convergence of issue-positions held by various actors, including the PLO, was developed to demonstrate an aspect of the mobilization process that has culminated in the growth of support for the Palestinian cause going hand-in-hand with a redefinition of the objectives of the PLO along lines more acceptable to most governments. It will be the purpose of the following section to reconsider certain aspects of the core of the mobilization process model.

Reconsidering the mobilization process model

When preparing the mobilization process model we began with Mansbach and Vasquez's definition of politics as the raising of and the authoritative resolution of issues. Of particular interest to our research was their and Cobb and Elder's contributions to the understanding of how actors bring issues of high salience to the forefront of a political agenda. We noted that Mansbach and Vasquez identified two sets of factors as crucial determinants of an agenda-setting process. They were 'the nature and variety of access routes' available to actors who want to put an issue on the agenda and 'the salience of an issue to key actors' in the 'system of interest'.

In our model these two sets of factors constituted the basis for two of the three central variables called 'accessibility' and 'cognitive linkage'. In the light of the contribution made by the mobilization theory to the study of the aggregation of support for social protest movements these two variables were supplemented by a variable called 'conducive environment'. The purpose of this section is to strengthen the core of the mobilization process model by re-examining the nature of this variable and also its relationship to the other two variables.

In someways it is possible to argue that without even having to go into the literature on mobilization theory, in Mansbach and Vasquez one can find a partial basis for the concept of a 'conducive environment'. This is evident in their argument which makes allowance for the fact that some issues 'never reach the global agenda because those who are satisfied resist their inclusion'.[33] They argue that 'the capacity of elites to keep items off an agenda is primarily a function of the nature of formal and informal access points, a structural variable'.[34] In such a situation it becomes rather difficult to talk of a 'conducive environment' for raising new issues by actors who lack access to the agenda. This structural variable, which Mansbach and Vasquez do not treat separately, constitutes a major aspect of the concept of a 'conducive environment'.

Hence, it seems certain structural conditions need to be present before mobilization at any level can start. Those structural conditions can be determined by the presence or absence of certain types of actors who have a say over the composition of a political agenda, as well as the existence or absence of communication networks between these actors and the initiator. For example, when our system of interest is centred around the UN, a change in the structure of the organization precipitated by the growth of Third World membership will make the promotion of certain outputs more likely than before. Similarly, at the Palestinian level the emergence of a Palestinian resistance movement was a necessary structural change to start the mobilization of support for the Palestinian cause. It opened up, for example, the way for using violence as an access route to raise the salience of the Palestinian Problem and also to attract the attention of the Palestinian community to their approach.

There is another dimension to the concept of a 'conducive environment' beside structural matters that needs to be taken into account. This concerns the nature of processes that are dominant in the 'system of interest'. It is these processes that will determine what kind of issues stand a better chance of being recognized and admitted to a political agenda. These cognitive processes will often be dominated by a 'belief system' which will condition how a problem is perceived and how it is treated by the participants.

For example since the adoption of Resolution 1514 at the UN attitudes towards colonialism and related issues have dramatically changed. The development of a new 'belief system' with its separate values, norms and expectations based on principles enunciated in this resolution generated a different set of criteria for determining the salience of an issue to the United Nations and the acceptability of various issue positions compared those dominating the UN prior to 1960. This process meant that decolonization was separated from processes that used to treat it within Cold War thinking. It also enabled issues such as apartheid to be treated as problems of international concern and, hence, not subject to the 'domestic jurisdiction' principle. At the Palestinian level events of high salience to the Palestinian community such as the Algerian and Vietnamese wars of liberation provided the basis for ideas advocating a Palestinian national struggle to develop and gain ground. This occurred against the prevailing wisdom which stressed Arab unity as the only means to liberating Palestine.

In the light of the above discussion, a 'conducive environment' for the actor trying to put items on the global political agenda can then be seen as the product of changes in the structure and processes characterising our 'system of interest' making the promotion of certain outcomes more likely at the systemic as well as the sub-systemic level.[35] The chances for a mobilization process to begin depend on the existence of such an 'environment'; the absence of a 'conducive environment' constitutes an obstacle for the mobilization process to commence. Yet the existence of a 'conducive environment' does not necessarily culminate in an immediate expression of support within the 'system of interest'. The mobilization of support will only commence when the central actor, the initiator, begins to utilize access routes that become potentially available to it, as a result of earlier structural changes, and to exploit existing thought processes to articulate and legitimize its issue-position.

It is in this light that 'accessibility' and 'cognitive linkages' have to be seen. 'Accessibility' becomes the variable that accounts for the exploitation of favourable structural features of a 'conducive environment' by an initiator to promote its cause. 'Cognitive linkage' on the other hand accounts for the perceptual similarities drawn between existing issues supported by a recognized belief system and the problem of concern to an initiator. The major purpose behind these linkages is to alter other actors' perceptions of the problem in such a way as to result in the extension of their support to the new issue.

Some limitations of this study

The purpose of this research was to study how the PLO raised the Palestinian issue to the global agenda and mobilized support for the Palestinian cause across the communal, regional and global levels of analysis. At the communal level we examined how the PLO gained the support of the Palestinian community in favour of the Palestinian cause as defined by the decisions of the PNC. At the regional and global levels the mobilization process model was employed with a view to understanding how the PLO came to modify world governmental perceptions of the nature of the Palestinian Problem and their attitudes towards the Palestinian cause.

One major limitation of this study is that throughout this analysis all actors, governments and the PLO alike, were treated as though they were unified. This should not be seen as the weakening of an earlier determination, as expressed in chapter two, to base this analysis on a paradigm that did not recognize the Realist assumption. Instead, it should be seen as the only practical solution to dealing with the decisions of more than one hundred governments. Hence, it was practical rather than theoretical considerations that culminated in the black-boxing of governmental decision-making processes. This, naturally, gives the impression that governmental decisions were straightforward coherent responses to PLO demands and also that these decisions were actually representative of the country as a whole. This is basically the consequence of having chosen a low level of resolution for the analysis.

This level of resolution, however, is a rather crude and incomplete representation of the real world. The views of governments have also been influenced by the activites of certain non-governmental actors such as trade unions, student groups, political parties and various pressure groups for whom the Palestinian issue became highly salient. Some of these actors who became supportive of the Palestinian cause went as far as developing direct relations with the PLO; such actors became active participants in efforts for the development of attitudes supportive of the Palestinian cause at various levels. Naturally, to develop a complete picture of the influence that non-governmental actors have had on governmental attitude formation one also has to assess the impact of such actors supportive of the Palestinian cause against those who have worked to prevent any changes to the status-quo.

Beside the influence that various domestic groups can have on the decision of a government there is also the need to take into consideration the role that different parts of a government can have on an eventual outcome. It is not unusual that differences arise between positions taken by the government and, for example, the ministry of foreign affairs of a country. Such a situation it seems would call for the treatment of a ministry of foreign affairs as a separate and important actor who also brings considerable influence to bear upon the eventual outcome as well as the impact that other ministries such as trade, energy, religious affairs may have on issues of salience to them.

To achieve a more complete understanding of how the world at large came to change its perception of the Palestinian Problem and how the PLO mobilized support for its cause, it would be necessary to include in the analysis the role of the above actors. It would be interesting to apply the mobilization process model to the world of non-governmental actors and then examine the interaction between the two worlds in respect to attitude formation on the Palestinian Problem.

Notes

1 *Arab Report and Record* (1976: 333); *ARR* (1976: 239).
2 Stebbins, R. and Adam, E. (eds) *American Foreign Relations 1973: A Documentary Record* (New York University Press, New York, 1976), p. 279.
3 Golan, G. *The Soviet Union and the Palestine Liberation Organization: An Uneasy Alliance* (Praeger, New York, 1980), pp. 58–9.
4 Frangi, A. *The PLO and Palestine* (Zed Books, London, 1983) p. 185.
5 *Report to Congress on Voting Practices in the United Nations* (United States Department of State, 24 February 1984) p. 3. Also see Claude, A. 'Collective legitimization as a political function of the United Nations', *International Organization*, vol. 10, no. 3, pp. 367–79, for an early study of this aspect of the United Nations.
6 Fisher, R. 'Following in Another's Footsteps: The Acquisition of International Legal Standing by the Palestine Liberation Organization', *Syracuse Journal of International Law and Commerce* vol. 3 (Spring 1975), p. 237.
7 Ibid., footnote 97.
8 Lilienthal, A. *The Zionist Connection II* (North American, New Brunswick, New Jersey, 1982) pp. 266 and 589.
9 See statement by Andrew Young quoted in Nicol, D. *Paths to Peace: The UN Security Council and its Presidency* (Pergamon Press, New York, 1981) pp. 324–5.
10 *Towards Peace in the Middle East: Report of a Study Group* (The Brookings Institution, Washington D.C., December 1975); Buheiry, M. 'The Saunders Document', *Journal of Palestine Studies*, vol. VIII (Autumn 1978), no. 1, pp. 28–40.
11 *ARR* (1973: 331); Amos, J. *Palestinian Resistance Organization of a Nationalist Movement* (Pergamon Press, New York, 1980) p. 125.
12 *ARR* (1973: 573).
13 Amos (1980: 126).
14 Cobban, H. *The Palestinian Liberation Organization* (Cambridge University Press, Cambridge, 1984) p. 173.
15 See chapter 5, pp. 60–1.
16 *ARR* (1973: 285).

17 Gresh, A. *The PLO: The Struggle Within* (Zed Books, London, 1985) pp. 151–2; Yodfat, A. and Arnon-Ohanna, Y. *The PLO Strategy and Tactics* (Croom Helm, London, 1981) pp. 61–2. In Algiers the decision was a secret one and Jordan had entered reservations whereas in Rabat the PLO was publically proclaimed sole and legitimate representative of the Palestinians in any part of liberated Palestine territory.

18 *ARR* (1973: 527).

19 Golan (1980: 232–3).

20 Yodfat *et al.* (1981: 90).

21 *ARR* (1974: 337).

22 Golan (1980: 57); Yodfat *et al.* (1981: 62–3) for a discussion of the reasons behind the preference for using the label 'authority' rather than 'state'.

23 Golan (1980: 56–8).

24 Coban (1984: 94–5).

25 *ARR* (1977: 276).

26 *ARR* (1977: 141, 145).

27 *ARR* (1977: 276, 806).

28 Carre, O. 'Steps Towards Peace' in Rodinson, M. *Israel and the Arabs* (Peguin Books, London, 1982) p. 285.

29 Amos (1980, 123).

30 Gresh (1985, 152).

31 UN Doc. S/PV.1870, 12 January 1976.

32 Correspondence and interview with a Palestinian representative of a Gulf state delegation at the United Nations.

33 Mansbach, R. and Vasquez, J. *In Search of Theory* (Colombia University Press, New York, 1981) p. 97.

34 Ibid.

35 What is to be considered as the system depends on what one is interested to explain. If the focus is on trying to examine how an actor raises an issue on an agenda then the actor might be regarded as the system and the wider political process would be occurring in that actor's environment. Whereas when one is focusing on the contention over the issue then the environment of the actor becomes the system for analysis.

Appendix I
Operationalizing the Concept of 'Political Support' for the Palestinian Cause

The purpose of this section is to introduce a framework for operationalizing the concept of 'political support for the Palestinian cause'. Countries' voting behaviour at the United Nations General Assembly on resolutions pertaining to the Middle East and Palestine will be used as indicators to construct an index of political support. The purpose of this index will be to measure the level of support for the Palestinian cause throughout the period under study and answer the following type of question: who forms the pool of support for the Palestinian cause and at what levels? How, or in what way, did this pool of support change during the period under study?

UN General Assembly voting behaviour

It was decided that voting at the General Assembly would be a satisfactory representation of member governments' attitudes on the issue under study. Votes on resolutions adopted by the General Assembly can be assumed to reflect the final position taken by a governmental delegation at the end of a political process on an issue. Bearing in mind its limitations, voting analysis can then enable the analyst to observe and measure the changing perceptions and attitudes of member governments on a variety of issues. It is with this in mind that Russett notes, 'Roll call votes in the General Assembly provide a unique set of data wherein many national governments commit themselves simultaneously and publicly on a wide variety of major issues ... Voting behaviour ... remains one of our best sources of replicable information on the policies of its ... members'.[1]

From the start it might be useful to note some of the limitations inherent in voting analysis. First, most of the methods employed in voting behaviour are not explanatory techniques. They do not necessarily explain causes and consequences of member countries' voting behaviour. They can only be descriptive rather than explanatory.

Voting analysis simply summarizes a delegation's stand on roll-calls and does not try to account for all the various factors that can influence a particular vote. Second, voting analysis cannot account for the differences in the intensity of a country's commitment to a vote and treats every delegation's vote equally. Third, United Nations' voting can also be seen as being highly symbolic and not necessarily carrying high costs.[2] Therefore some might argue that it does not necessarily reflect the 'true' attitude of the state. However, particularly on controversial and salient issues, the fact that such voting is publicly recorded and highly visible can have political ramifications, both within and outside the United Nations, inducing the delegation to cast a 'meaningful' vote.

Constructing an index of political support from United Nations' voting behaviour

The various techniques and methodological problems associated with United Nations' voting analysis have been examined elsewhere.[3] However, it should be noted that in this study 'absence' from voting was treated as lack of data while 'non-participation', as conventional practice suggests, was treated as a 'No' vote.

The scope of the analysis and methodology employed

During the normal sessions of the General Assembly member delegations find themselves voting on a great number of draft resolutions covering a wide range of issues. One such issue has been the Palestinian Problem. The problem in one form or the other has been a part of the General Assembly's agenda since the early years of the United Nations. During the period under study, from 1967 to 1980, various aspects of the Palestinian problem have come to the attention of the General Assembly. However, in this study three aspects of the Palestian problem, the rights of the refugees, the individual human rights of the Palestinians in the occupied territories and the collective political rights of the Palestinians, will form the basis for the definition of the scope of the 'Palestinian cause'. As can be seen from Table A1.1 a total of 66 roll-calls during 8 sessions were studied in an effort to measure support for the Palestinian cause.[4]

Table A1.1: Distribution of roll-calls by sessions and by sub-issue

Issues	1969 24th	1970 25th	1971 26th	1972 27th	1973 28th	1974 29th	1978 33th	1980 35th	Total
Refugee problems	—	1	3	4	2	2	2	2	16
Human rights	1	2	1	3	3	4	2	6	22
Political rights	2	4	3	2	4	3	5	5	28
Total	3	7	7	9	9	9	9	13	66

The origins of the methodology employed in this study, known as cluster-bloc analysis, can be traced to the late 1950s and early 1960s when scholars such as Reiselbach[5], Hovet[6] and Lijphart[7] became interested in studying voting behaviour at the United Nations in a systematic and comprehensive manner. It was by employing a modified version of Lijphart's Index of Agreement, which measures the degree of agreement between pairs of states at the General Assembly, that an index of support for the Palestinian cause was constructed. Lijphart's Index, in its original form, was defined as:[8]

$$I_A = \frac{(f + (1/2)g)}{t} \times 100$$

where f = the number of roll-calls with identical votes;
g = the number of roll-calls in which states showed 'partial agreement' (yes-abstain or no-abstain combinations)
t = the total number of roll-calls in which each pair jointly participated.

This index treats all roll-calls as being of equal value. However, to use the index in this form would not account for the differences in the political importance of the content of roll-calls being studied. Earlier it was pointed out that the Palestinian Problem included an amalgamation of roll-calls ranging from ones seeking solutions to the problems of the Palestinian refugees to ones calling for the establishment of a Palestinian homeland and the recognition of the PLO. It should not be difficult to note that the resolutions referring to the above matters carry political messages of rather different significance. A 'yes' vote cast on a resolution calling for an increase in voluntary contributions to the budget of UNRWA would have less significance than a 'yes' vote cast for a resolution inviting the PLO to participate in the work of the United Nations.

To be able to account for the differences in the political importance of the content of roll-calls being studied the above index was modified to incorporate a weighting scheme. Hence, the Index of Agreement was redefined as:[22]

$$WI_A = \frac{\sum_i^t w_i(f_i + (1/2)g_i)}{\sum_i^t w_i} \times 100$$

where w_i = the weight of the roll-call under study, the ith roll-call
f_i = the value of a dummy variable for the ith roll-call, a value of 1 indicates full agreement while 0 means a disagreement or partial agreement.
g_i = the value of a second dummy variable for the ith roll-call, a value of 1 indicates partial agreement and 0 indicates full agreement or disagreement.

Weighting roll-calls

The literature on United Nations voting behaviour takes a very cautious approach on the problem of weighting and, in general, follows the position taken by Turner. Reiselbach[9], Lijphart[10], Willetts[11] and Chai[12] all agree with Turner's argument[13] that it is impossible to weight issues, resolutions or, for that matter, votes in a way that is both objective and meaningful—mainly because the assignment of weights is regarded as a subjective task varying not only from person to person but also from time to time. What might be important to one may be less important, if not trivial, to another. Similarly, what might be regarded as an important issue at one time may be judged as less important at a different period.

It may be difficult to weight the importance of roll-calls objectively, but it may still be possible to make a meaningful effort and establish some acceptable degree of inter-subjectivty to the weighting process. In the case of this study it might be reasonable to introduce a weighting scheme to lend the Index of Support a greater degree of validity in relation to the concept it is trying to measure (see note 14 for a comparison of unweighted and weighted results). The purpose of this weighting scheme is to capture the different levels of political importance that roll-calls addressing the three aspects of the Palestinian problem carry. In order for the

Index of Support to reflect these differences, it was decided that such resolutions would be weighted according to the level of controversy generated by the draft resolution being voted.[15] In an effort to reduce the element of arbitrariness in the construction of a scale to differentiate between the importance of various sets of roll-calls the method outlined below was followed.

Three empirical factors seemed to call for the separation of the period under study into two. First, the agenda of the General Assembly between 1952 and 1974 did not have an item on the Palestinian Question. Various issues pertaining to the Palestinian problem were dealt with during deliberations on three agenda items entitled 'Assistance to refugees in the Near East', 'The Situation in the Middle East' and 'Situation regarding Israeli practices Affecting the Human Rights of the Population of the Occupied Territories'.

Second, the situation drastically changed at the 29th Session when a separate agenda item looking solely at the political rights of the Palestinians was included. Furthermore, this item was allocated directly to the plenary rather than to one of the main committees, reflecting the Assembly's feeling about the urgency and importance of this issue. Third, there was a significant change in the content and nature of both debates and decisions between these two periods. While in the first period references to the inalienable rights of the Palestinians and their right to self-determination became frequent and elaborate, it was at the 29th Session and thereafter that the political rights of the Palestinians were unambigiously interpreted to mean the right to independence. This conspicuous difference in the political content of the resolutions was also coupled by an authorization of the PLO to participate in debates as the sole representative of the Palestinians. Prior to the 29th Session, only individuals from various Palestinian organizations were allowed to put their case to the Special Political Committee of the General Assembly, with little effect.

Having separated the period into two, the 66 roll-calls included in the analysis were grouped into three, depending on whether they mainly addressed the problems of the refugees and their 'right to return', the individual human rights of the population in the occupied territories or the collective political rights of the Palestinians. Taking the first group of roll-calls as a reference point of lowest importance, the other two groups of roll-calls were assigned separate weights for the first and second periods on the basis of the degree of controversy involved.

The degree of controversy involved on each roll-call was calculated by the formula;

$$D_c = \frac{N + (1/2)A}{t}$$

where N = the number of 'No' votes
A = the number of abstentions
T = the total number of votes cast.

Then by employing

$$W_x = \frac{\sum D_c}{N}$$

the average value for each group of roll-calls was calculated for each of the two periods. Subsequently by assigning a value of '1' to the first group of roll-calls on matters pertaining to the refugees, the weights as shown in Table A1.2 were obtained for the other two groups of roll-calls. Thus the individual roll-calls were weighted according to the time and subject matter set in which they fell.

Table A1.2: Distribution of weights by period and by issues

Issues	1967–73			1974–80		
	No. of r-cs	W_x	Weights	No. of r-cs	W_x	Weights
Refugee matters	10	0.14	1	13	0.04	1
Human rights	10	0.25	1.8	25	0.07	1.8
Political rights	10	0.33	2.4	27	0.19	4.8

Results

Having determined the type and the number of roll-calls to be studied, the data for the two periods was processed with a computer package, VOTASS[16] that calculates, among other statistics, the degree of agreement between pairs of members of legislative assemblies. Ideally, it would have been preferable to use the degree of agreement between the PLO and the other members of the United Nations. However, the PLO was not recognized by the General Assembly as the sole representative of the Palestinians until 1974 and even then the observer status accorded to the PLO did not entitle it to cast a vote, a right reserved solely for member states.

At first the possibility of using the Arab group as a reference point for a pro-Palestinian position and calculating the Index of Inter-Group Agreement[17] of other groups with the Arabs was considered. For this to be meaningful a 100 percent cohesion within the Arab group[18] would have been required. Furthermore only scores for pre-specified groupings could have been calculated. It would have not been possible to measure the Index of Agreement between the Arab group and individual member states. In view of these problems, agreement scores between eligible[19] members and Israel were calculated. In this way, for example, if a score of I_A = 90.0 was obtained for the degree of agreement between Israel and the United States, this was interpreted as a 90 percent support for the Israeli position. The degree of support for the Palestinian cause was then calculated by subtracting the score obtained from 100 ;

$$I_{SP} = 100 - I_{SI}$$

where I_{SP} = Index of Support for the Palestinian cause
I_{SI} = Index of Support for the Israeli position.

Interpreting the results

The modified Lijphart Index gives scores ranging from 0.0 to 100.0 for the degree of agreement between Israel and each member of the Assembly. A score of 0.0

indicates complete disagreement with the Israeli position while, at the other end of the scale, a score of 100.0 suggests full agreement with Israel. The scores lying between these two extremes represent the varying degrees of support that Israel receives from each country.

In view of the large number of scores generated for approximately 140 countries per session and the need to differentiate between one level of support and another, the scale given below was introduced;

$\geqslant$ 0.0 and < 20.0 = Highly pro-Palestinian
$\geqslant$ 20.0 and < 40.0 = Medium pro-Palestinian
$\geqslant$ 40.0 and $\leqslant$ 60.0 = Intermediate
> 60.0 and $\leqslant$ 80.0 = Medium pro-Israeli
> 80.0 and $\leqslant$ 100.0 = Highly pro-Israeli

These cut-off points were determined intuitively on the basis of their political significance. However, it is possible to determine statistically significant levels of high agreement.[20] This can be done by employing a test of signifance against the null hypothesis of random voting. This test establishes the statistically high levels of agreement and disagreement between pairs of states. The scores lying between the two cut-off points are then treated as ones that could have been obtained by random voting. Although such a method is statistically very rigorous it was felt that for the purpose of this study it would be more appropriate to consider politically significant levels of agreement.

Two factors played a role in this decision. First, it seemed that employing intuitively determined categories of agreement levels would make a richer use of the information particularly for the scores lying between the statistically determined cut-off points. Second, strictly speaking one employs a test of significance to establish whether the sample one is using in an analysis to make inferences about the whole is actually representative of the whole or not. In this study all member states and all the roll-calls central to the research question were included in the analysis. Hence, it was felt that in this case a test of significance did not appear to be necessary and the validity or appropriateness of the cut-off points for the different categories of support was left to the test of 'reasonableness' to the judgement of the scholars in the field.

Notes

1 Russett, B. *International Regions and the International System* (Chicago: Rand McNally, 1967), pp. 60–1.
2 The Realists regard United Nations voting as relatively insignificant because there is no cost attached to it in real-value terms (such as territory lost, battle casualties etc . . .). Whereas the position of the transnationalists or the Global Politics Approach is that symbolic values can, in the minds of participants, be translated into real values. This process of attaching real costs to symbolic acts can take the form of, for example, loss of prestige and status, of being associated with a losing or illegitimate vote or the cost arising from the erosion of one's position at home when accounting for a vote to an unsatisfied/critical domestic constituency etc. The position taken in this analysis is that such considerations on the part of United Nations' delegations will ensure that the final vote is 'meaningful' and does represent that delegation's attitude on the issue.
3 See Appendix I in Kirisci, K. *Mobilization of Support for the Palestinian Cause: A Comparitive Study of Political Change at the Communal, Regional and Global Levels* (Ph.d. Thesis, The City University, London, 1986).
4 Roll-calls concerning the 'question of sovereignty over natural resources in occupied

Arab territories', 'relations between Israel and South Africa' and 'arms sales to Israel' were not included in the analysis. Also not included were 'near unanimous' roll-calls, that is roll-calls that received no opposition at all or had less than five abstentions. The data on roll-calls were made available by the Inter-University Consortium for Political Research.

5 Reiselbach, L. 'Quantitative Techniques for Studying Voting Behaviour in the U.N. General Assembly', *International Organization*, vol. 14 (Spring 1960).
6 Hovet, T. *Bloc Politics in the United Nations* (Harvard University Press, Cambridge, 1960).
7 Lijphart, A. 'The Analysis of Bloc Voting in the General Assembly', *American Political Science Review*, vol. 57 (1963).
8 Lijphart (1963: 910).
9 Reiselbach (1960: 292).
10 Lijphart (1963: 911).
11 Willetts, *The Non-Aligned Movement* (Frances Pinter, London, 1978) p. 93.
12 Chai, T. 'Chinese policy towards the Third World and the Super Powers in the U.N. General Assembly, 1971–1977: a voting analysis', *International Organization*, vol. 33 (Summer 1979) p. 393.
13 Turner, J. *Party and Constituency; Pressures on Congress* (The John Hopkins Press, Baltimore, 1951), pp. 20–1.
14 Weighting is a treacherous exercise. However in this particular case it can be said that not weighting the roll-calls is in effect actually weighting them. Table A1.3 compares the unweighted and weighted results for the distribution of support at the 29th Session. The difference between unweighted and weighted results is particularly evident in the case of the Western group. Not applying any weighting makes the Western group appear much less pro-Israeli.
   The average level of support for both Latin American and Western Europe is higher while the average values for Africa, Asia and East Europe indicate a more pro Palestinian position although the distribution across different levels of support remains the same.
15 With 'degree of controversy [contention]' here, we mean the amount of controversy or disagreement that the contents (or for that matter controversy over the Assembly procedures that govern a roll-call) of a draft resolution carry in the eyes of the delegate.

Table A1.3: Unweighted and weighted versions of the distribution of support by groups at the 29th Session

	Western Bloc %		Latin America %		Africa %		Asia %		Eastern Europe %		Assembly Total %	
	I_A	WI_A	I_A	WI_A	I_A	WI_A	I_A	WI_A	I_A	WI_A	I_A	WI_A
Highly pro-Israel	5	4	25	19	—	—	—	—	—	—	6	5
Medium Israel	5	29	—	—	—	—	—	—	—	—	1	6
Intermediate	33	24	13	19	4	4	—	—	—	—	11	10
Medium Palestinian	38	24	25	19	—	—	12	12	—	—	16	11
Highly pro-Palestinian	19	19	38	43	96	96	88	88	100	100	66	66
Mean value in %	40	48	39	41	13	7	14	11	11	8	22	24
No. countries	21		16		23		17		11		88	

(The first column for each group gives the unweighted values)

We assume that the more a draft resolution refers specifically to the political rights of the Palestinians the more controversial [contentious] it will be. The advantage of this index is that it is dynamic and empirical, that it captures the perception of what delegates regard to be controversial and important at one particular time. However, establishing the importance of a roll-call naturally can not be captured completely simply by looking at the distribution of votes on a roll-call. This will vary by the salience that is attached by a delegation to a particular issue. Ideally, one would construct an index that could possibly measure this intensity of commitment to an issue by examining the length of speeches made prior and/or after a vote, as well as by looking for certain key words. Russett too notes the problem of whether every vote is of equal importance and has sought to use amounts of discussion on the floor as a weighting device (Russett (1967: 59–93). In this case such an approach was found rather impractical in the face of limited resources. For the purposes of this analysis it was felt that the procedure followed in measuring the degree of controversy is adequate. The procedure employed at least reduces the element of arbitrariness in assigning weights to roll-calls by introducing a rationale behind the scheme that is easily reproducable.

16 VOTASS is a computer package written by Dr P. Willetts for legislative roll-call analysis. The unit of analysis can be a member of a legislative assembly such as a senate or a country at the General Assembly.

17 For a detailed description of this Index see Willetts (1978: 269).

18 The Arab group, to be able to represent the Palestinian cause as a whole, would have had to agree among themselves on all roll-calls. This was not the case particularly during the sessions which adopted resolutions critical of the Camp David Accords.

19 Members eligible for the analysis are those who met the required minimum attendance level normally set at 90 percent.

20 For a detailed examination of the role of the test of signifance in accounting for the effect of random voting on cluster-bloc analysis see Willetts, P. 'Cluster-Bloc Analysis and Statistical Inference', *American Political Science Review*, vol. 66, June 1972, pp. 569–82 or Willetts (1978: Appendix 6).

Appendix II
List of Membership of Regional and Political Groups

This appendix provides a list of countries in the various regional and political groupings used in the construction of the index of support as discussed in Appendix I. The basis of regional group membership is the same as the membership of geographical groupings used for the purposes of elections within the United Nations, with two exceptions. First, Arab countries are taken out of the African and Asian groups to form a separate Arab group based on Arab League membership. Secondly, the Western European group, which within the United Nations is formally known as the 'Western European and Others' group was enlarged to include the United States.[1]

The list below also includes two major political groupings. The two groupings are listed separately because unlike the Latin Americans and African political groupings their membership does not coincide with any one regional group. The Non-Aligned and the Islamic group both overlap with several of the regional groups. The membership of the Non-Aligned group, for the General Assembly sessions studied, was determined by whether a country had attended a Non-Aligned summit in the year of or preceding a General Assembly session.[2] In the case of the Islamic group, which did not come into existence until March 1971, the 1980 membership of the Islamic Conference Organization was used as a basis for all the General Asssembly sessions included in the study. The Arab countries have been included in both the Non-Aligned and Islamic groups. Afghanistan and Egypt were included in the Islamic group throughout in spite of their suspension from membership in 1980 and 1979 respectively. Egypt was re-admitted to the ICO in January 1984.

The Arab group includes all members of the Arab League, including, for the purposes of this study, Egypt after its suspension in March 1979. Even though Mauritania and Somalia were not admitted to the Arab League until 1973 and 1974 respectively, they were included in the Arab group for the sessions preceding these dates because of their close ties with the Arab world.

Regional[3] Groups	Political Groupings					
	NAM64	NAM70	NAM73	NAM76	NAM79	ICO
Africa						
Angola	—	—	—	M	M	—
Botswana	—	M	M	M	M	—
Burundi	—	M	M	M	M	—
Cameroon	M	M	M	M	M	M
Cape Verde	—	—	—	—	M	—
CAR	M	M	M	M	M	—
Chad	M	M	M	M	—	M
Comoros	—	—	—	M	M	M

Regional[3] Groups	Political Groupings					
Congo	M	M	M	M	M	—
Dahomey	M	—	M	M	M	—
Eq. Guinea	—	M	M	M	M	—
Ethiopia	M	M	M	M	M	—
Gabon	—	—	M	M	M	M
Gambia	—	—	M	M	M	M
Ghana	M	M	M	M	M	—
Guinea	M	M	M	M	M	M
G.Bissau	—	—	—	M	M	M
Ivory Coast	—	—	M	M	M	—
Kenya	M	M	M	M	M	—
Lesotho	—	M	M	M	M	—
Liberia	M	M	M	M	M	—
Madagascar	—	—	M	M	M	—
Malawi	M	—	—	—	M	—
Mali	M	M	M	M	M	M
Mauritius	—	—	M	M	M	—
Mozambique	—	—	—	M	M	—
Niger	—	—	M	M	M	M
Nigeria	M	M	M	M	M	—
Rwanda	—	M	M	M	M	—
Sao T.&P	—	—	—	M	M	—
Senegal	M	M	M	M	M	M
Seychelles	—	—	—	M	M	—
Sierra Leone	M	M	M	M	M	M
Swaziland	—	M	M	M	M	—
Tanzania	M	M	M	M	M	—
Togo	M	M	M	M	M	—
Uganda	M	M	M	M	M	M
Upper Volta	—	—	M	M	M	M
Zaïre	—	M	M	M	M	—
Zambia	M	M	M	M	M	—
Zimbabwe (N=41)	—	—	—	—	—	—
Asia						
Afghanistan	M	M	M	M	M	M
Bangladesh	—	—	M	M	M	M
Bhutan	—	—	M	M	M	—
Burma	M	—	M	M	M	—
Cambodia	M	—	M	M	—	—
China	—	—	—	—	—	—
Cyprus	M	M	M	M	M	—
Fiji	—	—	—	—	—	—
India	M	M	M	M	M	—
Indonesia	M	M	M	M	M	M
Iran	—	—	—	—	M	M
Japan	—	—	—	—	—	—
Laos	M	M	M	M	M	—
Malaysia	—	M	M	M	M	M
Maldives	—	—	—	M	M	—
Mongolia	—	—	—	—	—	—

Nepal	M	M	M	M	M	—
Pakistan	—	—	—	—	M	M
Papua New Guinea	—	—	—	—	—	—
Philippines	—	—	—	G	O	—
Samoa	—	—	—	—	—	—
Singapore	—	M	M	M	M	—
Solomons	—	—	—	—	—	—
Sri Lanka	M	M	M	M	M	—
Thailand	—	—	—	—	—	—
Vietnam	—	—	—	M	M	—
(N=26)						

Latin America

Argentina	O	O	M	M	M	—
Bahamas	—	—	—	—	—	—
Barbados	—	O	O	O	O	—
Bolivia	O	O	O	O	M	—
Brazil	O	O	O	O	O	—
Chile	O	O	M	—	—	—
Colombia	—	—	—	—	O	—
Costa Rica	—	—	—	—	O	—
Cuba	M	M	M	M	M	—
Dominica	—	—	—	—	O	—
Dominican R.	—	—	—	—	—	—
Ecuador	—	O	O	O	O	—
El Salvador	—	—	—	O	O	—
Greneda	—	—	—	O	M	—
Guatemala	—	—	—	—	—	—
Guyana	—	M	M	M	M	—
Haiti	—	—	—	—	—	—
Honduras	—	—	—	—	—	—
Jamaica	O	M	M	M	M	—
Mexico	O	—	O	O	O	—
Nicaragua	—	—	—	—	M	—
Panama	—	—	O	M	M	—
Paraguay	—	—	—	—	—	—
Peru	—	O	M	M	M	—
Saint Lucia	—	—	—	—	O	—
Surinam	—	—	—	—	M	—
Tri.& To.	O	M	M	M	M	—
Uruguay	O	O	O	O	O	—
Venezuela	O	O	O	O	O	—
(N=29)						

Western Group

Australia	—	—	—	—	—	—
Austria	—	G	G	G	G	—
Belgium	—	—	—	—	—	—
Canada	—	—	—	—	—	—
Denmark	—	—	—	—	—	—
Finland	O	G	G	G	G	—
France	—	—	—	—	—	—
Germany (West)	—	—	—	—	—	—
Greece	—	—	—	—	—	—
Iceland	—	—	—	—	—	—
Ireland	—	—	—	—	—	—

Regional[3] Groups	Political Groupings					
Italy	—	—	—	—	—	—
Luxembourg	—	—	—	—	—	—
Malta	—	—	M	M	M	—
New Zealand	—	—	—	—	—	—
Netherlands	—	—	—	—	—	—
Norway	—	—	—	—	—	—
Portugal	—	—	—	G	G	—
Spain	—	—	—	—	G	—
Sweden	—	—	G	G	G	—
Turkey	—	—	—	—	—	M
UK	—	—	—	—	—	—
USA	—	—	—	—	—	—
(N=23)						
Eastern Europe						
Albania	—	—	—	—	—	—
Bulgaria	—	—	—	—	—	—
Czechoslovakia	—	—	—	—	—	—
Germany (East)	—	—	—	—	—	—
Hungary	—	—	—	—	—	—
Poland	—	—	—	—	—	—
Romania	—	—	—	G	G	—
Soviet Union	—	—	—	—	—	—
Yugoslavia	M	M	M	M	M	—
(N=9)						
Arabs						
Algeria	M	M	M	M	M	M
Bahrain	—	—	M	M	M	M
Djibouti	—	—	—	—	M	M
Egypt	M	M	M	M	M	M
Jordan	M	M	M	M	M	M
Kuwait	M	M	M	M	M	M
Lebanon	M	M	M	M	M	M
Libya	M	M	M	M	M	M
Iraq	M	M	M	M	M	M
Mauritania	M	M	M	M	M	M
Morocco	M	M	M	M	M	M
Oman	—	—	M	M	M	M
Qatar	—	—	M	M	M	M
P.D.R.Y.	M	M	M	M	M	M
Saudi A.	M	—	M	M	M	M
Somalia	M	M	M	M	M	M
Sudan	M	M	M	M	M	M
Syria	M	M	M	M	M	M
Tunisia	M	M	M	M	M	M
Y.A. Rep.	—	—	—	—	M	M
UAE	—	—	M	M	M	M
(N=21)						

Key

M Member   O Observer   G Guest—Not Member

Notes

1 For a discussion of the membership of the formal United Nations geographical groupings as it stood in 1960 see Bailey, S. *The General Assembly* (Stevens and Sons, London, 1960) pp. 29–41.
2 For the complete list see Willetts, P. *The Non-Aligned in Havana* (Frances Pinter, London, 1981) pp. 65–7.
3 The Table includes 149 countries: the 153 UN members in 1980 except for Belorussia, The Ukraine, Israel and South Africa.

Appendix III
List of Palestinian National Council Meetings

	Place	Dates
1st	Jerusalem	28 May–2 June 1964
2nd	Cairo	31 May–4 June 1965
3rd	Gaza	20–24 May 1966
4th	Cairo	10–17 July 1968
5th	Cairo	1–4 February 1969
6th	Cairo	1–6 September 1969
7th	Cairo	30 May–4 June 1970
Extraordinary Session	Amman	27–28 August 1970
8th	Cairo	28 February–5 March 1971
9th	Cairo	7–13 July 1971
10th	Cairo	11–12 April 1972
11th	Cairo	6–12 January 1973
12th	Cairo	1–9 June 1974
13th	Cairo	12–20 March 1977
14th	Damascus	15–23 January 1979
15th	Damascus	15–19 April 1981
16th	Algiers	14–22 February 1983
17th	Amman	22–28 November 1984

Appendix IV
List of PLO Offices Abroad by Early 1980s

This list was prepared from information confidentially provided by a British diplomat and from a survey of the *Arab Report and Record*.[1] The list provides information on the status of PLO offices abroad. The information has been sub-divided into four classifications: first, those countries that extend the PLO some form of diplomatic status;[2] second, those countries that allow only information offices without formally recognizing the PLO; third, those countries who appear to have consented to an office, but about which there is insufficient information to determine whether or not it is a diplomatic mission. Such occurrences have been labeled as 'unclear'; finally there are those countries for which no information was available.

Country	Status of Office	Country	Status of Office
Africa (N=41)			
Angola	diplomatic	Madagascar	non-diplomatic
Botswana	—	Malawi	—
Burundi	non-diplomatic	Mali	diplomatic
Cameroon	unclear	Mauritius	diplomatic
Cape Verde	—	Mozambique	diplomatic
CAR	—	Niger	—
Chad	non-diplomatic	Nigeria	diplomatic
Comoros	—	Rwanda	—
Congo	non-diplomatic	Sao T. & P.	—
Dahomey	—	Senegal	diplomatic
Eq. Guinea	—	Seychelles	unclear
Ethiopia	diplomatic	Sierra Leone	—
Gabon	—	Swaziland	—
Gambia	diplomatic	Tanzania	diplomatic
Ghana	—	Togo	—
Guinea	diplomatic	Uganda	diplomatic
G. Bissau	diplomatic	Upper Volta	—
Ivory Coast	—	Zaïre	—
Kenya	diplomatic	Zambia	unclear
Lesotho	—	Zimbabwe	diplomatic
Liberia	—		
Asia (N=28)			
Afganistan	diplomatic	Maldives	diplomatic
Bangladesh	diplomatic	Mongolia	diplomatic
Bhutan	—	North Korea	diplomatic
Burma	unclear	Nepal	—
Cambodia	—	Papua New Guinea	—
China	diplomatic	Pakistan	diplomatic
Cyprus	diplomatic	Philippines	—

Country	Status of Office	Country	Status of Office
Fiji	—	Samoa	—
India	diplomatic	Singapore	—
Indonesia	unclear	Solomons	—
Iran	diplomatic	South Korea	—
Japan	non-diplomatic	Sri Lanka	diplomatic
Laos	diplomatic	Thailand	—
Malaysia	diplomatic	Vietnam	diplomatic

Latin America (N=29)

Country	Status of Office	Country	Status of Office
Argentina	—	Guatemala	—
Bahamas	—	Guyana	—
Barbados	—	Haiti	—
Bolivia	diplomatic	Honduras	—
Brazil	diplomatic	Jamaica	—
Chile	—	Mexico	diplomatic
Colombia	—	Nicaragua	diplomatic
Costa Rica	—	Panama	—
Cuba	diplomatic	Paraguay	—
Dominica	—	Peru	diplomatic
Dominican R.	—	Saint Lucia	—
Ecuador	non-diplomatic	Suriname	—
El Salvador	—	Tri. & To.	—
Greneda	—	Uruguay	—
		Venezuela	unclear

Western Bloc (N=24)

Country	Status of Office	Country	Status of Office
Australia	—	Luxembourg	non-diplomatic
Austria	diplomatic	Malta	diplomatic
Belgium	non-diplomatic	New Zealand	—
Canada	non-diplomatic	Netherlands	non-diplomatic
Denmark	non-diplomatic	Norway	—
Finland	non-diplomatic	Portugal	non-diplomatic
France	non-diplomatic	Spain	diplomatic
Germany (West)	non-diplomatic	Sweden	non-diplomatic
Greece	diplomatic	Switzerland	non-diplomatic
Iceland	—	Turkey	diplomatic
Ireland	—	UK	non-diplomatic
Italy	non-diplomatic	USA	non-diplomatic

Eastern Europe (N=9)

Country	Status of Office	Country	Status of Office
Albania	—	Poland	diplomatic
Bulgaria	diplomatic	Romania	diplomatic
Czechoslovakia	diplomatic	Soviet Union	diplomatic
Germany (East)	diplomatic	Yugoslavia	diplomatic
Hungary	diplomatic		

Table A4.1: Distribution of PLO offices by regions

	East Europe	West Europe	Latin America	Asia	Africa	Total
Diplomatic	8	5	6	14	14	47
Non-Diplomatic	—	14	1	1	4	18
Unclear	—	—	1	2	3	6
Missing data	1	5	21	11	20	60
No. of countries	9	24[a]	29	28[b]	41	131[c]

[a] Includes Switzerland
[b] Includes North and South Korea
[c] Excludes Arab countries. All Arab governments have allowed diplomatic offices for the PLO except Oman.

Notes

1 On numerous occasions Palestinian and Arab circles were approached to obtain information on the PLO offices abroad. Similarly attempts were made to circulate a questionnaire to the PLO offices. This questionnaire was designed in such a way that it was hoped it would have led to information on not only the location of the PLO offices but also on developments and changes in the diplomatic status of these offices. However, these efforts did not bear any fruit. The list that was finally obtained where possible was crosschecked and expanded.

2 One problem with the information on offices with diplomatic status is that it is often not detailed enough to determine the actual level of the mission. So it becomes rather difficult to tell whether one particular PLO diplomatic mission benefits from a status similar to an embassy or whether it is set at a lower status.

Appendix V

This appendix provides a list of specialized agencies and United Nations' institutions that have extended observership to the PLO and/or maintain regular and formal contacts with PLO representations in New York, Geneva and Vienna. Two United Nations sources were used in preparation of this appendix: the yearly reports prepared by the secretary general of the United Nations in accordance with Resolution 3300 (XXIX) of December 1974 adopted in relation to the agenda item entitled 'Implementation of the Declaration on the Granting of Independence to Colonial Countries and Peoples by the Specialized Agencies and the International Institutions associated with the United Nations'; reports prepared in accordance ECOSOC Resolution 2100 (LXIII) of 3 August 1977 and Resolution 34/133 of 14 December 1979 specifically urging specialized agencies to consult and cooperate with the PLO.

Specialised agencies

International Labour Organization (ILO)
Food and Agriculture Organization of the United Nations (FAO)
United Nations Educational, Scientific and Cultural Organization (UNESCO)
World Health Organization (WHO)
International Civil Aviation Organization (ICAO)
Universal Postal Union (UPU)
International Telecommunication Union (ITU)
World Meteorological Organization (WMO)
Inter-governmental Maritime Consultative Organization (IMCO)
World Intellectual Property Organization (WIPO)
International Fund for Agricultural Development (IFAD)

Other institutions and programmes

United Nation Conference on Trade and Development
United Nations Industrial Development Organization
United Nations Environment Programme
World Food Programme
UN document numbers for the reports used,
A/10080 and Add. 1-4, A/31/65, A/31/238, A/32/87 and Add. 1-3, A/32/286, A/33/109 and Add. 1-4, A/34/208 and Add. 1-3, A/35/178 and Add1-4, E/1978/55, A/35/227 and A/36/305.

Bibliography: Theory and Methodology

Books

Alker, M. and Russett, B. *World Politics in the General Assembly* (Yale University Press, New Haven, 1965).

Allison, G. *Essence of Decision* (Little Brown, London, 1971)

Beichman, A. *The 'Other' State Department, The United States Mission to the United Nations, Its Role in the Making of Foreign Policy* (Basic Books, New York, 1967).

Brecher, M. *The Foreign Policy System of Israel: Setting, Images, Process* (Oxford University Press, London, 1972).

Burton, J. *International Relations: A General Theory* (Cambridge University Press, Cambridge, 1965).

Burton, J. *World Society* (Cambridge University Press, Cambridge, 1972).

Carr, E. H. *The Twenty Year's Crisis, 1919–1939* (Macmillan, London, 1946).

Cobb, R. and Elder, C. *Participation in American Politics: The Dynamics of Agenda Building* (Allyn and Bacon, Boston, 1972).

Easton, D. *A Framework for Political Analysis* (Prentice Hall, Englewood Cliffs, N.J., 1965).

Elder, C. and Cobb, R. *The Political Use of Symbols* (Longman, New York, 1983).

Festinger, L. *A Theory of Cognitive Dissonance* (Row Peterson, Evanston, Ill., 1957).

Gamson, W. in *The Strategy of Social Protest* (The Dorsey Press, Homewood, Ill., 1975).

Gurr, T. *Politimetrics: An Introduction to Quantitative Macropolitics* (Prentice-Hall, Englewood Cliffs, 1972).

Hovet, T. *Bloc Politics in the United Nations* (Harvard University Press, Cambridge, 1960).

Jacobson, H. *Network of Interdependence: International Organizations and the Global Political System* (Alfred A. Knopf, New York, 1979).

Jacobsen, K. *The General Assembly of the United Nations; A Quantitative Analysis of Conflict, Inequality and Relevance* (Universitets-forlaget, Oslo, 1978).

Jones, B. and Willetts, P. *Interdependence on Trial* (Frances Pinter, London, 1984).

Jonsson, C. (ed.) *Cognitive Dynamics and International Politics* (Frances Pinter, London, 1982).

Keohane, R. and Nye, J. *Transnational Relations and World Politics* (Harvard University Press, Cambridge, 1971).

Keohane, R. and Nye, J. *Power and Interdependence* (Little Brown and Company, Boston, 1977).

Knorr, K. and Rosenau, J. (eds.) *Contending Approaches to International Politics* (Princeton University Press, Princeton, 1970).

Kuhn, T. *The Structure of Scientific Revolutions* (University of Chicago Press, Chicago, 1970).

Lakatos, I. and Musgrave, A. *Criticism and the Growth of Knowledge* (Cambridge University Press, Cambridge, 1970).

Mansbach, R., Ferguson, I. and Lampert, D. *The Web of Politics: Non State Actors in the Global System* (Prentice Hall International, London, 1976).

Mansbach, R. and Vasquez, J. *In Search of Theory; A New Paradigm for Global Politics* (Colombia University Press, New York, 1981).

Mitrany, D. *The Functional Theory of Politics* (Martin Robertson, London, 1975).

Morgenthau, H. *Politics Amongst Nations* (Alfred A. Knopf, New York, 5th edition, 1973).

Nicholson, M. *The Scientific Analysis of Social Behaviour* (Frances Pinter, London, 1983).

Oberschall, A. *Social Conflict and Social Movements* (Prentice Hall, Englewood Cliffs, 1973).

Reynolds, J. (ed.) *An Introduction to International Relations* (Longman, London, 1980).
Rosenau, J. (ed.) *Linkage Politics* (Free Press, New York, 1969).
Rosenau, J. *The Study of Global Interdependence* (Frances Pinter, London, 1980).
Rosenau, J. *The Scientific Study of Foreign Policy* (Revised edition, Frances Pinter, London, 1980).
Russett, B. *International Regions and the International System* (Rand McNally, Chicago, 1967).
Sauvant, K. *Changing Priorities on the International Agenda* (Pergamon Press, New York, 1981).
Smelser, N. *Theory of Collective Behaviour* (Free Press, New York, 1963).
Snyder, G., Bruck, H. and Sapin, B. *Foreign Policy Decision Making* (Free Press, New York, 1962).
Vasquez, J. *The Power of Power Politics; An Empirical Evaluation of the Scientific Study of International Relations* (Rudgers University Press, New Brunswick, 1981).
Wallace, W. *The Foreign Policy Process in Britain* (George Allen and Unwin, London, 1977).
Waltz, K. *Theory of International Politics* (Addison-Wesley, Reading, Mass., 1979).
Willetts, P. *The Non-Aligned in Havana* (Frances Pinter, London, 1981).
Willetts, P. *Pressure Groups in the Global System: The Transnational Relations of Issue-Orientated Non-Governmental Organizations* (Frances Pinter, London, 1982).
Zald, M. and McCarthy, J. (eds) *The Dynamics of Social Movements* (Winthrop, Cambridge, Mass., 1979).

Articles

Alger, C, 'Comparision of Intranational and International Politics', *American Political Science Review*, Vol. 57 (June 1972), pp. 40–9.
Alger, C. and Brams, S. 'Patterns of Representation in National Capitals and Inter-Governmental Organisation', *World Politics*, Vol. 19 (July 1967), pp. 646–63.
Banks, M. 'Ways of Analyzing the World Society' in Groom, J. and Mitchell, C. (eds) *International Relations Theory: a Bibliography* (Frances Pinter, London, 1978).
Beal, R. 'A Contra-Kuhnian View of the Discipline's Growth' in Rosenau, J. (ed.) *In Search of Global Patterns* (The Free Press, New York, 1976).
Cameron, D. 'Towards a Theory of Mobilization', *Journal of Politics*, Vol. 36 (February 1974), pp. 138–71.
Chai, T. 'Chinese policy towards the Third World and the Super Powers in the U.N. General Assembly, 1971–1977: a voting analysis', *International Organisation*, Vol. 33 (Summer 1979), No. 3, pp. 391–403.
Claude, I. 'Collective Legitimization as a political function of the United Nations', *International Organization* Vol. 10 (Summer 1966), No. 3, pp. 367–79.
Cobb, R., Ross, J. and Ross, M. 'Agenda Building as a Comparative Political Process', *American Political Science Review*, Vol. 70 (1976), No. 1, pp. 126–38.
Easton, D. 'The Current Meaning of "Behavioralism"', in Charlesworth, J. *Contemporary Political Analysis* (Free Press, New York, 1967).
Lijphart, A. 'The Analysis of Bloc Voting in the General Assembly', *American Political Science Review*, Vol. 57 (December 1963), pp. 902–17.
Lindblom, C. 'The Science of muddling through' *Public Administration Review*, Vol. 29 (1959), No. 2, pp. 79–88.
Little, R. 'Power and Interdependence: A Realist Critique', in Jones, B. and Willetts, P. (eds) *Interdependence on Trial* (Frances Pinter, London, 1984).
Mansbach, R. and Vasquez, J. 'The issue cycle: conceptualizing long-term global political change', *International Organisation* Vol. 37 (Spring 1983), No. 2, pp. 257–79.
Marx, G. and Wood, J. 'Strands of Theory and Research in Collective Behaviour', *Annual Review of Sociology* Vol. I (1975), pp. 364–420.
Masterman, M., 'The Nature of a Paradigm', in Lakatos, I. and Musgrave, A. (eds), *Criticism and the Growth of Knowledge* (Cambridge University Press, Cambridge, 1970).

O'Leary, M. 'The Role of Issues', in Rosenau, J. (ed.) *In Search of Global Patterns* (Free Press, New York, 1976).

Reiselbach, R. 'Quantitative Techniques for Studying Voting Behaviour in the UN General Assembly', *International Organisation*, Vol. 14 (Spring 1960), No. 2, pp. 291–306.

Rosenau, J. 'Introduction: Political Science in a Shrinking World', in Rosenau, J. (ed.) *Linkage Politics* (Free Press, New York, 1969).

Rosenau, J. 'Puzzlements in Foreign Policy', in *The Scientific Study of Foreign Policy* (Revised and Enlarged Edition, Frances Pinter, London, 1980).

Taylor, T. 'Power Politics', in Taylor, T. (ed.), *Approaches and Theory in International Relations* (Longman, London, 1978).

Vasquez, J. 'Colouring It Morgenthau: New Evidence for an Old Thesis' *British Journal of International Studies*, Vol. 5 (1979), pp. 210–28.

Walsh, E. 'Mobilization Theory vis-à-vis a Mobilization process: The Case of The United Farmers Workers Movement' in Kriesberg, L. (ed.) *Research in Social Movements, Conflicts and Change Volume 1* (JAI Press, Greenwich, Conn, 1978).

Willetts, P. 'Cluster-Bloc Analysis and Statistical Inference', *American Political Science Review*, Vol. 66 (June 1972), pp. 569–82.

Willetts, P. 'The United Nations and the Transformation of the Inter-State System' in Buzan, B. and Jones, B. (eds) *Change and The Study of International Relations: The Evaded Dimension* (Frances Pinter, London, 1981).

Wiletts, P. 'The Impact of Promotional Groups on Global Politics' in Willetts, P. (ed.) *Pressure Groups in the Global System* (Frances Pinter, London, 1982).

Willetts, P. 'The Politics of Global Issues: Cognitive Actor Dependence and Issue Linkage' in Jones, B. and Willetts, P. *Interdependence on Trial* (Frances Pinter, London, 1984).

Willetts, P. 'Introduction', in Chetley, A. *The Politics of Baby Foods* (Frances Pinter, London, 1980).

Wilson, K. and Orum, A. 'Mobilizing People for Collective Action', *Journal of Politics and Military Sociology*, Vol. 14 (1976), pp. 187–202.

Zald, M. and McCharthy, J. 'Social movement organizations: growth, decay and change', *Social Forces* Vol. 44 (March 1966), pp. 327–41.

Bibliography: Substantive

Books

Abu-Lughod, *Transformation of Palestine* (Northwestern University Press, Evanston, 1971).

Adams, J. *The Unnatural Alliance* (Quartet Books, London, 1984).

Allen, D. and Pijpers, A. *European Foreign Policy-Making and The Arab-Israeli Conflict* (Martinus Nijhoff, The Hague, 1984).

Amos, J. *Palestinian Resistance: Organization of a Nationalist Movement* (Pergamon Press, New York, 1980).

Bailey, B. *The General Assembly of the United Nations; A study of Procedure and Practice* (Stevens and Sons, London, 1960).

Bovis, H. *The Jerusalem Question 1917–1968* (Hoover Institution Press, Stanford, 1971).

Cobban, H. *The Palestinian Liberation Organisation* (Cambridge University Press, Cambridge, 1984).

Becker, J. *The PLO: The Rise and Fall of the Palestine Liberation Organization* (Weidenfeld and Nicolson, London, 1984).

Bethell, N. *The Palestinian Triangle: The Struggle between the British, the Jews and the Arabs 1935–48* (Andre Deutsch, London, 1979).

Cattan, H. *Palestine and International Law* (Longman, London 1976).

Chibwe, E. *Arab Dollars for Africa* (Croom Helm, London, 1976).

Chibwe, E. *Afro-Arab Relations* (Julian Friedmann, London, 1977).

Curtis, M. and Gitelson, S. *Israel in the Third World* (Transaction, New Brunswick, New Jersey, 1976).

Davis, J. H. *The Evasive Peace: A Study of the Zionist-Arab Problem* (John Murray, London, 1968).

Dupuy, T. N. *Elusive Victory: The Arab Israeli Wars* (Harper and Row, London, 1978).

El-Ajouty, Y. (ed.) *The Organization of African Unity, After Ten Years* (Praeger, New York, 1975).

El-Rayyes, R. and Nahas, D. *Guerrillas for Palestine* (Croom Helm, London, 1976).

Finger, M. *Your Man at the United Nations: People, Politics and Bureaucracy in the Making of Foreign Policy* (New York University Press, New York, 1980).

Frangi, A. *The PLO and Palestine* (Zed Books, London, 1983)

Fraser, T. G. *The Middle East, 1914–1979* (Edward Arnold, London, 1980).

Gilmour, D. *Dispossessed: The Ordeal of the Palestinians* (Sphere Books, London, 1982).

Glick, E. *Latin America and the Palestine Problem* (Theodor Herzl Foundation, New York, 1958).

Glick, E. *The Triangular Connection: America, Israel and American Jews* (George Allen and Unwin, London, 1982).

Goodwin, G. *Britain and the United Nations* (Oxford University Press, London, 1957).

Golan, G. *The Soviet Union and The Palestine Liberation Organization: An Uneasy Alliance* (Praeger, New York, 1980).

Gresh, A. *The PLO: The Struggle Within* (Zed Books, London, 1985).

Hardie, F. and Hermann, I. *Britain and Zion: The fateful entanglement* (Blackstaff, Belfast, 1980).

Harkabi, Y. *Fedayeen Action and Arab Strategy* (Adelphi Papers No. 53, Institute of Strategic Studies, 1968)

Harkabi, Y. *Palestinians and Israel* (Wiley, New York, 1975).

Hirst, D. *The Gun and the Olive Branch* (Faber and Faber, London, 1977).

Horowitz, D. and Lissak, M. *Origins of the Israeli Polity* (University of Chicago Press, Chicago, 1978).

Hurewitz, J. C. *The Struggle for Palestine* (W. W. Norton, New York, 1950)

Jansen, G. *Afro-Asian and Non-Alignment* (Faber and Faber, London, 1966).

Jansen, G. J. *Zionism, Israel and Asian Nationalism* (The Institute of Palestine Studies, Beirut, 1971).

Kadi, L. *Arab Summit Conferences and The Palestine Problem* (Research Centre, PLO, Beirut, 1966).

Kaufman, E., Shapira, Y. and Barromi, J. *Israel-Latin American Relations* (Transaction Books, New Brunswick, 1979).

Kaufmann, J. *United Nations Decision Making* (Sitjhoff and Noordhoff, Alphen aan den Rijn, 1980).

Kayyali, A. W. *Palestine: A Modern History* (Croom Helm, London, 1978).

Kayyali, W. (ed.) *Zionism, Imperialism and Racism* (Croom Helm, London, 1979).

Khalidi, W. *From Heaven to Conquest: Readings in Zionism and the Palestine Problem until 1948* (Institute for Palestine Studies, Beirut, 1971).

Khalidi, A. W. *Palestine: A Modern History* (Croom Helm, London, 1978).

Landau, J. *The Arabs in Israel* (Oxford University Press, London, 1969).

Lall, A. *The United Nations and the Middle East Crisis, 1967* (Columbia University Press, New York, 1968).

Laquer, W. *The Israeli-Arab Reader: A documentary history of the Middle East conflict* (Penguin Books, Harmondsworth, 1970).

Laufer, L. *Israel and the Developing Countries; New Approaches to Cooperation* (Twentieth Century Fox, New York, 1967).

Legum, C. *Pan-Africanism: a short political guide* (Pall Mall Press, London, 1965).

Lilienthal, A. M. *The Zionist Connection II* (North American, N.J., 1982).

Ma'oz, M. *Palestinian Arab Politics* (Jerusalem Academic Press, Jerusalem 1975).

Migdal, J. *Palestinian Society and Politics* (Princeton University Press, Princeton, 1980).

Macdonald, R. *The League of Arab State: A Study in the Dynamics of Regional Organization* (Princeton University Press, Princeton, 1965).

Nakhleh, E. *The West Bank and Gaza: Towards the making of a Palestinian State* (American Enterprise Institute for Public Policy Research, Washington, D.C., 1979).

Nicol, D. (ed.) *Paths to Peace; The UN Security Council and its Presidency* (Pergamon Press, New York, 1981).

Nweke, G. *Harmonization of African Foreign Policies 1955-1975: The Political Economy of African Diplomacy* (African Studies Center, Boston University, 1980).

O'Ballance, *Arab Guerilla Power, 1967-1972* (Faber and Faber, London, 1974).

O'Neill, B. *Armed Struggle in Palestine: A Political-Military Analysis* (Westview, Boulder, 1978).

Ovendale, R. *The Origins of the Arab-Israeli Wars* (Longman, London, 1984).

Quandt, W., Jabber, F. and Lesch, A. *The Politics of Palestinian Nationalism* (University of California Press, London, 1973).

Rodinson, M. *Israel and the Arabs* (Penguin Books, London, 1982).

Rowley, G. *Israel into Palestine* (Mansell, London, 1984).

Rubenberg, C. *The Palestine Liberation Organization; Its Institutional Infrastructure* (Institute of Arab Studies, Belmont, Mass., 1983).

Sachar, H. M. *Europe Leaves The Middle East, 1936-1954* (Cox and Wyman, London, 1972).

Schichor, Y. *The Middle East in China's Foreign Policy 1949-1977* (Cambridge University Press, Cambridge 1979).

Schiff, Z. and Rothstein, R. *Fedayeen, The Story of the Palestinian Guerrillas* (Vallentine Mitchell, London, 1972).

Schleifer, A. *Search for Peace in the Middle East* (Fawlett Publications, Greenwich, Conn., 1970).

Sharabi, H. *Palestine and Israel: The Lethal Dilemma* (Pergasus, New York, 1969).

Sharabi, H. *Palestine guerrillas, their credibility and effectiveness* (Georgetown University Press, Washington D.C., 1970).
Snetsinger, J. *Truman the Jewish Vote and the Creation of Israel* (Hoover Institution Press, Stanford, 1974).
Stevens, R. *American Zionism and U.S. Foreign Policy (1942–1947)* (Pageant, New York, 1962).
Sykes, C. *Cross Roads to Israel* (Collins, London, 1965).
Thiam, D. *The Foreign Policy of African States* (Phoenix House, London, 1965).
Tibawi, A. L. *British Interest in Palestine* (Oxford University Press, London, 1961).
Vital, D. *The Origins of Zionism* (Clarendon Press, Oxford, 1975).
Vital, D. *Zionism, The Formative Years* (Clarendon Press, Oxford, 1982).
Yodfat, A. and Arnon-Ohanna, Y. *PLO Strategy and Tactics* (Croom Helm, London, 1981).
Zuijdwijk, T. *Petitioning the United Nations* (St.Martin's Press, New York, 1982).
Zureik, E. *The Palestinians in Israel: A Study in Internal Colonialism* (Routledge and Kegan Paul, London, 1979).

Articles

Abegunrin, O. 'The Arabs and the Southern African Problem', *International Affairs*, Winter 1983/84, pp. 97–105.
Akinsaya, A. 'The Afro-Arab Alliance: Dream or Reality', *African Affairs*, October 1976, Vol. 75, No. 301, pp. 501–29.
Allen, D. 'The Euro-Arab Dialogue', *Journal of Common Market Studies*, Vol. XVI, No. 4, 1978, pp. 323–42.
Artner, S. 'The Middle East: A Chance for Europe?', *International Affairs*, Summer 1980, pp. 420–42.
Buheiry, M. 'The Saunders Document', *Journal of Palestine Studies*, Vol. VIII (Autumn 1978), No. 1, pp. 28–40.
Campell, J. 'The Middle East: A House of Containment Built On Shifting Sands', *Foreign Affairs*, Vol. 60 (1981), No. 3, pp. 593–628.
Chhebra, H. 'The Competition of Israel and the Arab States for Friendship with the African States', *India Quarterly*, 1975–6, No. 31–32, pp. 362–70.
Cervenka, Z. 'Afro-Arab relations: exploitation or cooperation ?', *Africa*, June 1974, No. 34, pp. 47–8.
Decalo, S. 'Israeli Foreign Policy and The Third World' *Orbis*, Vol. 2 (1967), No. 3, pp. 724–45.
Decalo, S. 'Israel and Africa: A Selected Bibliography', *The Journal of Modern African Studies*, Vol. 5 (1967), No. 3, pp. 385–99.
Decraence, P. 'Is the Romance with Israel over ?', *African Report*, May–June 1973, pp. 20–3.
El-Ayouty, Y. 'Legitimization of national liberation: United Nations and Southern Africa', *Issue*, Vol. 10 (Winter 1972), No. 2, pp. 36–45.
El-Ayouty, Y. 'O.A.U. mediation in the Arab-Israeli conflict', *Geneve-Afrique: Acta Africa*, Vol. 14 (1975), No. 1, pp. 5–29.
El-Khawas, M. 'African and The Middle Eastern Crisis', *Issue* (Spring 1975), pp. 220–52.
Fisher, R. 'Following in Another's Footsteps: The Acquisition of International Legal Standing by the Palestine Liberation Organisation', *Syracuse Journal of International Law and Commerce*, Vol. 3 (Spring 1975), pp. 221–53.
Freedman, R. 'Soviet policy towards International Terrorism', in Alexander, Y. (ed.) *International Terrorism* (Praeger, New York, 1976).
Freudenschuss, H. 'Legal and Political Aspects of the Recognition of National Liberation Movements' *Millenium: Journal of International Studies*, Vol. 11 (1980), No. 2, pp. 115–29.
Feuer, G. 'La politique de la France', *Revue Française de Sciences Politique*, Vol. 19 (1969), No. 2, pp. 414–28.

Finger, S. 'International Terrorism and the United Nations' in Alexander, Y (ed.) *International Terrorism; National, Regional and Global Perspectives* (Praeger, New York, 1976).

Gitelson, S. 'Israel's African Setback in Perspective', *Jerusalem Papers on Peace Problems, The Hebrew University of Jerusalem*, May 1974, No. 6, pp. 1–27.

Gross, L. 'Voting in the Security Council and the PLO" *American Journal of International Law*, Vol. 70, (1976), No. 3, pp. 470–91.

Hamid, R. 'What is the PLO?' *Journal of Palestine Studies*, Vol. IV (Summer 1975), No. 4, pp. 90–109.

Herzl, T. 'From "The Jewish State"' in Laquer, W. (ed.) *The Israel-Arab Reader: A documentary history of the Middle East Conflict* (Penguin Books, Harmondsworth, 1970).

Hudson, M. 'The Palestinian Arab Resistance Movement: Its Significance in the Middle East Crisis' in Moore, J. (ed.) *The Arab-Israeli Conflict, Volume I* (Princeton University Press, New Jersey, 1974).

Hudson, M. 'Developments and Setbacks in the Palestinian Resistance Movement, 1967–1971' *Journal of Palestine Studies*, Vol. 1 (Spring 1973), No. 3, pp. 64–84.

Hudson, M. 'The Palestinian Arab Resistance Movement: Its Significance in the Middle East Crisis' in Moore, J. (ed.) *The Arab-Israeli Conflict*, Volume II (Princeton University Press, Princeton, 1974).

Hurewitz, J. 'The Middle East: A Year of Turmoil', *Foreign Affairs*, Vol. 59 (1980), No. 3, pp. 540–77.

Klick, I. 'Latin America and the Palestine Question' *IJA Research Report*, Nos 2 and 3 (January 1986).

Kassim, A. 'The Palestine Liberation Organization's Claim to Status: A Juridical Analysis Under International Law', *Denver Journal of International Law and Policy*, Vol. 9 (1980), No. 1, pp. 1–33.

Lazarus, C. 'Le statut des movements de liberation nationale à l'organisation des nations unies', *Annuaire Français de Droit International*, Vol. 20 (1974), pp. 173–200.

Mallison, T. and Mallison, S. 'The National Rights of the People of Palestine', *Journal of Palestine Studies*, Vol. IX (Summer 1980), No. 4, pp. 119–30.

'Mandate of Golan Heights Force Renewed; PLO invitation to Mid-East Favored', *UN Monthly Chronicle*, No. 11 (December 1975).

Meron, T. 'The Composition of the UN Regional Economic Commissions and the PLO', *International and Comparative Law Quarterly*, Vol. 28 (January 1979), pp. 52–64.

Metz, R. 'Why George Habash turned Marxist', *Mideast* (August 1970), pp. 30–6.

Miller, J. 'African-Israeli Relations: Impact on Continental Unity', *Middle East Journal*, Vol. 29 (1975), pp. 393–408.

Miller, J. 'Black viewpoints on the Mid-East Conflict', *Journal of Palestine Studies*, Vol. X (Winter 1981), No. 2, pp. 37–49.

Moisi, D. 'La France de Mitterand et le conflict du Proche-Orient comment concilier émotion et politique', *Politique Etrangère*, Vol. 47 (1982), No. 2, pp. 395–402.

Peres, Y. 'Modernization and Nationalism in the Identity of the Israeli Arabs', *Middle East Journal* (Autumn 1970), pp. 479–92.

Peritz, R. 'Israel and Asia', *New Outlook* Vol. 12 (1969) No. 4, pp. 38–43.

Reich, B. 'Israel's Policy in Africa', *Middle East Journal*, Vol. 18, (1964), No. 1, pp. 14–26.

Rudebeck, L. 'Nordic Policies Towards the Third World', in Sundelieus, B. (ed.) *Foreign Policies of Northern Europe* (Westview, Boulder, Colorado, 1982).

Sayegh, F. 'The Camp David Agreement and the Palestine Problem', *Journal of Palestine Studies*, Vol. VIII (Winter 1979), No. 2, pp. 3–40.

Sawant, A. 'Rivalry between Egypt and Israel in Africa South of the Sahara, 1956–1970' *International Studies* Vol. 17 (April–June 1978), No. 2, pp. 259–329.

Sharif, R. 'The United Nations and Palestinian Rights, 1974–1979', *Journal of Palestine Studies*, Vol. IX (Autumn 1979), No. 1, pp. 21–45.

Shuaibi, I. 'The Development of Palestinian Entity-Consciousness: Part I' *Journal of Palestine Studies*, Vol. IX (Autumn 1979), No. 2, pp. 67-84.

Shuaibi, I. 'The Development of Palestinian Entity-Consciousness-Party II' *Journal of Palestine Studies* Vol. IX (Winter 1980), No. 2, pp. 50–70.

Shuaibi, I. 'The Development of Palestinian Entity-Consciousness: Part III' *Journal of Palestine Studies* Vol. IX (Winter 1980), No. 3, pp. 97–124.

Silverburg, R. 'The Palestine Liberation Organisation In the United Nations: Implications for International Law and Relations', *Israeli Law Review*, Vol. 12 (1977), No. 3, pp. 365–92.

Stone, J. 'Palestinian Resolution: Zenith or Nadir of the General Assembly' *International Law and Politics*, Vol. 1 (1975), No. 1, pp. 1–18.

Suleiman, M. 'Attitudes of the Arab Elite Toward Palestine and Israel', *American Political Science Review* Vol. 67 (1973), No. 2, pp. 482–9.

Suleiman, M. 'Development of Public Opinion on the Palestinian Question', *Journal of Palestine Studies*, Vol. XIII (Spring 1984), No. 3, pp. 87–116.

Taylor, A. 'The Euro-Arab Dialoque: Quest for Interregional Partnership', *The Middle East Journal*, Vol. 32 (Autumn 1978), No. 4, pp. 429–43.

Tessler, M. 'Israel's Arabs and the Palestinian problem', *The Middle East Journal*, Vol. 31 (Summer 1977), No. 3, pp. 313–29.

Tomeh, G. 'When the UN Dropped the Palestinian Question', *Journal of Palestine Studies*, Vol. IV (1974 Autumn), No. 1, pp. 15–30.

Travers, P. 'The Legal Effect of United Nations Action In Support of the Palestine Liberation Organization and the National Liberation Movements of Africa', *Harvard International Law Journal*, Vol. 17 (Summer 1976), No. 3, pp. 561–80.

Wallace, W. and Allen, D. 'Political Cooperation: procedure as a substitute for policy', in Wallace, H. and Webbs, C. (eds.), *Policy Making in the European Communities* (Wiley, London 1977).

Documents and other sources

African Contemporary Record, Legum, C. (Ed.).

African Research Bulletin.

Arab Reports and Analysis, in issues of *Journal of Palestine Studies*.

Arab Report and Record

Conference of Heads of Government of Non-Aligned Countries, Belgrade, September, 1–6 1961 (The Publishing House, Beograd, undated).

Documents and Source Material in issues of *Journal of Palestine Studies*.

Facts on File.

Jankowitsch, O. and Sauvant, K. *The Third World Without Superpowers; The Collected Documents of the Non-Aligned Countries-Volume I–IV* (Oceana Publications, Dobbs Ferry, New York, 1978).

Keesings Comtemporary Archives.

League of Nations Documentation.

Middle East Magazine.

Le Monde.

The Economist.

The Europa Yearbook.

The Guardian.

The Jewish Yearbook.

The Times.

The Yearbook of the United Nations.

Views from Abroad, in issues of *Journal of Palestine Studies*.

United Nations General Assembly Official Records (GAOR) (UN Doc. A/-).

United Nations General Assembly Official Records (SCOR) (UN Doc. S/-).

Other UN Documentation.

Index

accessibility variables 27–8
  and Palestinian nationalism 45–8, 59–61, 77–81, 105–12, 132–5
  and terrorism 111–12, 134–5
  direct 133–4
  indirect 132–3
  non-violent 106–11
  see also variables
active actors 23–5
actors
  active 23–5
  high status 20, 22–5
African countries
  and Palestinian nationalism 71–7
  see also OAU, Third World countries
agenda building 25
agenda politics 20–3, 25–31
ALF 37–8, 66
Algeria 40
  and Palestine 54, 55, 75
  war of independence 59
  see also Arab League, OAU
America see USA
analytical techniques 20–30
  active actors 23–5
  agenda building 25
  agenda politics 20–3, 25–31
  behaviourism 15
  high status actors 20, 22–5
  mobilization theory 17, 26–7, 30, 41–51, 55–66
  paradigms 11–17, 21–2, 104–5
  research models 25–31, 40–3
ANM 36–7
anti-colonialism 74–5, 76, 88, 98–100, 136
anti-imperialism see anti-colonialism
anti-Zionism 48
  see also Zionism
Arab Agency 6
Arab League 6
  and PLO 8, 38, 54–68, 80
  history 4, 70
  see also individual countries
Arab Liberation Front see ALF
Arab Nationalist Movement see ANM
Arab unity 34, 37, 40, 44–5, 54, 59
Arab–Israeli war 22, 38, 56, 62, 82, 95
  effects in Europe 96–7, 98
  effects in Palestine 42, 43, 49
  effects in UN 137–8
  Jordan river diversion 41, 55

Arabs
  and Jews 1, 5
  in Israel 35, 47–8, 49–50
  personal identity 45, 48, 64–5
  refugees 35, 36, 41, 47, 49, 58, 81, 132–3
  see also Palestine
Arafat, Y. 38, 50
  and Al-Fatah 36, 58–9, 60–1
  and Nasser 63, 108
  and PLO 61, 79, 108, 110
  and USSR 108, 109, 114
  at UN 66
Asian countries
  and Palestinian nationalism 71
  see also Third World countries
Austria
  and Palestinian nationalism 107
  see also
    European Community
    European countries
Australia
  and Palestinian nationalism 119, 120

Balfour Declaration 1–2
Bandung Conference 70, 71, 72, 74, 78–9
bargain linkages
  and Palestinian nationalism 73–7, 101–2
  see also linkage variables
Begin, M. 97
behaviourism 15
Biltmore programme 3
Britain
  and Palestine 2–4, 5, 34, 107
  and PLO 107, 115
  and Suez 57
  and USA 3
  and Zionism 1–3, 4
  Balfour declaration 1–2
  see also European Community, European countries
Brussels declaration (1973) 101, 106

Camp David agreement 65, 97, 115, 119
Canada
  and Palestinian nationalism 119–20
Casablanca Group 74–5, 82
Chad
  and PLO 80
  see also OAU

China
    and Palestinian nationalism 79
    and PLO 79
cognitive dissonance 44
cognitive linkages 29
    and Palestinian nationalism 43–5, 57–9, 72–7,
        98–100, 134–7
    see also linkage variables
Cold War 70
colonialism *see* anti-colonialism
Common Market countries *see* European Com-
    munity
communication networks 27–8
community service 38–9, 47
conducive environment *see* environmental
    variables

Democratic Front for Peace and Equality 48
diaspora
    Arab 35
    Jewish 2, 3, 34
diplomatic relations
    by Israel 7, 73, 77–8, 80, 87
    by PLO 79–80, 102, 181–3
    see also international relations
direct access 133–4
    see also accessibility variables

economic aid
    by Israel 73
economic sanctions 76, 77, 101–2
Egypt
    and Israel 65
    and OAU 73–4, 75, 78
    and Palestine 6, 41, 54
    and Syria 40
    and USSR 96, 109
    see also Arab League
environmental variables 26–7
    and Palestinian nationalism 40–3, 55–7, 69–
        72, 94–8, 126–32
EPC
    and Palestinian nationalism 95
European Community
    and Palestinian nationalism 93, 95, 97–8, 99,
        101–2, 105–12
    and PLO 96, 106–8, 111–12, 112–21
    see also European countries, individual
        countries
European countries
    and Arab–Israeli war 96–7, 98
    and Israel 96–7, 100–1, 109–10
    and PLO 106–12, 112–21
    see also European Community, individual
        countries
European Jews 1, 4, 6
European Political Cooperation *see* EPC

Al-Fatah 57–9, 60–1
    Arab criticism of 58, 62
    community services 47
    history 7, 36, 37, 38, 42, 55

ideology 44–5, 49
    membership 46–7
    see also resistance movements
Finland
    and Palestinian nationalism 99
    see also Nordic Council, Scandinavian coun-
        tries
France
    and Palestinian nationalism 96
    and PLO 106, 115
    see also European Community, European
        countries

Gaddafi, W. 63
Germany
    and Palestine 3
global politics paradigm 11, 13–17, 104–5
Graham, J. 107
Great Britain *see* Britain
Greece
    and Palestinian nationalism 95, 99
    see also European Community, European
        countries
Group of 77, 87–8
guerrilla warfare 56, 60, 62, 66
    see also resistance movements, terrorism

Habbash, G. 36–7
Hawatmeh 37
Herzl, T. 1
high status actors 20, 22–3
hijackings *see* terrorism
Hungary
    and Palestinian nationalism 113
    see also European countries

ICO 71
    and Palestine 8, 71, 87
    and PLO 80, 87
ideology
    Arab 40, 42
    Baathist 37, 38
    Al-Fatah 44–5, 49
    Israeli 102–3
    Non-Aligned 71, 74
    Third World 70
imperialism *see* anti-colonialism
indirect access 132–3
    see also accessibility variables
international relations 11–17, 102–5
    see also diplomatic relations
Iraq
    and Palestine 6, 37–8, 54, 55
    see also Arab League
Ireland
    and Palestinian nationalism 99, 115
Islamic Conference Organization *see* ICO
Islamic countries
    and Israel 86
    and Palestinian nationalism 86–7, 99
    and PLO 86–7
    see also Third World countries

Israel
  and Egypt 65
  and European countries 96–7
  and Islamic countries 86
  and Jerusalem 86, 97
  and Lebanon 97–8, 111
  and Libya 80
  and OAU 72, 73, 76
  and South Africa 73
  and Third World countries 72–7, 77–8, 80–1
  and UN 80, 132
  and USA 108, 118
  and USSR 96
  diplomatic relations 7, 73, 77–8, 80, 87
  economic aid by 73
  history 3, 5, 6–8, 34
  Palestinians in 35, 47–8, 49–50
  political activities 48
  Suez War 71
  see also Arab–Israeli War, Jews, Zionism
Israeli Arabs 35, 47–8, 49–50
Israeli Communist Party *see* Maqi
Israeli Labour Party 48

Jamaica
  and PLO 88
Jerusalem
  status of 86, 97
Jewish Agency 4, 133
Jewish nationalism *see* Zionism
Jews
  and Arabs 1, 5
  and Britain 1
  anti-Zionist 48
  diaspora 2, 3, 34
  European 1, 4, 6
  in USA 3, 102–3
  see also Israel, Zionism
Jordan
  and Palestine 41, 54
  and PLO 63–4
  civil war 61
  see also Arab League
Jordan river diversion scheme 41, 55

Kaddoumi, F. 107, 108
Korea *see* North Korea
Kreisky, B. 107

Latin American countries
  and Israel 87
  and Palestinian nationalism 70, 87–9, 145–6
  see also Third World countries
League of Nations
  and Palestine 2
Lebanon
  and Palestine 6, 54
  Israeli invasion 97–8, 111
  see also Arab League
legal linkages 100–1
  see also linkage variables

Libya
  and Israel 80
Lijphart formula 81–2, 168–9
linkage variables 27, 28–30
  bargain 73–7, 101–2
  cognitive 29, 43–5, 57–9, 72–7, 98–100
  legal 100–1
  penetrative 103
  political 102–3
  strategic 103–5

Malta
  and Palestinian nationalism 99
  see also European Community, European
    countries
Maqi 48
Marxist paradigm 11
mobilization theory 17, 26–7, 30
  and Palestinian nationalism 41–51, 55–66
models *see* paradigms, research models

Nasser, G. A. 40, 41, 49, 55, 56, 57, 58, 60, 64, 82
  and Arafat 63, 108
  and USSR 108
NATO 99
New Communist List *see* Rakah
New Zealand
  and Palestinian nationalism 119, 120
  and PLO 120
Non-Aligned Movement
  and Palestinian nationalism 71, 75, 76, 79–81,
    82–4, 87–8, 99
  and PLO 79–81, 83–4
  and South Africa 75, 76
  anti-colonialism 74, 76
non-violence
  and accessibility 106–11
Nordic Council 117
  see also Scandinavian countries
North Korea
  and PLO 79

OAS 70, 71
OAU
  and Egypt 73–4, 75, 78
  and Israel 72, 73, 76
  and Palestine 8, 71–7, 78–81, 84–6
  and PLO 80, 86
  history 70
  see also individual countries
oil supplies 95–6, 101–2
  OPEC 87–8
Oman 61
  see also Arab League
OPEC 87–8
  see also oil supplies
Organization of African Unity *see* OAU
Organization of American States *see* OAS
organizational theory 27–8
  see also research models

Palestine
   and Algeria 54, 55, 75
   and Australia 119, 120
   and Britain 2–4, 5, 34, 107
   and Canada 119–20
   and China 79
   and Egypt 6, 41, 54
   and ICO 8, 71, 87
   and Iraq 6, 37–8, 54, 55
   and Jordan 41, 54
   and League of Nations 2
   and Lebanon 6, 54
   and Nazi Germany 3
   and New Zealand 119, 120
   and Non-Aligned Movement 71, 75, 76, 79–81, 82–4, 87–8, 99
   and OAU 8, 71–7, 78–81, 84–6
   and Syria 6, 37, 54, 79
   and UN 3, 4, 6–7, 8, 56, 61, 83–4, 126–51, 167–74
   and USA 3, 5, 99–100
   and USSR 5, 37, 96, 105
   and Warsaw Pact 98
   Arab–Israeli war 42, 43, 49
   community of 35, 36
   European support for 93–126, 143, 145
   history 1–8, 34, 55
   Islamic support for 86–7, 99
   Jewish attitudes to 1, 2
   Latin American support for 70, 87–9, 145–6
   leadership 42–3
   local support for 6, 25–31, 34–53
   modernization 42–3
   national support for 54–68
   nationalism 7–8, 34–53, 55–66, 69–81, 93–112, 119–20, 126–32, 132–5
   partition of 2, 3, 5, 99
   politics 1–8
   resistance movements 36–9, 42, 45, 66
   Scandinavian support for 99
   Third World support for 69–92
   see also Arabs, Al-Fatah, PLO
Palestine Liberation Army *see* PLA
Palestine Liberation Organization *see* PLO
Palestine National Council *see* PNC
Palestinian National Front *see* PNF
pan-Arabism *see* Arab unity
paradigms 11–17
   global politics 11, 13–17, 104–5
   Marxist 11
   power politics 11
   realist 11, 12–13, 14, 16, 21–2, 104–5
   world society 11
   see also analytical techniques, research models
Paris Declaration (1979) 97
Partition Plan 3, 99
Passfield Paper 2, 3
PDFLP 36–7, 42, 45, 66
Peel partition plan 2
penetrative linkages
   and Palestinian nationalism 103
   see also linkage variables

personal identity
   for Arabs 45, 48, 64–5
PFLP 37, 38, 42, 45, 47, 66
PLA 56, 60, 75
PLO
   and Arab League 8, 38, 54–68, 80
   and China 79
   and European Community 96, 106–8, 111–12, 112–21
   and ICO 80, 87
   and Jordan 63–4
   and New Zealand 120
   and Non-Aligned Movement 79–81, 83–4
   and OAU 80, 86
   and PNF 48
   and terrorism 8, 21, 46, 60, 81, 111–12, 134–5
   and UN 133–4, 143, 158–60, 167–74, 184
   and USA 107–8, 117–19
   and USSR 105, 108–11, 112–14
   Arafat as Chairman 61, 79, 108, 110
   community services 38–9, 47
   control of 49
   diplomatic relations 79–80, 102, 181–3
   European support for 106–12, 112–21
   history 7–8, 38, 55–6
   international support for 126–51, 152–66
   Islamic support for 86–7
   local support for 25–31, 34–53, 156–7
   National Covenant 44
   national support for 54–68, 153
   politicization of 38
   recognition of 8, 102
   Scandinavian support for 107, 116–17
   Third World support for 69–92, 153–4
   see also Palestine, resistance movements
PNC 38, 44, 47, 56, 58–9, 60, 63, 66, 180
PNF 48, 50, 66
Poland
   and Palestinian nationalism 113
   see also European countries
political linkages
   and Palestinian nationalism 102–3
   see also linkage variables
political theory 11–17, 20–33
   agenda building 25
   agenda politics 20–3, 25–31
Popular Front for the Liberation of Palestine *see* PFLP
Portugal 74, 75
   and PLO 107
power politics paradigm 11
Pym, F. 107

racism 73, 74, 76
Rakah 48
Reagan plan 119
realist paradigm 11, 12–13, 14, 16, 21–2, 104–5
refugees 6–7, 8
   Arabs 35, 36, 41, 47, 49, 58, 81, 132–3
   Jewish 4, 6
research models 25–31
   limits of 31

see also analytical techniques, organizational
theory, paradigms, variables
resistance movements
ALF 37–8, 66
and UN 131, 134
ANM 36–7
in Palestine 36–9, 42, 45, 66
membership 46–7
PDFLP 37, 38, 42, 45, 66
PFLP 37, 38, 42, 45, 47, 66
PLA 56, 60, 75
PNF 48, 50, 66
Al-Saiqa 37, 38, 46
support for 39–51
see also Al-Fatah, guerrilla warfare, PLO,
terrorism
Rogers' Plan 41, 56, 63
Russia *see* USSR

Al-Saiqa 37, 38, 42
sanctions
economic 76, 77, 101–2
Scandinavian countries
and PLO 107, 116–17
see also individual countries, Nordic Council
Schumann Report 97, 101
Shukairy, A. 56, 59, 60, 62, 79
social services 38–9, 47
Socialist International 72, 103
South Africa
and Arab countries 75
and Israel 73
and Non-Aligned Movement 75, 76
Soviet Union *see* USSR
Spain
and Palestinian nationalism 99
see also European Community, European
countries
strategic linkages
and Palestinian nationalism 103–4
see also linkage variables
students 37
Suez War 57, 71, 72, 79
Sweden
and Palestinian nationalism 99
see also Nordic Council, Scandinavian countries
Syria
and Egypt 40
and Palestine 6, 37, 54, 79
see also Arab League

territorial integrity 82–3
terrorism 46–7
and PLO 8, 21, 46, 60, 78, 81, 111–12, 134–5
and Zionism 2
see also guerrilla warfare, non-violence, resistance movements
Third World countries
and Israel 72–5, 77–8, 80–1
and Palestinian nationalism 69–92
and PLO 69–92, 153–4

and UN 70, 126–8, 130, 131–2
see also Asian countries, individual countries
Turkey
and Palestinian nationalism 99

UAR *see* United Arab Republic
Uganda
and PLO 80
see also OAU
UN
and Arab–Israeli war 137–8
and Israel 80, 132
and Palestine 3, 4, 6–7, 8, 56, 61, 83–4, 126–
51, 167–74
and PLO 133–4, 143, 158–60, 167–74, 184
and refugee problem 6–7, 36, 41, 42, 132–3
and resistance movements 131, 134
and Third World countries 70, 126–8, 130,
131–2
Arafat at 66
membership 127–30
Partition Plan 3
political groupings 130–1
structure 129–30, 131–2
United Arab Republic 40, 59
United Kingdom *see* Britain
United Nations *see* UN
United Nations Relief Works Agency *see*
UNRWA
United Nations Special Committee on Palestine
see UNSCOP
United States *see* USA
UNRWA 36, 42, 132–3
UNSCOP 4–5
USA 70
and Britain 3
and Israel 108, 118
and Palestine 3, 5, 99–100
and PLO 107–8, 117–19
and USSR 103–5
and Zionism 3
Cold War 70
Jews in 3, 102–3
Reagan plan 119

variables 26–9
accessibility 27–8, 45–8, 59–61, 71–81, 105–
12, 132–5
environmental 26–7, 40–3, 55–7, 69–72, 94–
8, 123–32
linkage 27, 28–30, 43–5, 57–9, 72–7, 98–105
Vatican
and Zionism 2
Venice Declaration (1980) 97, 115–16
violence *see* terrorism

Warsaw Pact
and Palestinian nationalism 98
weighting
of UN votes 169–71
Weizmann, C. 1

world society paradigm 11
World Zionist Organization 3

Young, A. 103, 108

Zionism 1–8
  and Britain 1–3, 4

and terrorism 2
and Vatican 2
anti-Zionism 48
in USA 3
  see also Israel, Jews
Zionist Congress (1897) 1
Zionist Congress (1911) 1